Higher Education Privatization in Kuwait

HIGHER EDUCATION RESEARCH AND POLICY (HERP)

VOLUME 9

The *Higher Education Research and Policy* (HERP) series is intended to present both research-oriented and policy-oriented studies of higher education systems in transition, especially from comparative international perspectives. Higher education systems worldwide are currently under multi-layered pressures to transform their funding and governance structures in rapidly changing environments. The series intends to explore the impact of such wider social and economic processes as globalization, internationalization and Europeanization on higher education institutions, and is focused on such issues as the changing relationships between the university and the state, the changing academic profession, changes in public funding and university governance, the emergent public/private dynamics in higher education, the consequences of educational expansion, education as public/private goods, and the impact of changing demographics on national systems. Its audience includes higher education researchers and higher education policy analysts, university managers and administrators, as well as national policymakers and the staff of international organizations involved in higher education policymaking

PETER LANG

Ahoud Al-Asfour

Higher Education Privatization in Kuwait

A Study in the Processes of Policy Production

PETER LANG

Bibliographic Information published by the Deutsche Nationalbibliothek
The Deutsche Nationalbibliothek lists this publication in the Deutsche Nationalbibliografie; detailed bibliographic data is available in the internet at http://dnb.d-nb.de.

Library of Congress Cataloging-in-Publication Data
A CIP catalog record for this book has been applied for at the Library of Congress.

ISSN 2193-7613
ISBN 978-3-631-77296-6 (Print)
E-ISBN 978-3-631-77297-3 (E-PDF)
E-ISBN 978-3-631-77298-0 (EPUB)
E-ISBN 978-3-631-77299-7 (MOBI)
DOI 10.3726/b15463

Peter Lang – Berlin · Bern · Bruxelles · New York · Oxford · Warszawa · Wien

This publication has been peer reviewed.

www.peterlang.com

Abstract

Like most countries around the world, the State of Kuwait has over the past two decades experienced a rapid growth in student demand for higher education. Lacking public resources, most emerging systems of higher education have turned to privatization policies as a way of meeting this demand. Similar financial pressures do not however apply to Kuwait, since it enjoys a surplus of revenue from its oil exports. Financial arguments explaining the adoption of privatization policies are therefore not compelling in the case of Kuwait. This research project aims to analyse some of the key reasons for Kuwait to pursue a privatization policy in higher education. More broadly, the project seeks to examine how various local and global processes have influenced the production of national policies of higher education in Kuwait. Using qualitative methods of policy research, this project examines some of the internal and external pressures that led to the production of a privatization policy in the Kuwaiti system of higher education in 2000. Particular reference is made to the Private Universities Law (PUL) (34/2000) in an attempt to explain how this policy was developed, who were its main architects, and what interests does the policy now serve. The research supports the conclusion that privatization is not a necessary outcome of globalization, but that the production of higher education privatization policies in Kuwait has involved a complex interplay of both local and global factors, with contextual realities playing a crucial role not only in the introduction of these policies but also in defining the form of privatization that is currently being implemented.

Contents

Chapter One: Introduction

Privatization has, over the past few decades, become a common policy preference worldwide. Savas (2000) argues that the trend towards the private sector and away from the state can be observed in most institutions. However, its introduction in higher education is the main focus of this book. The adoption of privatization has not been excluded in any specific country or territory; it is happening in one way or another in all of the world's regions. Savas (2000), while commenting on the widespread implementation of privatization in practice among different political systems of the world, notes that:

> Privatization is now commonplace throughout the world, in communist, socialist, and capitalist countries, in developed and developing countries, in democracies and dictatorship; more than one hundred countries have officially endorsed privatization and more [in] considering it. ... It is no longer a partisan or ideological issue but a pragmatic and increasingly routine approach to governing and managing public services. (p. 315)

The spread of privatization is justified on a wide variety of grounds, in particular in terms of the now dominant neoliberal ideology that advocates increasing the role of the market over the role of the state. It is also supported by the widespread notion that states tend to fail in meeting public demands, and by the belief that rapid government growth will lead to increasing inefficiency (Savas, 1982, 1987, 2000). Accordingly, privatization in its various forms has been promoted with the assumption that it will provide more efficient and better quality public services.

Savas (2000) identifies several major influences that have propelled the privatization movement globally. These influences include pragmatic, economic, philosophical, commercial, and populist rationales. While pragmatists look for better and more efficient government, the economists' standpoint is that economic affluence should reduce people's dependence on the state and increase their acceptance of the more effective privatized approaches. The goal of those who approach the matter philosophically is to achieve 'less government', with governments playing a smaller role vis-à-vis the provision of goods and services. This goal accords with the Jeffersonian view that the 'government which governs least governs best' (as cited in Savas, 2000, p.5). The goal of the commercial interests, on the other hand, is to generate more business opportunities by directing more government spending towards private firms, as they believe that public resources and government enterprises are better run by the private sector. The populist rationale is that privatization creates a better society that empowers people by offering them more choices in public services and by abolishing the power of distant state bureaucracies. In this way, the government's ability to fulfil public needs has been questioned by most advocates of privatization. This scepticism of government ability is used by privatization advocates in justifying their preference for increasing the role of the market over the public by the assumption of more efficiency and better quality.

Broadly speaking, privatization can be defined as shifting the responsibility of delivering the services that were once provided by the public sector to private institutions, thus decreasing the role of the state and increasing the role of the market in meeting social needs. It is the act of reducing the role of the state and increasing the role of the market in providing goods and services. The idea of privatization is not a modern innovation. The utilization of the private sector to satisfy people's need is not a recent practice. What is new in the contemporary context, however, is the contemporary deliberate use of privatization as a tool to improve the functions of the government. Over the last few decades, under the influence of the ideology of neoliberalism, the principles of privatization have been introduced into policy debate as a method to improve the performance of the public sector and to provide alternative financial resources in providing public services.

In their recent manifestations, privatization measures were initially introduced by the United Kingdom and the United States in 1979 and 1980, respectively. Palley (2004) has argued that, 'the elections of Margaret Thatcher in 1979 and Ronald Reagan in 1980 can be viewed as inaugurating the formal period of neoliberal economic policy dominance' (p. 6), and the trend towards privatization initiated, with the practice of selling government assets to the private sector. Since then the contemporary political utilization of the concept has been promoted broadly through a 'neoliberal imaginary' (Rizvi & Lingard, 2010), which advocates economic liberalization, deregulation, free trade, and open markets. Neoliberalism supports the privatization of public institutions, deregulation, and the enhancement of the role of the private sector generally in modern societies. It involves reducing state control, based on the ideological belief that unregulated market capitalism will deliver growth and widespread prosperity for all.

Undoubtedly, privatization has been promoted and implemented widely in various public arenas around the world, including higher education systems. At present it is rare to find any countries without a version of private higher education. Even rich welfarist countries such as the Arab Gulf States have witnessed a boom in private higher education over the past two decades. The focus of this book is on its introduction in higher education in the state of Kuwait.

Privatization and Higher Education

Traditionally most higher education has been provided mainly by the state. However, recently the emergence of the private sector or the application of market principles into higher education sector has been increasing. Despite the historical precedent of privatization in the United States in particular, the introduction of privatized higher education in most developing systems is a relatively recent phenomenon. In these systems, in contrast to the situation a couple of decades ago, the share of private higher education has grown significantly across all world regions, creating dual systems of higher education.

James (1987) sums up the growth of private education into two categories: *excess demand* and *differentiated demand* for higher education (as cited in Tilak, 1991). The first indicates increased social demand for higher education that exceeds the public supply, where the private sector seeks to meet the unsatisfied demand. The second indicates the demand for different quality (presumably high quality) and content (for example, religious education) in education which also contributes to the growth of privatization. On the supply side, Tilak (1991) notes that 'private entrepreneurs are ready to provide higher education either for philanthropic or other altruistic motives, or for profit … The dividends could be social and political gains, or quick economic profits' (pp. 227–228).

Nowadays private higher education is well-established and is still growing significantly in most countries, although some noted stagnation or only a slight increase in private shares of higher education, such as in some Central and Eastern Europe countries (Levy, 2009). The growth is illustrated not only in enrolment rates but also in the number of institutions across most of the world regions. Many scholars have documented the expansion of private higher education across regions, including Altbach (1991, 1999b, 1999c), Levy D. (2009) & (2010), Altbach & Levy (2005). Altbach (1999c), for instance, notes that 'private higher education is one of the most dynamic and fastest-growing segments of post-secondary education at the turn of the 21st century' (p.1). Umakoshi (2004) also visualized the phenomenon, across Asian states in particular, describing the rapid expansion of the private sector as a force 'squeezing' the public sector to a degree that eliminates any further public expansion.

Levy (2009) has developed a global typology that shows the reality of private higher education to be 'wide-ranging' and 'multifaceted' (p. 7). Asia comes first, having the largest concentration of countries with proportionally the largest private sectors. For instance, Japan, the Philippines, and the Republic of Korea, which are over 70 percent private (Levy, 2009), with different variations across countries. Latin America shares the summit with Asia, although widespread private higher education has a longer history there. By the late 1970s Latin America was already approaching 40 percent privatization (Levy, 1986) and data indicates that this has reached 47 percent today (Levy, 2009). The United States, on the other hand, has the world's most prestigious and long-standing tradition of private higher education, which excels in graduate education, research, funds and impact. It has retained a stable share of privatized higher education for decades, remaining between 20 and 25 percent (Levy, 2009). In Central and Eastern Europe, since the first half of the 1990s, the growth has been dramatic, from zero to substantial. This expansion and dramatic changes in enrolments is of course associated with the collapse of Communism. Privatization in Western European higher education, on the other hand, has mostly been in relation to changes in the finance and the management of public institutions, as in the case of the UK (Clark, 1998; Salter & Tapper, 1994). Sub-Saharan Africa has been late to modern expansion of private higher education, but the growth there is notable as well (Varghese, 2006). In Kenya, for example, the practice of public universities taking in private-paying students has increased to the point where one-fifth of all students are private-paying (Levy, 2009; Varghese, 2006). Most of the growth in privatization in Africans countries came during the 1980s and 1990s.

Apart from the long-existing private American universities in Egypt, Lebanon, and Jordan since the 1950s, Levy (2009) has noted that in most Arab regions private higher education 'is just beginning to register significant enrolment' (p. 14). He also noted that 'The Arab Middle East stands out as the region in which [private higher education] emergence is mostly planned and promoted by governments, often in partnership with European and United States universities [in addition to a number of Australian universities] as well as with occasional World Bank support' (p. 14). He notes that the emergence of private education has become a widespread reality in a relatively short period of time, covering the great majority of countries in the region (United Arab Emirates, Bahrain, and Saudi Arabia, to name few).

Privatization in higher education is a general concept that encompasses a range of different policies and practices. In the higher education system, there are various practices that can be regarded as an exercise of privatization. Marketization, commercialization, decentralization, corporatization, deregulation and internationalization are all different practices that can fall under the general notion of privatization. However, in one way or another they are all functioning as a shift away from the state towards the market. These various practices produce a heterogeneous collection of institutions that can be described as private higher education. The most appropriate typology, I believe, is one that represents the existing private institutions on a continuum extended between two extremes of purely public and purely private provision and funding. In between these two extremes are various forms that include the participation of both public and private firms in ownership, administration, and funding of higher education institutions.

Private higher education can also be classified based on its function, ownership, and student population. Levy (2011) talks about identity institutions (religious and beyond), elite/semi elite institutions, and demand-absorbing/non-elite institutions. Several factors have shaped the diverse structure of private higher education. Ownership, source of funds, and regulations are three factors that can, to a large extent, identify the nature and the function of any private institution. Thus, the variation in the implementation of privatization across different countries is based on several factors that define the nature of privatization.

Generally speaking, declining public budgets for higher education, and the lack of public funds to meet the rapidly growing demand for higher education, have greatly contributed to the rapid growth of privatization, although growing national and international market forces have also played a role. The costly nature of higher education, to a great extent, has stimulated governments' policy choices to privatize their higher education and abandon a commitment to its 'publicness'. From a theoretical perspective, the classification of the benefits provided by higher education for individuals and society as a whole has been considered in terms of a contrast between a public good and a private good. Advocates of privatization regard higher education as a private good, since they argue that higher education offers individual returns. That is to say, individuals should be expected to pay for their own education since they are the main beneficiaries of this education. Opponents of privatization, on the other hand, view higher education as a public good, and appeal to the positive benefits that higher education provides to the society as a whole.

In recent years, the advocates of private higher education have also relied upon other rationales. They have argued that rapid technological developments have placed a huge financial burden on the higher education sector when it comes to preparing human resources for the knowledge economy. It is claimed that the public sector is mostly incapable of coping with these rapid changes due to an inherent lack of flexibility and excess of bureaucracy.

Since rapid technological developments have changed the nature of higher education, technologically intensive higher education requires extensive resources that most governments either lack or prefer not to spend on, thereby making some degree of privatization both desirable and perhaps even inevitable.

From a policy perspective, privatization has been promoted globally through various means. International or transnational organizations have played a crucial role in the global spread of privatization policies. The role of organizations such as the World Bank (WB) and the International Monetary

Fund (IMF), the World Trade Organization (WTO), the Organisation for Economic Cooperation and Development (OECD), and the United Nations Educational, Scientific and Cultural Organization (UNESCO) in the promotion of privatization policies has been frequently discussed and debated in the literature (Rizvi & Lingard, 2010; Tilak, 2009a). Furthermore, privatization has often been imposed by international agencies on developing countries through structural adjustments plans (Rizvi, 2006), often involving 'coercive strategies' in the negotiation of financial settlements in the granting and repayment of loans to those agencies who mostly act as lenders.

What this short discussion suggests is that financial pressure is often the primary explanation for the adoption of privatization in higher education around the world. On this account, privatization is introduced as a way of reducing the requirements from the public budget for the higher education sector. This reduction is rendered necessary due to the increased demand that exceeds the public provision in many countries. This explanation, however, does not apply to the Kuwaiti context. Kuwait is one of the richest countries in the world (Kuwait's GDP per capita is about US$40,000), mainly due to its oil wealth, with a small population of citizens that roughly exceeds one million. Thus, Kuwait has no financial limitations that would result in any shortages in the budget required to expand the public supply for higher education. Nor does it face any financial crises that would place it under the control of the international organizations that promote privatization policies through coercive strategies such as structural adjustment programs. Nevertheless, privatization has also been implemented in Kuwait. The Kuwaiti government has followed the global trend in seeking to privatize its system of higher education. The question arises then as to why, how, and in what form privatization has been implemented in Kuwait.

Higher Education Privatization in Kuwait

Traditionally and since the establishment of Kuwait University (KU) in 1966, five years after independence, higher education was provided publicly, free from any charges – as a right secured for citizens by the state's Constitution. As stated in article 40:

> Education is a right for Kuwaitis, guaranteed by the state in accordance with law and within the limits of public policy and morals. Education in its preliminary stages shall be compulsory and free in accordance with law.

In the Constitution explanatory note (article 40) has been explained:

> … Nothing in this constitutional text that prevents the free provision to extend to all other levels of education as it is now the case in Kuwait and as it always hoped to remain.

In addition to free education, in most cases the government pays student allowances to citizens enrolled in any kind of higher education as well. Kuwait University was the one and only public university. It was aligned with another, mainly vocational, institution, the Public Authority for Applied Education and Training (PAAET), which was established in 1982 to accommodate and regulate all vocational and polytechnics programs and colleges in the country. Thus, prior to the production of the Private Universities Law (34/2000), public higher education has been only provided locally by the government through those two public institutions. It was in 2000 that Kuwait first witnessed the introduction of the private sector of higher education, following rapidly increasing demand for higher education, as illustrated by the thousands of high school graduates without higher education spaces, which was only made possible by the produced privatization policy (34/2000).

Over the past two decades or so, Kuwait has witnessed a surge in the number of private higher education institutions. Taking into account the small size of the country and its small population (roughly three million with only one third of that being citizens), the emergence of nine private institutions and the licensing of twenty in total represents an enormous change in the provision of higher education (PUC, 2018). The passage of the Private Universities Law (34/2000), in particular, now allows for the establishment of completely new private universities.

However, it is worth mentioning that the government has not only granted permission for the private sector to provide higher education services, it has also greatly subsidized the private sector in many ways, including free lands (government facilities) and the Counter-Trade Offset Program (BOT) established in 1992, a programme by the Ministry of Finance that helped several private institutions to set up their initial infrastructure, such as the case of the Australian College of Kuwait (ACK), which has obtained major engineering, aviation and marine science equipment from offset obligations, valued at more than 12 million Kuwaiti Dinar (roughly equivalent to US$40 million) (Al-Atiqi & El-Azma, 2007).

Also worth noting is the introduction of the internal scholarship program (activated in 2006) that directs public students to the private sector. Currently this scholarship program is supporting, in part, up to 80 percent of the private institutions' student enrolments. In this program the government is responsible for paying 80 percent of the student's tuition fees, with 20 percent left to the private educational institutions to pay (Al-Atiqi, Al-Rashed, & Al- Ali, 2010). Thus, government expenditure on higher education is still huge, and higher education is still a public right for all eligible citizens (although, due to lack in transparency and poor dissemination of data, there is no concrete data available). However, according to the Twenty-Fourth

Report of the Investment Climate in Arab Countries (2008), Kuwait has the highest percentage of expenditure on higher education of the total public education expenditure (32.6 percent), followed by the UAE (27.6 percent) and Tunisia (24 percent) (as cited in Sabre, 2009). The report also noted that Kuwait has the highest per student expenditure as a percentage of the per capita gross domestic product (80 percent of income per capita) (Sabry, 2009). This reality raises the question of what form of privatization is being practiced in Kuwait if higher education is still mostly publicly funded.

Most established private institutions in Kuwait are affiliated with American, British, and Australian universities or colleges. Sometimes the affiliation is by program or courses, resulting in institutions coordinating with more than one system. This affiliation is required by the Private Universities Council (PUC)'s policies, which oblige those private institutions to be affiliated with top universities in the world in any program they wish to offer. Rules and Procedures for Private Educational Institutions License Applications (Branches of Foreign Educational Institutions) (PUC 2/30-4/ 2007), stated that:

> The (Parent) Educational Institution is qualified in accordance with the adopted Standards and Criteria of the Private Universities Council no. (PUC16/d 25-02/2006) which stipulates that the institution must be among the best 200 universities listed in the latest appendix of the Times Educational Magazine. Educational Institutions have the capacity to grant Diploma degrees are qualified according to PUC resolution (PUC 4 26-3/2006) which requires the parent educational institution to be distinguished in its domain in conformity with the standards laid down by the licensing committee.

However, the nature of this affiliation is determined by the broader rules of foreign investment in Kuwait and ownership that to a great extent define the nature of the affiliation.

As in public higher education colleges, the main language of instruction in most courses and programs in private institutions is English, while in public institutions English is only used in scientific and business colleges, not in most social sciences and humanities. This brief overview of the form of higher education privatization implemented in Kuwait results from the Private Universities Law (PUL 34/2000), which in short period of time has significantly changed the structure of higher education in the country, in line with similar higher education reforms happening in the region (the Gulf Cooperation Council (GCC) countries) and in most other developing countries. It is in this broader context in which this study is located, with its research questions and approach defined.

Research Questions

With regard to private higher education, Clark suggests that the following questions need to be asked: (i) *why do private sectors exist?* (ii) and *what do they do?* (as cited in Geiger, 1986). This study adds a third question with respect to privatization of higher education in Kuwait: how and under what influences has higher education privatization been promoted in Kuwait? The salience of this question lies in the fact that, in meeting the rapid growth in demand for higher education, the State of Kuwait does not appear to have similar financial pressures as other developing systems pursuing privatization policies. Despite the country's rich economy higher education privatization has been implemented – why and how?

The study is thus structured around four key questions:

1. **How might we explain Kuwait's adoption of a privatization policy in higher education in the year 2000?**
2. **Why was this policy developed in Kuwait; who were the main policy players; and what interests does the policy serve?**
3. **What were some of the local and global pressures that led to the production of a privatization of higher education policy in Kuwait?**
4. **How does this case study of Kuwait illustrate the ways in which global processes influence the production of national policies in higher education?**

The first research question – how might we explain Kuwait's adoption of a privatization policy in higher education in year 2000? – is based on a number of considerations. Given the diverse ways in which privatization has been implemented in different higher education systems across different contexts, it is important in order to analyse the processes of the production of the privatization policy in Kuwait to deeply understand the context, the dynamics of its policy processes and its historical highlights, which to a great extent shaped the power that steered its national policy processes and subsequent public policy decision, these questions will be the focus of Chapter Three. Accordingly, the answer to this first question will help to locate the Kuwaiti local experience in the global trend of higher education privatization in a global comparative perspective, and also provide a solid ground for the argument(s) of the study. However, an adequate explanation will not be possible without answering the rest of the questions.

Reviewing the literature illustrates how higher education privatization policies in different countries – rich and poor, developed and developing – have developed in different, as well as similar, policy processes, producing a varied private higher education sector. Accordingly, we have arrived at the second research question asking why this policy was developed in Kuwait; who were the main policy players; and what interests does the policy serve?

Tracking the development of the policy is significant in order to form a conceptual historical understanding about the processes concerning the production of the privatization law and relate them to the social, economic and political conditions of the period under investigation. The reference years of the policy development will shed light on and identify the key policy players involved. It will also clarify the main beneficiaries of the policy. The answer to this question will be answered across Chapters Five, Six and Seven.

Stephen Ball (2006) argues that policy texts are framed by broader discourses. Accordingly, there must be preconditions that serve as triggers that promote privatization policy in Kuwait. Given the influence globalization mostly has on national policy decisions today we asked (3) what were some of the local and global pressures that led to the production of a privatization of higher education policy in Kuwait? Although some of the local pressures can be drawn out from answering the first and second research questions, it is still important to conduct an in- depth investigation of both local and global factors that promote the production of privatization policy in separate chapters (Five and Six), in order to differentiate between what is local and what is global in national perspectives. Often similar pressures can be identified differently in different contexts, as contexts do matter. For example, demand pressure can be identified differently in different contexts.

Despite the separate examination of what constitutes local pressures and what constitutes global or external, in action both are happening at the same time in conjunction with each other. Based on this assumption and in linking the global with local concerns, I asked the question of (4) how does this case study of Kuwait illustrate the ways in which global processes influence the production of national policies in higher education? Globalization has changed our understanding of different phenomena. Its processes have influenced policy creation in many different countries; however, its influence has not been the same in all local contexts. Rather, its impact is modified and shaped by the different histories, cultures, and political systems of each locality. I have assumed that global influences have been mediated in response to local pressures. Thus, the main purpose of this question is to provide an illustration of the influence of globalization processes on a country like Kuwait, which, as an Arab Gulf State, has economic, religious, and social conditions that differ significantly from most other countries around the world where privatization has been implemented and whose implementation of globalization has mostly been under-researched.

In order to answer the questions raised above and to realize the aims and objectives of the study, a mainly qualitative approach has been undertaken, relying heavily on data collected from interviews and policy documents. To broaden the scope of the data, I followed a 'continuum qualitative approach', or mixed methods approach, as proposed by Laura L. Ellingson (2011), which encourages the utilization of multiple tools and methods to add depth, richness, and complexity in understanding the phenomenon under investigation.

Ellingson (2011, p. 595) also proposed a continuum qualitative approach that loosens some of the unproductive methodological constraints highlighted by K. I. Miller (2000):

> [Researchers] do jump across traditions, we do straddle metatheoretical camps, and (unfortunately) we do let pragmatic 'definitions' constrain our work. … [I want to] allow for comfortable jumps and straddles and to loosen some of these constraints. (as cited in Ellingson, 2011, p. 595)

Taking this viewpoint into consideration, I added a student survey, using Survey Monkey software, in order to allow the examination of the policy from below, from a user perspective.

This study is primarily a case study of Kuwaiti higher education privatization policies that were initiated in 2000. In order to answer the above research questions, both qualitative and quantitative data is used in this study. Qualitative data was derived from documentary sources and semi-structured interviews, while quantitative data mainly consist of statistics from various official national and international bodies and an electronic survey of students in local public and private higher education institutions. Methods used in this study therefore include documentary analyses of policies and legislation and 30 interviews of key policy figures in the field of higher education, including members of the PUC and both councils of the KU and the PAAET. Interviews were conducted among key policy players, including presidents of private universities and board members. The survey was circulated electronically among students at KU and two other private universities: the Australian College of Kuwait (ACK), and the Gulf University of Science and Technology (GUST). The survey mostly comprises seven closed questions, one matrix question of twelve statements to be rated, and two open-ended questions. Content thematic analyses were conducted on data from interviews, as well as policy documents.

Research Approach

Privatization has been pursued by different countries with diverse histories, traditions, capacities, and political systems. Not surprisingly therefore it is pursued or implemented differently in various contexts. The variations in the way that privatization has been promoted, adopted, and implemented make it necessary to conduct context-specific studies that focus on analysing the emergence of the phenomenon in different local and national settings, even as it is important to interpret local practices within a framework of regional and global comparative conceptualizations. This investigation cannot be conducted in isolation from the world practices, since these practices provide local policymakers with an overarching view regarding higher education privatization. Marginson and Rhoades (2002) suggest a 'glonacal agency heuristic' that emphasizes the simultaneous significance of global, national, and local dimensions and forces (p. 281). Regarding globalization, they stress that higher education studies must take into account the simultaneous interaction between the three dimensions, emphasizing the role of the local and national in shaping the global. They explain:

> In presenting our glonacal agency heuristic, we emphasize the intersections, interactions, mutual determinations of these levels (global, national, and local) and domains (organizational agencies and the agency of collectivities). We do not see a linear flow from the global to the local; rather, we see simultaneity of flows. In the stories that we want to offer and facilitate about higher education we do not see global agencies and agency as fully defining national and local agencies and agency. National and local entities and collective efforts can undermine, challenge and define alternatives to global patterns; they can also shape the configuration of global flows. (p. 289)

Such context-specific studies make us aware of the usefulness of comparative research in higher education, especially when conducted on a closed system such as Kuwait, isolated as it is by language barriers, lack of research culture, and poor systems of knowledge dissemination. Teichler (1996) argues that comparative studies on higher education policy processes provide fruitful cross-national insights into national patterns. They are also

> ... indispens[a]ble for understanding a reality shaped by common international trends, reforms based on comparative observation, growing trans-national activities and partial supra-national integration in higher education. (Teichler, 1996, p. 431)

Modern trends in higher education comparative research have challenged the conventional underlying rationale of previous comparative higher education research that presumed that 'we can reasonably analyse and compare national systems which are defined as relatively closed'(Enders, 2004, p. 370). The complexity of the phenomenon under investigation requires us as researchers to keep an open mind and try to construct a more differentiated picture of the causes, implications, and 'effects of the emerging secular trends at stake' (Enders, 2004, p. 370). The researcher must also take into account the multiplying actors and stakeholders involved and the noted 'rise of the Stakeholder Society' (Maassen, 2000, p. 462).

Rizvi (2006) suggested that there are 'global drivers of privatization', a set of globalization processes that contributes to the wide spread of privatization and constitutes a key to understanding the dissemination of it globally (p. 72). Nevertheless, those processes are never uniform and do not necessarily lead to uniform outcomes. We should bear in mind that the context of higher education privatization varies substantially from one country to another. As we all know 'context matters', and the point from which we started always leaves its stamp on wherever we may arrive (Stinchcombe,

1965; as cited in Enders, 2004, p. 369). I agree with Enders when he stresses that '... the economic and political power of a country, its size and geographic location, its dominant culture, the quality and typical features of its higher education system, [and] the role its language plays internationally, ... have all to be taken into consideration' (Enders, 2004, p. 369), in order to have a broad understanding of the phenomenon under investigation. Not so many years ago privatization policies would never have been considered, even as a possibility, for the higher education system of a rich country such as Kuwait.

Enders (2004) also noted the transformation in the vision of policy analysis researchers and how comparative studies are being valued nowadays in contrast to previously widespread uncertainty of their usefulness. He comments:

> For policy analysts working in comparative higher education it is, of course, particularly interesting to see how a previously widespread and entrenched scepticism about the possibility of learning anything useful from foreign experiences is being overtaken by an equally insouciant optimism as to the transferability of specific elements of other higher education systems. (p. 367)

He maintains that: 'The outcomes of this development, however intriguing, are far from clear' (Enders, 2004, p. 367). Although there may be some uncertainty as to the ultimate value and transferability of such studies, they do nonetheless provide valued insights that are lacking in overarching global studies, which are mostly superficial and touch only the surface of phenomena. This is the case in most of the reviewed literature that focuses on the Arab Gulf States, including Kuwait.

Broadly speaking, a great deal of the literature on privatization attributes the widespread emergence of higher education privatization policies in developing countries to a neoliberal determinism carried out by the power of international organizations such as the World Bank (WB) and the International Monetary Fund (IMF). On this account, developing countries are more or less forced into privatization by the financial pressure that these agencies can exert. Many studies have investigated the adoption of privatization measures into different higher education systems, which mainly attributed its commonality to the influence of financial international agencies (Degefa, 2011; Ginsburg, Espinoza, Popa, & Terano, 2005; Jamshidi, et al., 2012; Tilak, 2009a; and Wangenge-Ouma, 2008). However, the differences in Kuwait's circumstances as a rich state open the door for new research to investigate how these processes are taking place in a country such as this, which is free from such financial pressures exerted by international organizations.

However, it is not the purpose of this book to map the broad landscapes of these studies, nor to introduce a new theory of privatization. My intention is a rather modest one – to contribute, from a certain perspective on higher education privatization studies, to the analysis of the processes of the production of privatization policies in the state of Kuwait and, specifically, investigating the sources of influence that steer national policy processes in general and higher education policy decisions in particular. I am not going to set a clearly defined hypothesis to be tested as, according to Teichler (1996), this approach will purchase a simplicity for the comparative study only at the price of disregarding the complex context in comparative settings. He contends that most comparative studies are 'exploratory and most productive in providing unexpected insight' (p.431).

Another contribution of this study is the information gained from extensive interviews and other data about Kuwait private higher education, the analysis of which produces several significant findings with major policy implications. This analysis highlights crucial issues that need to be taken into account in policy review and policy formulation. Among these issues are the importance of planning and research, the importance of considering the suitability of the policy to the local context, and the importance of avoiding the blind policy of borrowing without evaluating local needs. The analysis also explores the various factors to be taken into account when building a local private higher education system.

The phenomenon of higher education privatization in the state of Kuwait is a recent phenomenon. It is one reason why the phenomenon is understudied. Even the few studies found in the literature refer to the phenomenon in the wider region of the Gulf Cooperation Council (GCC) (such as Donn & Al Manthri, 2010), and the Middle East and the Broader Middle East and North Africa (BMENA) (such as OECD, 2008; The World Bank, 2000, 2008). Although Kuwait shares many common features with those regions, it also differs significantly in its culture, history, political system, and economy. Thus, the study of the context of Kuwait will contribute a unique perspective on the phenomenon. On the other hand, the lack of adequate literature on the topic might be as the result of problems of practical nature. Major obstacles concerning my object of study are language barriers and poor dissemination of reliable data, information, and statistics. These obstacles limit access to field knowledge in such a way that often leads to a poor provision of information. Teichler (1996) also pointed to similar obstacles facing comparative research of a practical nature, which often lead to poor provision of information, resulting in 'International collaborative research teams tending to be vulnerable due to, among other things, a heterogeneity of schools of thoughts, spiralling costs, and different work styles' (p. 431). In addition to these obstacles, there are two problems specific to the Kuwaiti context – namely, the lack of a research culture that pushes scholars to do more research and the absence of researchers who are not overly burdened by teaching loads.

Levy (2006) talks about the unanticipated explosion of private higher education globally, referring to the often 'surprise emergence' of the sector (p. 220). He notes that 'for the most part, central policy does not create, design, or even anticipate emerging private sector roles' (p. 220). In another study, Levy (2011) further argues that it is not common that the introduction of private higher education is deliberately introduced by public policies (p. 384). In contrast to Levy's findings, the emergence of the private higher education sector in Kuwait was not in existence prior to the production of the public policy (PUL 34/2000) that allowed its establishment, with high government involvement. Therefore, this study of the Kuwaiti context will provide insights into the deliberate emergence of higher education privatization policies, opposite to the case in most countries as noted by Levy above.

Book Structure

Chapter Two broadly reviews the privatization literature, its theories and intellectual foundations. It illustrates expansion and diversities of the private higher education sector across the world's regions. The chapter also mirrors global debates, both for and against, the introduction of privatization to higher education. After examining most of those arguments that explain the introduction of privatization to higher education systems in different contexts, it is apparent that most justifications are financially driven. Taking into account the lack of similar financial pressures in Kuwait, the chapter argues that financial arguments explaining the adoption of privatization policies are not compelling in the case of Kuwait.

Chapter Three discusses the context of the study – the State of Kuwait. It provides a historical overview of the country and its socio-economic texture, which are significant in order to understand the country's current policy processes. By reviewing major historical insights experienced during the formation of the modern state of Kuwait, conceptual understanding can be formed of the nature of the foreign influence on its policy decisions. Lastly it will give an overview of the tradition of higher education in Kuwait, describing its traditional public higher education sector.

Chapter Four presents the research design and methods of this study. It describes the participants in the study, the sources of data, and the methods used in data collection and analysis. It attempts to account for the phenomena leading to the emergence of higher education privatization policies in Kuwait. These are the types of data analysis: documentary analysis of policy and legislation and international consultation reports by the IMF; as well as content analysis of data drawn from the interviews. In an attempt to provide a bottom-up understanding of the phenomenon, an electronic survey was circulated among students in both private and public higher education sectors. Triangulation is made between all data collected, as well as references to reports published by international agencies concerning Kuwait specifically and the region generally. Based on the analysis of the data, relevant themes and interpretation are presented.

Drawn from Marginson and Rhode's (2002) 'glonacal heuristic approach', which stresses the need for comparative educational studies to emphasize the simultaneous significance of global, national, and local dimensions and forces in any comparative policy analysis research, the following chapters of the book are structured accordingly. Chapters Five, Six and Seven report and discuss the analysis of the data.

Chapter Five investigates major internal (local) pressures that influenced the policy decision of higher education privatization in Kuwait. It identifies those pressures in relation to the almost universal pressures promoting higher education privatization policies, but discusses them entirely in local settings. It also argues that those local pressures have been outcomes of the unsystematic and random policy processes being practised for years in Kuwait.

Chapter Six investigates the major external influences that promoted higher education privatization policies in Kuwait. The term 'external' here refers to both the global and regional influences on local Kuwaiti higher education policy decisions. This chapter identifies the major external factors that have influenced national policy decisions in Kuwait and explains the nature of this influence. It argues that privatization has been promoted externally using different tools of soft governances, illustrated in the role of international organizations in promoting privatization policies.

Since neither endogenous (local) nor exogenous (global) factors occur in isolation from each other, a separate chapter will be needed to examine these interrelations. Thus, **Chapter Seven** investigates that interplay between both local and global pressures in promoting higher education privatization policy in Kuwait. It will illustrate how the interaction between those dimensions (local, regional and global) creates a private higher education system with a national identity, which has been mediated and recontextualized in response to legislative requirements, and influenced by the local conditions, religion, culture, and traditions, and that emphasizes the existence of the power of the nation-state, even under the inevitable forces of globalization. This private education system will exemplify what might be called 'privatization from below', where global pressures have been localized.

Finally, **Chapter Eight** is the conclusion chapter that will answer most of the research questions and present the key findings of the study. It will also discuss the current debate about higher education in Kuwait and speculate on the performance and the sustainability of the private higher education sector, providing suggestions and principles that may improve the current practices and inform new policies to organize the overall higher education sector in Kuwait.

Chapter Two: Privatization and Higher Education

Privatization as a concept is not new. In practice the action of selling state owned enterprises to a private individual or individuals happened centuries ago. Adam Smith (1776) noted that, two centuries ago:

> In every great monarchy in Europe the sale of the crown lands would produce a very large sum of money, which, if applied to the payment of the public debts, would deliver from mortgage a much greater revenue than any which those lands have ever afforded to the crown. When the crown lands had become private property, they would, in the course of a few years, become well improved and well cultivated. (as cited in Yarrow 1986, p. 324)

Thus, the assumed efficiency of decentralizing and shifting decision-making to a smaller organization dates back centuries. What is new, however, is the political utilization of the concept 'privatization', presumably to improve efficiency and then quality. The historical practice of the concept cannot be compared to the modern popularity of privatization, in all of its definitions, as a policy choice in providing public services.

In 1989 Mengistu and Hail-Mariam noted that privatization was a fairly recent term that was lacking in most 'lexicons' and missing from all but the most recent textbooks, with only a few works having given it a full treatment – notably Emanuel Savas's work (1982), *Privatizing the public sector: how to shrink government* and Madsen Pirie's (1985), *Dismantling the state: The theory and practice of privatization* (p.43). However, over the last two decades privatization has become a growing field in the literature. Its widespread practices attracted many scholars to study, investigate, and evaluate (praise or criticize) the phenomenon. For example, Savas himself, who is one of the advocates of privatization, has written extensively on the topic in the following books: *Privatization, the key to better government* (1987), *Privatization and public-private partnerships* (2000), and *Privatization in the city: successes, failures, lessons* (2005). The contemporary political conception of the concept has been promoted broadly by neoliberal views that advocate economic liberalization, free trade, and open markets. Broadly, neoliberalism supports privatization of public institutions, deregulation, and the enhancement of the role of the private sector in modern societies. Its central goal is to reduce state control; based on the belief that unregulated market capitalism will deliver growth and widespread prosperity for all. The introduction of privatization as a policy solution is particularly associated with the government of Margaret Thatcher in the UK and Ronald Reagan in the US (Savas, 2000). Palley (2004) has argued that:

> The elections of Margaret Thatcher in 1979 and Ronald Reagan in 1980 can be viewed as inaugurating the formal period of neoliberal economic policy dominance. The last quarter century has seen an expanding application of neoliberal ideas within both industrialized and developing-country economies. (p. 6)

Today privatization has become a common policy choice for many countries and it is rare to find any nation-state without some form of privatization. It is its introduction to higher education, however, that is the concern of this book. The introduction of privatization and market principles to the provision of the different public services might in some cases be the best solution to improve both quality and efficiency. However, when it comes to education in general and higher education in particular, it is a different issue. Providing higher education through market mechanisms or leaving it entirely to be controlled by the market power is highly disputed. The unique role and function of higher education makes it quite different from other areas that might be privatized. As centres of knowledge creation and dissemination and as socio-political entities, universities differ considerably from the market in terms of its functions, goals and objectives.

There are many questions that can be legitimately asked about privatization. What is privatization and what does higher education privatization mean? Who promotes the concept of privatization and on what rationale? Is it suitable for higher education provision? What is the global debate around the phenomenon? Is privatization good or bad for higher education? What are its advantages and disadvantages? What forms of higher education privatization are there? This chapter aims to provide a conceptual understanding of privatization by exploring its intellectual foundations. The chapter also discusses various theories of privatization. By reviewing the theoretical debates about privatization and the provision of public services, it argues that higher education is more of a public than a private good. The chapter then further mirrors arguments for and against higher education privatization. It also explains the role of globalization in the proliferation of higher education privatization policies globally. It concludes by arguing that most financial arguments that explain the adoption of privatization policies, as well as the role of international agencies, are not compelling in the case of Kuwait, due to the lack of the kind of financial pressures that forced many governments to adopt privatization policies for their higher education.

The Idea of Privatization

In the past fifty years there has been a shift in economic paradigms from Keynesianism to neoliberalism. The decline of Keynesianism, in the mid-1970s, after reigning as the dominant paradigm for understanding the determination of economic activities since the end of the Second World War

(1945), resulted mainly from the internal intellectual divisions between the American neo-Keynesians and the European (British) post-Keynesians, a conflict that weakened its position and bastardized Keynes's message (Palley, 2004). Palley (2004) argued that the divisions among Keynesians, along with other economic and cultural factors, enhanced the rise of neoliberalism. Accordingly, in the mid-1970s Keynesianism was replaced by neoliberalism, which can be understood in terms of free markets, deregulation, and the empowering of the private sector regarding the provision of goods and services at the expense of the role of the state.

For the last fifty years, economic policy and public thinking, have been dominated by neoliberalism as an economic philosophy. The reference to 'liberalism' reflects an intellectual lineage that connects with nineteenth-century economic liberalism associated with Manchester, England, where the system was predicated upon laissez-faire economics and was closely associated with free trade and the repeal of England's Corn Law, which restricted importation of wheat (Palley, 2004, p.1). Contemporary neoliberalism, however, is 'principally associated with the Chicago School of Economics, which emphasizes the efficiency of market competition, the role of individuals in determining economic outcomes, and distortions associated with government intervention and regulation of markets' (Palley, 2004, p.1).

The above paradigms have economic roots that apply generally to macroeconomic levels. In order to relate the economic discussion to higher education, an examination of the ideas of Milton Friedman, one of the key figures of the Chicago School, can be helpful. The classic modern statement on the importance of the market in (higher) education comes from Freidman (1962). In his reassessment of the economic and social role of the state he recommended the use of market mechanisms in many activities for which such use had previously been considered unusual, especially in education. Although he acknowledged the important externalities associated with education, and the financial role that the state should take in this sector, he challenged the provision of these services by the state (Teixeira, Dill, Amaral, & Jongbloed, 2004, p. 5). One of Friedman's (1962) classical criticisms of public provision of education by the state is the poor efficiency of a system monopolized or quasi- monopolized by the state, based on a situation of uniformity in wages that prevents performance payments. The system where government subsidies flow directly to the providers of education has – in Friedman's view – led to less responsive institutions that are underfunded and less adapted to the demands of society; a system of vouchers, where government funding flows directly to students (and from them to the institutions), would create more competition between institutions and lead to more efficient use of resources.

Such a system might be supplemented by students through fees and other private contributions. While the Friedman model primarily targeted basic education, it could easily be extended to higher education.

As a political construct, the idea of privatization emerged in the 1970s when a number of Western countries, such as the US and the UK, attempted to make the distinction between the decision-making in the areas of public policy and the execution of service provision. These processes led to what has become the privatization movement, which has been increasingly influential since the elections of Margaret Thatcher and Ronald Reagan in 1979 and 1980, respectively (Savas, 2000). Three decades later it has become globally pervasive, with an increased assumption that it is the best way to ensure the efficiency and effectiveness of public service provision (Rizvi, 2006). In *The general theory of employment, interest, and money*, John Maynard Keynes (1936) argued that:

> [T] he ideas of economists and political philosophers, both when they are right and when they are wrong, are more powerful than is commonly understood. Indeed, the world is ruled by little else. Practical men, who believe themselves to be quite exempt from any intellectual influences, are usually the slave of some defunct economist. (p. 383)

Keynes pointed to the intellectual influence economists and political philosophers have on creating and imposing ideologies on policymakers and eventually steering policy processes around the world, even if those ideas have no basis in fact. In the same context, and drawing on the classical Marxist tradition that led him to understand ideology in a new sense, Rizvi (2006) argues that 'the political context in which privatization is promoted is inherently ideological [and] it is based on an almost ontological assumption that the private sector is intrinsically more productive than the public sector' (p. 68). Rizvi (2006) convincingly explains how privatization as an ideology has attained a global dominance without adequate supporting empirical evidence as follows:

> Ideology is a highly contested theoretical construct. In popular parlance, it often refers to a set of ideas to which one is totally committed, even if those ideas have no basis in fact. Ideology is often also associated with theories that are impractical, abstract, and even fanatically held. In the classical Marxist tradition, it is viewed as a misrepresentation of reality, nothing more than the ideal expression of the dominant material relationships designed to obscure historical truths, encouraging subordinate groups to give assent to ruling ideas – in short, 'false consciousness'. [He] uses the term ideology in a neo-Marxist sense, stripped of its association with historical determinism but highlighting the material interests of the ruling classes it serves by obscuring their real interests. In this sense, [He] regards ideology as a contingent phenomenon employed by people to make sense of the world in ways that are never neutral but always interest-relative. Ideology thus has both

> discursive and material dimensions: it names 'mental frameworks-the languages, the concepts, categories, imagery of thought, and the systems of representation-which different classes and social groups deploy in order to make sense of, define, figure out, and render intelligible the way society works (Hall 1996, p.26)'. (pp. 71–72)

Tilak (1991) also talks about the 'politico-ideological' nature of the arguments made in favour of, as well as against, privatization. He argues that most of these arguments are 'myths' that should be open to empirical verification, 'without which they may be brushed aside by the opposing side as merely politico-ideological arguments' (Tilak, 1991, p. 230).

The notion of privatization is very broad and can embrace a wide variety of actions. Privatization does not refer to a single policy choice. Belfield and Levin (2002) argued that 'privatization is an umbrella term referring to different educational programs and policies' (p. 19). They define privatization as the 'transfer of activities, assets and responsibilities from government/public institutions and organizations to private individuals and agencies' (p.19). Many scholars define privatization based on their own personal and thus, limited, understanding of the phenomenon. The literature, in fact, is only clear on one point: that it means different things to different people. In the same vein, a number of the classifications that have been provided are based on particular practices of privatization. For this reason, many terms have been created for conceptually similar notions, such as: privatization, marketization, commercialization, deregulation, decentralization, corporatization, and internationalization. These are all different practices that can be subsumed under the general notion of privatization.

Despite the existing practical variations, privatization can be broadly understood as the process of shifting from public to private, from the state to the market generally in serving society's needs. Savas (2000) defines it broadly as 'relying more on the private institutions of society and less on government to satisfy people's needs' (p. 3). In other words, it is the act of reducing the role of the government and increasing the role of the other institutions of society in producing goods and services and in owning property. Similarly, Rizvi (2006) echoes Savas's definition, as he states: 'In very broad terms, the idea of privatization refers to the transfer of services provided by the public sector to a range of private sector interests' (p. 67). The concept of privatization seems easy to understand, however, it is difficult to have a consensus on a single unique definition, or even several clear definitions, due to the complexity of its various forms in practice, a complexity that creates ambiguity in the term privatization. Tilak (1991) illustrates this ambiguity of the term privatization, as in practice he found it very difficult to distinguish between what is public and what is private. Degefa (2011), from a different viewpoint, suggests that 'what is meant by privatization will vary according to the perspective that one uses to judge the phenomenon' (p. 14).

To Kolderie (1986), for example, privatization means no more than contracting out functions that were performed by the public sector to the private sector. If privatization is simply another name for contracting out functions to private entities then, again, the idea of privatization is not really new. On the other hand, Carrol (1987), in contrast with many writers, views privatization as a political economy component of an administration's approach to the conduct of public business (as cited in, Mengistu & Hail-Mariam, 2011).

Pirie (1985), who is one of the strongest advocates of privatization, defines privatization as a 'process by which the public sector is reduced by transferring its functions to the private sector' without apparently affecting ownership (p. 4).

Kolderie (1986), however, argued that it is useless to discuss 'turning over' a government function to the private sector, as he stresses that much of the discussion about privatization is unclear, largely because two quite different ideas are being expressed by using the same word and that very different interests with very different implications for public policy are represented by those different ideas. He distinguishes between provision of a service, a policy decision involving responsibility for the service, and the production of a service or its actual delivery. According to Kolderie (1986), services, then, can be considered as best belonging in one of four categories: public provision and public production; public provision and private production; private provision and public production; and private provision and private production. This 'four-part' concept, he suggests, is the only way to have a useful discussion about the role of public and private and the strategy of privatization, which he explains it as follows:

> The usefulness of much of the current discussion about privatization is impaired by a basic confusion about definitions and concepts. In particular, many observers fail to distinguish between the primary policy decision of government to provide a service and the secondary decision to produce a service. Either function or both may be 'turned over' to private parties. In the latter case, the efficiency and effectiveness of government may be improved. In the former, the objective of social equity may be put seriously at risk. (Kolderie 1986, p. 285)

Johnson and Watson (1991) also explore the differences between provision and production of public services by the public and the private sectors. The study concludes that the structure and process of privatization have a significant implication for the successful application of privatization in a local government setting. In the same vein, Savas (2000) also pointed to the significance of the distinction between the three participants involved in the act of service delivery in order to understand the core concept of privatization: the consumer, the producer, and the arranger or provider. He argues that this distinction – between providing or arranging for a service and producing it – is profound. It is at the heart of the entire concept of privatization and puts the role of government in perspective.

Degefa (2011) argues that any definition based on the distinction between public and private misses expressing the full picture of the multifaceted privatization policy, as it neglects the fact that privatization involves sharing the provision of higher education services between the state and the private sector. He explains:

> ... the definition of privatization on the basis of provision of funding and provision of higher education shows that the distinction between higher education as a public good and higher education as a private good is a zero-sum thinking. What can be clearly seen is that one can talk about the degree of privatization as existing along all modalities. For instance, there is a private contribution in the traditional publicly owned and run higher education when students have to sacrifice their time and families have to sponsor non-educational students' expenses. Conversely, in the other extreme where we have total private ownership and private provision of higher education, there is considerable public involvement as the state helps these institutions by putting in place the legal framework and by providing legal protection as well. (p.19)

Degefa (2011) also suggests that, considering the sources of inputs, the nature of outputs and the process of knowledge production might help to figure out what exactly is private higher education and what is privatization policy. Privatization in higher education, thus, generally means the withdrawal of control from the state and the transfer of it to the market.

Privatization can occur either gradually by changing the degree of participation of each sector or by the development in isolation of institutions that are established, managed and funded by the private sector. Ideally, privatization can be done without neglecting the state's role in producing the proper policies and overseeing their operation, in order to ensure the quality of provision.

Typologies of Privatization

The diversity of the privatization phenomenon has brought several typologies into being, as it is difficult to encompass the entire provision under a single classification system. Tilak (1991) points to the ambiguity of the term 'privatization' because of the different meanings it might have with reference to the source of funding or the degree of public/private role within the system. For example, if the source of funding were proposed as the sufficient criterion to differentiate between public and private higher education systems, then one could point out that private universities often receive substantial resources from the government, and that public universities can generate a significant amount of resources from private sources. Thus, a more sophisticated approach is needed. Tilak (2009b) classifies the phenomenon of the privatization of education based on 'Management-cum-finances' into four types:

a) **An extreme degree of privatisation**, where education is seen as a business, and profits – exorbitant profits – are made by private institutions.
b) **A strong form of privatization**, where a large proportion of the cost is recovered, but no profits are made.
c) **A moderate form of privatization** characterized by low-to-moderate levels of fees, which are set much below the cost levels.
d) **Pseudo privatization**, which includes private institutions managed completely privately, but financed nearly fully by the government (p. 52).

The privatization of higher education has also manifested itself in different practices such as marketization and commercialization that simply mean applying market principles to public higher education provision.

Tilak (2008) also provides a classification for private education provision, in a specifically Indian context, by distinguishing types of provision according to the sources of funding and the kinds of courses and programs provided. Based on the programs offered at Indian institutions, he identifies two types of institution: universities and non-universities. Regarding worldwide private higher education, Tilak argues that it can be classified into four categories: the US model, the Western European model, the Japan-Korea model (or the j-model as Umakoshi, 2004 calls it), and the developing countries model (Tilak, 2009b).

Although the above categorization seems universal and might incorporate most of the existing practices of higher education privatization, 'it is [still] difficult to generalize about international patterns of ownership and funding for private higher education. There is, and will continue to be, considerable diversity' (Altbach, 1999c, p. 7). As an example of emerging diversity, Altbach (1999c) points to the recent trend of exporting higher education. This trend is illustrated by branch campuses that have been established worldwide, resulting in a 'multinationalization' of private higher education (p. 10). He also distinguishes between the not-for-profit and for-profit institutions, regarding the latter as a recent phenomenon that only emerged in the 1980s and 1990s. Altbach (1999c) notes that their existence depends on the legal provisions of particular countries and that they are, without question, a major phenomenon worldwide, which only attained legitimacy in the 1990s (Varghese, 2006).

Thus, the heterogeneity that characterizes private higher education allows for various typologies to be presented in the literature. Each typology seems to have its strengths and weaknesses. However, as Levy points out, none are perfect or cover all cases.

Despite the diversity of privatization, I found that a better conceptualization of privatization is to examine the degree of participation of each public and private sector in the institution. Drawing on Johnstone's (1999) continuum conceptualization of privatization 'as a trend of moving from highly public to highly private higher education', Degefa (2011) introduces the practice of using degrees of privatization as the best way to classify privatization as it occurs in higher education. His classification of higher education institutions is based on the differences in the roles that the state and the market play in privatizing higher education institutions. Degefa (2011) perceives financing higher education and education provision as two distinct functions that can be carried out either by the state or the market or both.

Accordingly, he provides four possible modalities that move from pure public to pure private higher education (see Tab. 2.1 Trends towards private higher education, Degefa, 2011, p. 17). Those four modalities, with the exclusion of the pure public model, are:

a) **Privatization as cost-sharing** (public provision and private financing modality)
b) **Privatization by application of business-like management styles to public institutions** (corporatization of universities)
c) **Privatization through voucher system** (market provision and state financing)
d) **Privatization as emergence of non-state higher education sector** (market provision and financing)

For better illustration of Degefa's modalities, I draw the following diagram (Fig. 1) as an illustration of Johnstone's (1999) continuum (as cited in Degefa, 2011). It visualizes the concept of Johnstone's (1999) continuum that help in classifying private higher education institutions based on the share of provision and funding.

Theoretical Debates

Privatization in theory stands basically on the classification of goods and services according to two main properties 'exclusion' and 'consumption'. The nature of any good or service will be decided according to those two measures. Accordingly, the role of government and the market will be determined concerning the provision of those goods and services.

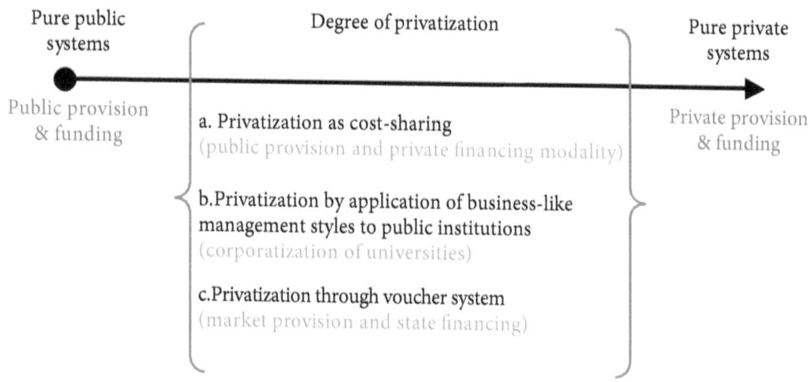

Fig. 1: Trends towards private higher education.

The classic economic definition of public and private good is that of Samuelson (1954). Public goods and services are ones that are 'non-rivalrous' and 'non-excludable'. 'Non-rivalrous' means that they can be consumed by any number of people without being exhausted. In other words, their consumption by some does not diminish other people's consumption levels of the same goods (Tilak, 2008). 'Non-excludable' means that the benefits cannot be confined to individual buyers. That is to say, such goods cannot be provided exclusively to some people, and others cannot be excluded from consuming them. In contrast, private goods are both rivalrous (exhaustible) and excludable.

In his theory of privatization Savas (2000) similarly classifies goods and services based on these two characteristics: exclusion and consumption. He argues that:

> The vast jumble of goods and services can be sorted and classified according to two characteristics: exclusion and consumption. The resulting classification determines the roles of government and of the nongovernmental [private] institutions of society in supplying the goods and services. (p.41)

According to him 'a good has the property of exclusion if its acquisition or use can readily be denied by the supplier' (e.g., a piece of clothing, but not fish in the sea) (p. 61), while 'a good is characterized as a joint consumption good or an individual consumption good depending on whether it can or cannot be consumed jointly and simultaneously by many users' (e.g., a TV broadcast is a joint consumption good, whereas a loaf of bread is not) (p. 61). He suggests that goods and services can be classified according to the degree to which they possess these two properties. Accordingly, he concluded with four ideal kinds of goods: individual goods (characterized by exclusion and individual consumption); toll goods (exclusion and joint consumption); common-pool goods (non-exclusion and individual consumption); and collective (or public) goods (non-exclusion and joint consumption). His conclusion is that both individual and toll goods can be supplied by the marketplace with public action playing a minor role through regulating market operations in general. Thus, Savas's theory of privatization depends on determining the proper roles of government and the private sector by the examination of goods and services needed in a modern society.

Savas (2000) also distinguishes between three basic participants of service delivery: the *consumer*, the *producer*, and the *arranger* or the *provider*. In order to understand the core concept of the privatization, he argues that 'this distinction between providing or arranging a service and producing it is profound [and] It is the heart of the entire concept of privatization and puts the role of government in perspective' (p. 65). He explains that if a government decides to provide a service at public expense, it does not have to produce it using its employees and equipment. Savas also contends that most of the opposition against privatization often comes from the 'false alarms' raised by those who do not 'appreciate' the difference between the two concepts *providing* and *producing* the service, and who have made the wrong assumption that, if the government will 'divest itself of the producer function', its role as provider must automatically be abandoned, particularly if the divesting concerns 'inherently governmental' services such as higher education. Accordingly, he proposes ten basic arrangements for service delivery that can be combined in multiple ways, creating a wide range of service delivery choices that differ in the roles played by the government, the private sector and the consumer (see Savas, 2000, pp. 88–89).

Higher education produces two principal products: education and research. Brown and Carasso (2013), in their recent book examining the marketization of the UK higher education, argue that teaching, for example, can be a predominantly public good or a predominantly private good, depending on which aspects of teaching and learning are uppermost in its social organization. According to Marginson (2011),

> Teaching and learning contain public good aspects: the knowledge learnt; general education unrewarded in labour markets that contributes to a shared knowledge base; education understood as a citizen entitlement to the common culture and to social opportunity; and the contribution of higher education to social tolerance and international understanding. (p. 426)

However,

> Teaching and learning also carry private good aspects: scarce credentials, from exclusive higher education institutions, providing entry to income-generating professions. (p. 426)

Thus the theoretical classification of goods and services is not absolute, as it is difficult to treat all goods and services alike. Some goods have social character that even though they are excludable such as education, since they have a positive collective effect on the society as a whole. Samuelson (1954) supports such argument assuming that:

> ... no mystical collective mind that enjoys collective consumption goods; instead ... each individual has a consistent set of ordinal preferences with respect to his consumption of all goods (collective as well as private). (p. 387)

According to this perception, all goods public as well as private provide a personal set of interests in regards to their consumption. In the same context, Savas (2000) developed the notion of 'worthy goods' – that is, goods that, although their private returns are for individuals (excludable), nonetheless do have positive externalities that benefit the society as a whole, such as education, which make them goods that all should have (p. 57). Similarly, Kanbur, Sandler and Morrison (1999) developed the notion of 'club goods' for products that are not rivalrous but are excludable, e.g., patents, copyright, etc.

Most of the theoretical debate held concerning the role of privatization in higher education rests on the conflict about the role higher education performs for individuals and societies. Regarding higher education as a private or public good is the key to understanding the discussion of privatization in higher education. Arguments advocating privatization in higher education are often based on the belief that it is an individual good, since it offers individual benefits to its participants. On the other side, opponents of privatization believe that higher education is a public good, since it produces many social benefits. Whether higher education is considered a private or public good has important implications for those responsible for providing it. If education is a public good, then it would seem that the public should be responsible for providing it. If, on the other hand, education is considered a private good, then it would seem that the burden of finding and paying for it should be on the individual, not the public. In this section, in order to answer the question of whether higher education is a private or a public good, it will be useful to adopt an economic perspective that regards higher education as a product or an enterprise that provides intangible goods or services to its recipients. The ultimate goal of this section is to clarify the lines of the conflict and determine who has the responsibility for providing higher education.

Privatization in higher education is one of the most controversial policies in the world, with avid proponents and equally avid opponents. Since higher education has become an area of interest for many disciplines, these connections with other disciplinary fields, such as economics and political economy, require an interdisciplinary mode for considering higher education issues. This mode and the mounting interest from educationalists, economists, sociologists, anthropologists, and even human right activists have produced an environment in which the field of higher education must draw heavily from these disciplines. Thus, in addition to the contextual factors and the global pressures of standardization, Degefa (2011) sees that the higher education 'locus' (presence) in multiple fields of study has obscured and/or complicated the way it is perceived and defined (p. 14). According to him, the complexity can be seen in the difficult differentiation between public and private higher education in terms of their activities, outputs and influences on society.

Since the conflict over privatizing higher education ultimately depends on the issue of whether to treat higher education as a public or private good, it is necessary to examine the outputs of education and determine whom they benefit. Some consider that both public and private benefits are produced by higher education. Friedman (1962), for example, justifies government intervention into education based on two grounds:

> The first is the existence of substantial '*neighborhood effects*', i.e., circumstances under which the action of one individual imposes significant costs on other individuals for which it is not feasible to make him compensate them, or yields significant gains to other individuals for which it is not feasible to make them compensate him – circumstances that make voluntary exchange impossible. The second is the *paternalistic concern* for children and other irresponsible individuals. (pp. 85–86)

He further differentiates between '*neighborhood effects*' and 'paternalism' based on their very different implications for general education for citizenship on the one hand and specialized vocational education on the other. Friedman (1962) states that 'the grounds for governmental intervention are widely different in these two areas and justify very different types of action' (p.86). Initially, He points out that:

> [I]t is important to distinguish between 'schooling' and 'education'. Not all schooling is education nor all education, schooling. The proper subject of concern is education … [and] the activities of government are mostly limited to schooling. (Friedman, 1962, p.86)

He argues that vocational and professional schooling [higher education] has no '*neighborhood effects*' of the kind attributed above to general education, arguing:

> It is a form of investment in human capital precisely analogous to investment in machinery, buildings, or other forms of non-human capital. Its function is to raise the economic productivity of the human being. … [Individual in return will be] rewarded in a free enterprise society by receiving a higher return for his services

> than he would otherwise be able to command. This difference in return is the economic incentive to invest capital whether in the form of a machine or a human being. In both cases, extra returns must be balanced against the costs of acquiring them. (Friedman 1962, p. 100)

Freidman (1962) further explains that:

> For vocational schooling, the major costs are the income foregone during the period of training, interest lost by postponing the beginning of the earning period, and special expenses of acquiring the training such as tuition fees and expenditures on books and equipment. For physical capital, the major costs are the expense of constructing the capital equipment and the interest foregone during construction. In both cases, an individual presumably regards the investment as desirable if the extra returns, as he views them, exceed the extra costs, as he views them. In both cases, if the individual undertakes the investment and if the state neither subsidizes the investment nor taxes the return, the individual (or his parents, sponsor, or benefactor) in general bears all the extra costs and receives all the extra returns: there are no obvious unborne costs or unappropriable returns that tend to make private incentives diverge systematically from those that are socially appropriate. (pp. 100–101)

Freidman's views are purely economic in that they neglect the important social benefits that acquiring higher education will produce. This type of view ignores the social character of higher education as a good that is discussed by both Marginson (2011) and Brown and Carasso (2013, p. 22). Marginson (2007), on the other hand, argues that instability, ambiguity, and blurred understanding of the public and private aspects of education are due to the continual changes in the roles of higher education and the state. Hence, an understanding of the sources of inputs, the nature of outputs, and process of knowledge production might help to figure out what exactly private higher education is and what privatization policy is.

From a purely economic perspective, higher education is both excludable and rivalrous. Accordingly, it is regarded as a private good. Savas (2000), for instance, explicitly states that, with respect to graduate school (higher education), accepting one applicant may mean rejecting another, consumption is more individual, and higher education is more of an individual good (p. 49). However, its positive externalities, or the '*neighborhood effects*' that benefit the society as a whole, cause higher education to become a 'worthy good' according to Savas (2000). Nevertheless, Savas (1987) maintains that the production should be contracted to the private sector, even for those services for which government must retain their provision responsibility such as education. He envisions the government's role as articulating the demand, acting as the purchasing agent, monitoring the contractor's performance, and paying the bill (Savas, 1987, p. 288).

Marginson (2012) noted that 'Knowledge is the unique claim of higher education [that is] at the core of every public and private good that is created in the sector' (p. 9). Stiglitz (1999) argues that knowledge, and thereby higher education and research, does satisfy all of the conditions attached to public goods – viz., non-excludability and non-rivalrousness. He further supports his argument with the illustrative example of a mathematical theorem, which is non-excludable (once it is published no one can be excluded from reading and enjoying the theorem), and non-rivalrous (one's enjoyment of the theorem will not affect another's enjoyment of the same). Thus, its utilization is equally available to all at the same time. There is zero marginal cost for making it available to an additional person. Johansson (1991), for the same reason, regarded higher education as a collective good, as the cost of excluding an additional person from benefiting from higher education can be infinite, while the cost of an additional person can be nil (pp. 63–64). Both Stiglitz (1999) and Johansson's (1991) arguments lack logical sense, however, as they neglect the material costs of being a participant in higher education. The full cost of the acquisition of the knowledge has not been accounted for. For example, acquisition of knowledge may require access to the Internet, which in turn requires service provider fees, not to mention the cost of the computer devices. These sorts of costs cannot reasonably be described as nil.

That externalities are produced by obtaining higher education has rarely been denied. Tilak (2008) suggests that if the consumption of higher education, interpreted as a consumption of its benefits, is not a consumption of good per se, then higher education satisfies both essential features of a public good, as 'the spread of benefits from an educated citizenry cannot be restricted to a small population, nor is the quantum of benefits received by some affected by the level of benefits others receive' (p.452). Accordingly, he criticizes this theoretical view that excludes higher education from being a public good, describing it as naïve and a very narrow interpretation of the technical attributes of public goods and the consumption of education. Stiglitz (1986) has noted that there are two critical properties of public goods: it is not feasible to ration public goods, nor it is desirable to do so (as cited in Tilak, 2008, p. 452). While it may be feasible to ration admissions to higher education, it is not feasible to ration the distribution of benefits that flow from higher education (Weisbrod 1988; as cited in Tilak, 2008). Thus education, higher education in particular, satisfies all three essential features of public goods: it is non-excludable, non-rivalrous, and it produces externalities.

Acquiring private benefits from the consumption of public goods is not a unique feature attached to higher education. Bloom et al. (2006) noted that public goods yield both private and public benefits. Thus, obviously, higher education produces private benefits to its participants. Tilak (2008), however, argues that, even though there are private benefits from higher education, it should be regarded as a public good, mainly because of its externalities that benefit the society as a whole, which outweigh those benefits individuals will gain. The 'public good' nature of higher education is well understood and can be easily recognized by viewing the traditional functions and social benefits produced through its institutions that benefit society as a whole economically and socially. Among these benefits are the creation, advancement, absorption and dissemination of knowledge, as well as the cultivation of the human capital required for the creation of knowledge societies etc. (Tilak, 2008). Higher education's objectives are not only economic; higher education also contributes significantly to nation building. The Task Force on Higher Education and Society (TFHES) (The World Bank, 2000) highlighted higher education's ability to serve the public interest, by: (1) unlocking the potential at all levels of society, (2) helping talented people to gain advanced training whatever their background; (3) creating a pool of highly trained individuals that attains a critical size and becomes a key national resource; (4) addressing issues for study whose long-term value to society is thought to exceed their current value to students and employers; and (5) providing a space for the free and open discussion of ideas and values.

Thus, we come to the question of whether the state or the market should provide higher education. Based on the above theoretical economic views, higher education is definitely a public good. Thus, the state should be responsible for its provision; or, as Tilak (2008) concludes, 'higher education is a public good beyond any doubt and the current controversy is ill-motivated and unwarranted' (p. 453). On the other hand, public goods cannot be provided by the market. Since profit cannot be a criterion in the production of public goods, private producers cannot profit from producing them. Tilak further added that it is better for public goods to be provided by the state than to be left to insecure and unstable market forces. Concerning efficiency of provision, he states 'the personal or market provision of public goods is not feasible, and even if feasible is inefficient' (p.451).

Therefore, public goods should not be subject to competition, as they should be available for all and are generally characterized by underproduction in market conditions, 'because private demand would fall severely short of socially optimal levels' (Tilak, 2008). Tilak (2008) further asserts his preference of government monopolies in providing public goods that are subject to economies of scale, explaining that:

> In fact, public goods that are subject to economies of scale are better provided by the state as a monopolist, than by many, as the economies of scale enjoyed by the single supplier far outweigh any efficiency gains from competition. To prevent the abuse of the monopoly power, and to ensure that any producer surplus is returned to the society, it is only natural that it is produced and supplied by the state. On the other hand, private goods are not available to all and they are subject to principles and laws of markets. (p. 451)

Supposedly, both public and private higher education provide similar functions for individuals and societies, and the classification of goods as public and private does not apply to the discussion of higher education, since the discussion will be about the ownership rather than the functions of higher education. Degefa (2011) argues that:

> This dichotomous classification of goods reflects the dualism of liberal theory. [The] zero sum approach to the distinction between public goods and private goods is inherently flawed when it comes to higher education. Higher education whether in the market or the public domain is basically engaged in similar activities leading to the creation of private goods and public goods. (p. 15)

Marginson (2007) has similarly argued that 'in the real world, the public and private elements are not necessarily zero sum' (p. 310). In publicly owned and financed higher education both public benefits and private benefits are available to both private participants and society at large. Likewise, privately owned and run higher education systems are supposed to offer both private and social benefits. This means that graduates of private higher education would enjoy as much personal benefit as their counterparts in public higher education do. Similarly, the whole society also benefits from the graduates of private higher education. In economic terms, similar externalities are accrued to the society either from graduates of private higher education or public higher education. Hence, the distinction that can be made between public good and private good will be in the ownership rather than in the basic functions of higher education. On the other hand, in the liberal political philosophy the term public is often associated with government/state whereas private refers to any non-state production.

Similarly, this approach treats the categories of public and private as mutually exclusive. Criticizing this classification of higher education as public good and private good, Marginson (2007) argues that 'the private or public education is a policy choice rather than determined by intrinsic nature of the good' (p. 313).

The distinction of goods and services between public and private has also been viewed by some as both 'technical' and 'ideological'. The classification of public goods is not absolute; it depends on government policies, market conditions, level of developments, and political realities (Tilak, 2008). If the distinction is to be regarded as a norm, Tilak (2008), argues that 'The concept of public goods needs to be interpreted, considering all aspects – the intrinsic nature of the given good, the public goods it produces, the social purpose it serves, and the limitations of markets or what is widely known as market failures in the production of such goods' (pp. 451–452). Moe (1987) noted that the problem is that the relationship between the public and the private sectors is often viewed as a 'zero-sum' game, where increased prosperity for one sector must be achieved at the expense of the other (p. 455). On the contrary, he argues that the reality of the modern nation-state is that the prosperity of the two sectors is inextricably linked (Moe, 1987, p. 455).

Arguments in Favour of Privatization

The general introduction of privatization into higher education provision has created a global debate around the idea, there being both proponents and opponents of the phenomenon. One main reason for this controversy is that higher education has traditionally been a public service provided and subsidized by the state in most countries. The shift of education provision to the market and the application of market mechanisms in providing higher education are trends that have caused much controversy, with some advocating the privatization of higher education and others opposing it. This section will incorporate the key arguments of the debate about higher education privatization and cover the main theoretical arguments, both those in favour of privatization and others against it.

Proponents of privatization generally advance a number of advantages in its favour, including reducing government costs, lowering public taxes, improving levels of service, and controlling the growth of government (Pirie, 1985). Although many of these benefits are not universally proven, numerous cases are cited in the literature where a changeover from public to private delivery of services has directly resulted in distinct and tangible advantages (Mengistu & Hail-Mariam, 1989). In regard to higher education, most arguments made in favour of privatization are ideological (Rizvi, 2006; Tilak, 1991). In fact, 'sophisticated arguments based on hard core evidence are rarely made in favour of privatization' (Breneman & Finn, 1978, p. 6). Tilak (1991) further argues that, 'without empirical evidence, all the arguments, however well-formulated and articulated, remain as myths' (p. 230).

Arguments in favour of privatization have been developed in different educational, economic, and political dimensions. However, advocates of privatization rely heavily on economic justifications of the market forces in the higher education sector. They draw heavily on the potential of market forces in enhancing efficiency of resources utilization. Rizvi (2006) has argued that, most reasons governments give in favour of privatization are 'couched in economic terms' and 'many of these [economic] arguments have become commonplace, even if most cannot be substantiated with any hard data' (p. 68).

Efficiency

The most readily visible and most often cited benefit of privatization is that it can provide immediate financial relief for reducing the state's expenses. Traditionally it seemed obvious that the government provide goods and services cheaper or free in comparison to the private sector, because government could operate without making profits. The pendulum, however, is now swinging back to a preference for the private provision and production of services. This is due, in part, to the belief that the public provision of goods and services over the past decades has generally been disappointing. As Samuel Paul of the World Bank observed at the international level, 'in country after country, unbridled state expansion has led to: economic inefficiency ..., ineffectiveness in the provision of goods and services ..., and rapid expansion of the bureaucracy ...' (Paul, 1985, p. M-4). Belfield and Levin (2002) also have pointed out that 'advocates of privatization emphasize efficiency ... and many of the pressures for privatization can be seen as pressures for a more efficient education system' (p. 35).

Privatization as a common remedial policy choice has been associated with a neoliberal ideology that claims the superiority of market principles in bringing efficiency and quality to state provision, since inefficiency and poor quality are often associated with government activities. Savas (2000) generally claims that dissatisfaction and persistent problems with government activities invite privatization as a possible remedy for the problems. In higher education particularly, privatization has become the easiest and fastest solution to deal with the two main categories of problems that concern the sector: 'excess demand' and 'differentiated demand' (Tilak, 1991).

Efficiency is about the challenge of doing more with less. As Savas (2000), maintains: 'The principle reason why privatization leads to increased efficiency is not lower wages and benefits but greater productivity; that is, fewer workers needed to do the same amount of work ...' (p. 287). Being imported from the business world, it focuses on the relationship between the production costs and the outputs of the production process (Degefa, 2011).

Advocates of privatization then claim that the market is inherently efficient in delivering such outputs because of its flexibility, competition, and responsiveness. The costly nature of higher education promotes the significance of efficiency in operating higher education services. Its operations require a great fraction of the educational budget because it employs a highly qualified faculty and demands expensive physical facilities. Thus, cost-effectiveness is considered to be the primary feature of market preference (ahead of flexibility, competition, and responsiveness) that should be implemented in the state higher education institutions, as a shortage of resources has been the main justification for privatization in higher education.

Even with regard to countries that are considered as financially capable, Savas (2000) argues that, 'Rich countries may be able to afford inefficient and ineffective government services, but they, too, are wasting resources that could be put to better use by society' (p. 289).

Nevertheless, while efficiency and cost-effectiveness are commonly attributed to private contractors, Boyer and Drache (1996) argue that it 'is a contention that has repeatedly been shown to be both groundless and perhaps unverifiable' (as cited in Rizvi, 2006, p. 68).

Samuelson (1954), discussing the impossibility of a decentralized spontaneous solution, assumes that if there were no collective consumption goods, the solution for private individuals would be enormously simplified. Because,

> on the one hand perfect competition among productive enterprises would ensure that goods are produced at minimum costs and are sold at proper marginal costs, with all factors receiving their proper marginal productivities; and on the other hand, each individual, in seeking as a competitive buyer to get to the highest level of indifference subject to given prices and tax, would be led as if by an Invisible Hand to the grand solution of the social maximum position. (Samuelson, 1954, p. 388)

Privatization is regarded as the 'invisible hand' that presumably is often the solution for public or government failures in providing more efficiency. The concept of invisible hand is a metaphor popularized in economic thought by Adam Smith (1977) to describe what we nowadays call the market mechanism. The metaphor has been elaborated by economists, particularly with respect to the most important characteristic of the market mechanism – that is, efficiency (Teixeira et al., 2004, p. 2). Considering the financial relief that privatization of higher education supposedly brings to governments, Tilak (1991), drawing on evidence from many different countries, demonstrates the great dependency of private institutions on government subsidies, whether explicitly or implicitly, in the way of student grants and scholarships. He argues that 'most private institutions are not totally private, at least from a financial stand point'. He also asserts that the claim that private institutions are truly private with respect to financing is one of the myths that have been attached to privatization, which lack empirical evidence (p.232). According to him, proponents of privatization rely on these 'myths' when they argue that the market model for higher education is more efficient than the state-supported one due to its greater *flexibility*, *competition*, and *responsiveness*.

Greater *flexibility* in pursuing alternative approaches to institutional goals is a quality advocates attribute to market provision of higher education. They argue that 'the decision making process in public higher education is costly and costs outrun the potential benefits' (Degefa, 2011, p. 25). Savas (2000), also talks about the bureaucratic cost of government. He claims that it is one of the problems that invite privatization and market principles into public services. It can be argued that decision-making in public higher education takes a long time and that any actual action requires the passage of a new law. In contrast to the lengthy process required by public higher education, developments and innovations can take place at a rapid pace in private higher education. Belfield and Levin (2002) comment:

> ... An open market encourages the development of new services and products. A government provider must write new laws and rules when it needs to introduce new or additional services. These laws take time to be approved and implemented. (p. 40)

In addition to flexibility, it has been argued that market forces can improve efficiency by introducing competition among institutions. In other words, privatization introduces competition by applying market principles. Savas (2000) argues that:

> Competition [is the] key ingredient for successful privatization. ... [He adds that] the primary goal of any privatization effort is, or should be, to introduce competition and market forces in the delivery of public services, in the operation of public enterprises, and in the use of public assets. (p. 122)

Accordingly, if higher education institutions operate in the market, competition will be introduced. As a consequence, these institutions will be competing to improve their performance so as to ensure their survival, since the unforgiving market forces will either punish or reward higher education institutions depending on their performance. Some institutions will face the threat of being eventually shut down. In this business/economic perspective, competition will improve production efficiency. In addition, Camilleri (2008) argues that this promoted competition is not restricted to the private sector. It can be promoted in public institutions as well, by getting rid of the 'lump-sum financing system' and implementing an effective incentive/disincentive structure. He suggests the 'hybrid funding system', where competition becomes a tool for the improvement of current conditions rather than one needed to ensure mere survival (see Camilleri, 2008).

In addition to flexibility, the private sector is also supposedly characterized by a quick *responsiveness* to economic needs and individual demands in providing various types of education. According to Tilak (1991), this alleged responsiveness is also a myth that lacks supporting empirical evidence. He argues that: 'The private sector responds to market demands, but only in the short term, while improvement of schools requires long-term planning – not the quick alteration of a commodity to meet changing fashions' (p.233). The unique academic nature of the higher education sector thwarts the market's ability to operate in such a sector. Degefa (2011) argues that efficiency, the strongest argument for privatization, is controversial, since it only focuses on the internal efficiency of the system. It focuses on the performance of a narrowly defined output and ignores education's larger importance and relation to society's needs. It is all about reducing the costs of production not about improving quality. Camilleri (2008), on the other hand, encourages capturing the best insights of market provision and then implementing them in public institutions. He argues that efficiency in private institutions is not due to ownership per se. The secret recipe, according to him, is the autonomy given to universities to govern their practices. He refers to Bruegel's report that was able to prove that 'universities with autonomous management boards perform better on the Shanghai ranking, a potential measure for quality, than universities without autonomous management' (p.9). To avoid confusing autonomous governance structure with self-governance, he pointed to Bruegel's definition, an autonomous university has: legal standing, its own assets, the capacity to contract, the ability to hire staff and set their pay level, the freedom to set budgets, and the freedom to develop policies of every kind. Thus, efficiency can be improved in public universities by implementing a proper autonomous governance structure without selling them off to the private market.

Equity

Proponents of privatization further argue that privatization can also promote equity in higher education provision. Equity in higher education can be understood as the equal distribution of enrolment opportunities for members of a society, irrespective of their socio-economic backgrounds. With regard to privatization and equality of educational opportunities, financial capability and the ability to pay are the most enduring factors. 'Proponents of privatization argue that state-supported higher education is unfair and inequitable when compared to market provision' (Degefa, 2011). Two main justifications have been made for this claim.

First, the increased demand and reduced budgets in state-supported higher education will result in poor quality of education and more exclusion. In this sense, by utilizing private resources, the poor will have a greater chance to access higher education. Increased enrolment is assumed to lead to more inclusion. The second justification appeals to proportional equity and fairness in financing. Privatization proponents argue that the cost- sharing mechanism between the state and participants of public higher education creates an unfair situation by distributing government money to rich and poor alike. They argue that the cost-sharing mechanisms of privatization will promote equality in higher education, particularly for the poor by making the rich pay for their own education. They criticize the idea that the state should pay for all higher education participants equally, as education is funded from general taxes. In this sense, they argue, fairness is not applicable since the poor pay for the education of the rich. They assume that by privatization and the application of tuition fees (cost-sharing), higher education will be more equitable.

The equity effects of privatization are more ambiguous and hypothetical than concrete and observable. This fact is convincingly summarized by a statement made by Levy (1986) on empirical research in Latin American countries. He argued that:

> The effects of privatization on equity are in practice less clear than they appear in much of the economics of education literature ... With their tough admissions standards and elevated costs, high-status private universities are bastions for society's privileged, mostly from elite private secondary schools. Socio-economic stratification is facilitated if not aggravated. (p. 316)

Freedom of choice

Advocates of privatization maintain that freedom of choice, as a means, should be regarded as an educational advantage for students and their families. Levin (1997) has claimed that choice allows them to choose the type of education they want for their children. This democratic vision regards freedom of choice as a human right. Competition will be promoted among higher education institutions as a result of participants being allowed to choose among them. In this sense, advocates of privatization assume that this sort of freedom can only be ascribed to market provision of higher education, since it functions according to 'natural selection theory' (Degefa, 2011). Marginson and Rhoades (2002), for instance, have said that the market is 'a terrain of natural freedom that is prior to the state and that functions according to natural laws' (p. 283).

Savas (2000) argues that this type of competition can be promoted in state-supported higher education institutions without transferring ownership, through vouchers that allow students to choose among institutions. Degefa (2011) argues that the freedom of choice argument is an ideological point of view that lacks educational value. Some think that 'freedom of choice is considered to be a value in itself, independent of other goals for an education system' (Friedman, 1993; as cited in Belfield & Levin 2002, p. 36). Friedman (1962) also argued that this approach (a voucher system) would create a more efficient school system by providing a wide range of choices to meet parental and student concerns and by using vouchers as an incentive for schools to compete for students. Friedman also maintained that educational vouchers would speed the advance of technological progress in education by building incentives for schools to find ways of getting a competitive edge in the marketplace.

The freedom of choice argument also assumes that higher education is a private good within the authority of individuals. More importantly, however, is how those individual choices are appropriated to fulfil the bigger societal goals and objectives allocated for higher education. As Tilak (1991) has argued, 'the stress upon individualism – upon individual preference – at the expense of social responsibility and cohesiveness must be a matter of concern' (p. 235). Making the choice in higher education particularly is costly at both psychological and financial levels. If families or students are subject to commercial advertisements, these advertisements might lead them to buy or undertake higher education courses that might not be in demand in the labour market. Education is a long-term investment, not only in financial terms, but also in terms of time devoted to such experience. Thus, the role of the government should be significant in steering that choice, even though there is a voucher system, in order to realize the general public objectives of higher education. Leading both students and parents to make informed choices is the responsibility of the state (Levin & Driver, 1997). On the same matter, Salter and Tapper (2013) argued that higher education offers a unique blend of two resources essential for economic and social development: knowledge and status. Because of this fact, understanding universities solely in terms of their contribution to the national wealth would be suboptimal. Accordingly, Brown and Carasso (2013) argue the inevitability of the growing exercise of state power in relation to higher education:

> In its [the state] dealings with higher education, the state is obliged to recognise that universities perform a key social function by controlling the individual and occupational mobility necessary for social change. But in addition, the universities' monopoly of the union of high-state knowledge and culture endows them with a third kind of socio-political power: the authority to promote particular sets of values. (p. 12)

Arguments Against Privatization

Many opponents of privatization challenge its purported advantages and raise additional issues that seem to be outside of the purview of the pro-privatization discussion. Opponents of higher education privatization mostly appeal to the academic and social nature of higher education to be handed or given away and controlled by the unstable market forces. They argue that most of the alleged advantages of privatization are 'myths' that mostly lack illustrative evidence (Tilak, 1991). Caillods (2002), on the other hand, notes that privatization occupies a large place in the education policy debate but that the debate is loaded with ideological considerations and that little evidence is available on privatization's effect in addressing educational problems so far (as cited in Belfield & Levin, 2002). Even Savas, who is promoting the idea of privatization, points to the criticality of its implementation. He notes that 'privatization is like dismantling a bomb – it must be done very carefully, for wrong decisions can have nasty consequences (Savas, 2000, p. 284).

A first objection to be made is against privatization to improve quality of provision in higher education institutions. Due to the absence of available data on quality differences between public and private higher education institutions, Tilak (2009b) suggests that one may look at the world university rankings for evidence as to the difference in results between the two types of institution. Despite their familiar weaknesses, world university rankings are based on a variety of qualitative and quantitative indicators of university systems. He noticed:

> In the world university ranking of the Times Higher Education Supplement (2006), it is interesting to note that very few non-US private universities figure. Out of the 138 non-US universities that the THES ranked, only six private universities can be found. ... They include one university in North America (Canada), four in Europe and one in Asia (South Korea); none of them, however, figures in the top 50 universities. (Tilak, 2009, pp. 61–62)

A major argument to be criticized is that privatization will reduce public expenditure on higher education, creating financial relief for the state. McEntee (1987) has argued that the idea that production and provision of services is performed at lower cost by the private sector is a misconception (as cited in Mengistu & Hail-Mariam, 1989). As he sees it, once all the different costs of 'going private' are considered, the bottom line cost may actually be higher with the private sector. This is so, McEntee (1987) insists, because '... private companies exist to make a profit and the necessity of a profit drives up costs, if not immediately, then eventually' (p. 48). McEntee points to the hidden costs of going private such as contract preparation, administration and monitoring of the contractor's performance, the appropriate use of public facilities, the expense of renegotiating the contract, public employee training of contractor work crews, and the contracting-out effect on the morale of the remaining public workers. Furthermore, McEntee contends that once dependency on private sector delivery of services is established, the eventuality of rising costs, much higher than would have been the case under the public sector delivery, is certain.

The most outstanding criticisms against privatization are economic arguments. Market imperfections and private entities' need for profit-generation are two major characteristics that would argue against privatizing higher education. Accordingly, the suitability of market mechanisms has been criticized in the managing and organizing of higher education. Tilak (1991) for example, argues that the market can be criticized in two aspects: its inability to insure an optimum social investment in the higher education that is a quasi-public good; and the lack of information that it provides for its consumers [students]. The market is incapable of ensuring a long-term social investment in higher education. According to economists, the market mechanism in relation to enhancing productive efficiency is based on the premise that the 'utility maximizing behaviour of persons and the profit-maximizing firms will, as through an invisible hand, distribute goods in such a way that no one could be better off without making someone else worse off' (Teixeira et al., 2004, p. 2). This original principle of the market forces raises opponents' concerns regarding its distributional efficiency in providing higher education services, which in turn raises equity concerns.

In addition to rising costs, there are also concerns about the impact of economic recessions on higher education if it has undergone privatization. Camilleri (2008) discusses the potential risks of handing higher education to the private sector and allowing it to be dominated by market forces. His major concern is the impact of economic recessions on privatized higher education. The question he asks is how we can ensure that those economic recessions will never 'strike' our universities if they undergo privatization. Camilleri (2008) explains:

> In the context of the debate on privatisation of Higher Education it means we need to ask why should we privatise and whether the benefits and opportunities acquired by such an exercise justify the risks – which, as we are being reminded of late [through the collapsing economy during the recession], can and do sometimes come true. (p. 2)

Palley (2004), in the same vein, noted the economic failure of neoliberalism,

> The last quarter century has seen an expanding application of neoliberal ideas within both industrialized and developing-country economies. Compared to the 1945-80 era, this recent period has seen substantially slower economic growth and widening income inequality, both within and between countries. (p. 6)

Although privatization might bring something good to services provision, the market is not secure enough to be given absolute autonomy in providing higher education. The role of the state is still necessary. Johnson and Watson (1991) argue that:

> It is essential for a city to maintain its responsibility for provision of public services. A city can contract the production of services to private firms but must maintain responsibility for their provision. The structure and process of a public-private partnership establish these relationships. (p. 88)

Privatization can be beneficial for both the public and private sectors, although success depends more on the structure of the privatization arrangement rather than on the nature of the service or the good. Privatization can be a successful venture for both the public and the private sectors; however, the state must play a significant role for a successful privatization. Johnson and Watson (1991) argue, based on their study of two cases of privatization, that the lessons to be learned are:

> In the provision of a public service it is essential that public and private sector goals be coaligned and that ultimate responsibility for the provision of the service remain

> in the public sector. In the private production of a public service it is essential that feedback (oversight) mechanisms be in place in order to assure public accountability. It is the responsibility of the public sector to assure that these requirements are in place before implementing a privatized project. (p. 88)

Opponents of privatization have also argued that it increases inequality. The introduction of tuition fees and, accordingly, profit generation associated with market principles as a result of privatization can negatively affect social equity. It can be argued that privatization in higher education perpetuates social inequality and social exclusion. Although policies stress the potentiality of market mechanisms in improving efficiency of higher education institutions, they rarely point to its role in addressing distributional equity. Equity in private higher education is linked with the ability to pay. The introduction of tuition fees plays a significant role in escalating social exclusion among citizens. In terms of privatizing the sources of funding, Camilleri (2008) argues that it is almost impossible to create an equitable system with private funding. Tuition fees create an obstacle in this form of privatization, as it increases disproportionally compared to family incomes. He supported his argument with an illustration from a report published in 2008 by the US National Centre for Public Policy and Higher Education that compared the costs of college tuition in the United States over the last 25 years. The data provided revealed that, over the last 25 years, excluding financial aid granted to students, college tuition has risen 435 percent, in comparison to only 145 percent rise in the median family income (Camilleri, 2008). He pointed to the potential negative effect these figures might have on equity in the higher education system. From the same data, he illustrated that there is a huge disparity between the costs of higher education relative to family income, which might lead to an increase in the financial burden on students and their families through student loans. Camilleri (2008) concluded that with private funding it is very difficult to structure a financial model for the higher education system that eliminates inequality and offer equal opportunities for all.

Tilak (1991) also points to the high tuition fees in the United States private higher education system, where the tuition prices are five times the tuition prices at public universities. Accordingly, he argues that private higher education helps in the perpetuation of the social class structure and inhibits access to higher education by lower-income groups, which are negatively affected by the rapid growth of privatization. He adds, that by charging fees private institutions create 'irreparable' socio-economic inequities between the rich and the poor. In another study, Tilak (2009a) argues that the increased reliance of higher education on student fees affects the composition of students in higher education institutions, which is considered as an important feature of higher education that needs to be 'safeguarded'.

Diversity in student composition is regarded as an important feature in higher education, which can be only achieved in private institutions by providing student aid programs such as scholarships and grants. This sort of student aid requires the allocation of a considerable amount from an institution's budget, which is a feature lacking in most private higher education institutions in developing countries since they are driven by the profit-making motive.

Indeed, for-profit higher education that primarily relies on student fees can be regarded as a huge problem for privatization, as this will facilitate inequality. Tilak (1996) contends that private universities, in general, 'are involved in disguised [hidden] profit making operations in almost all countries' (p. 66). This reliance on student fees means that participation in higher education is connected to the student's ability to pay. Altbach (1999c) argued that this will also affect the social class of student enrolment and the type of programs offered. For instance, institutions that are regarded as prestigious will charge students high fees in order to ensure the maintenance of high standards in the institution's educational courses. As a result, students from low socio-economic backgrounds will not be able to afford to pay.

Accordingly, enrolments in those institutions will be exclusive to the rich and students from low socio-economic backgrounds will be forced to enrol in poor quality institutions with less expensive programs, leading to low earnings in the labour market. In the same vein, Degefa (2011) argues that private institutions may exacerbate class or other divisions in society as well. He refers to the geographical bias of for-profit institutions noted by a World Bank study, since they always focus on localities where the purchasing power of citizens is above average. This study noted that private education turns out to be 'socially and economically divisive' (Tilak, 1991, p. 236). Tilak (2009a) also argues that, 'while equitable expansion of higher education may be difficult in the public sector, it is impossible in the private sector' (p. 73). Accordingly, 'knowledge capitalism' will be the natural outcome of these persistent inequalities in privatizing higher education. Tilak (2008) argues that:

> Treating higher education as a marketable [commodity] may severely affect knowledge production and will lead to knowledge capitalism. ... [which] makes higher education beyond the reach of large numbers of youth belonging to middle and lower socioeconomic strata. (p. 461)

Even more, it will keep many economically poor countries away from good quality higher education.

In the world economy **competition** will presumably improve the quality of a product. However, in higher education, opponents argue that this type of market competition will negatively affect academic quality. Higher education privatization is often associated with freedom of choice, created by way of its mechanism, the voucher system. A significant concern here is about the criteria used to make the choice between the institutions and courses available to the students, and between programs offered by the institutions. When higher education undergoes privatization, the choice relies heavily on market considerations. Rizvi (2006) argues that this 'affects curriculum and pedagogy, as well as research in ways more dramatic than is often realized' (pp. 78–79). He explains, 'pedagogic approaches are evaluated in terms of cost-effectiveness, efficiency, and marketability rather than in terms of the academic mission of universities. Research [on the other hand] is judged more in terms of its market-use value than of its academic contribution (Slaughter & Rhoads, 2004)'. Rizvi supported his argument with an illustration of privatization's influence on Australian higher education. Where privatization's freedom of choice is present, the profit-making motive will 'march' the academic decisions.

Privatization too, to a great extent, is motivated by profit-making, which is undoubtedly a feature characterizing most private higher education institutions that negatively affects their academic quality in general. Degefa (2011) argues that 'revenue generation per se is not bad in itself but the temptation to sideline the core goal of educational institutions – creation and dissemination of knowledge – is critical' (p. 74). Bok (2004) also argues that 'money making behaviour puts selfish interests and private pursuits above responsibilities to students and colleagues' (p.42). Tilak (2009) as well claims that the management of the private institution is more concerned about profit-making than providing quality education, a fact which explains the tendency of private higher education institutions towards market driven course delivery in Malaysia (as sited in Tan, 2002). In the Philippines, where private higher education is predominant, 90 percent of courses provided by private institutions are concentrated in vocational areas (Geiger, 1986). Private institutions focus on less expensive programs as well (Tilak, 2009b). Tan (2002) supports this observation as he argues, 'private higher education providers tend to avoid operating in high cost fields and technologies' (p. 58). This attitude, he argues, explains the inability of private higher education to fulfil the long-term manpower needs of a society, due to the mismatch between the type of students produced by private higher education institutions and the type of human resources needed in a country (Gonzalez, 1997). Savas (2000) referred to this obstacle as the 'Cream skimming' effect of privatization, where the private sector is only interested in the most profitable opportunities to provide service and not bidding on the others (p. 312). Kolderie also mentions creaming and describes it as a situation where the service provider provides services to only the easiest or most profitable customers, often neglecting the difficult or unprofitable customers. Thus, competition will lead to creaming problem. In considering possible solutions to the problem of a creaming, Kolderie (1986) concludes that 'a new concept, combining equity in the provision of services with competition in their production, has yet to be articulated politically' (p. 290).

Kolderie (1986), on his side, raises six major issues with privatization, all of which have the potential to create problems: competition, creaming, cost, control, community, and corruption. Although Kolderie was discussing privatization in general, all of the six issues have the potential to create similar problems if privatizing higher education. The first three issues have been mostly covered in the discussion in this section; however, the remaining ones have not yet been raised. The issue of control, according to Kolderie, refers to the general lack or decrease in overall control that a government may have when it privatizes public services. The lack of control by government may directly result in either lack of accountability or responsiveness by the private agency providing the service. Mengistu and Hail-Mariam (1989) argue that Kolderie's presentation of the issue of community is a theoretical and ideological construct rather than a practical or tangible disadvantage of privatization. The issue of community as regards privatization, Kolderie (1986) asserts, is the feeling, by some, that 'going private' loses the public purpose of the privatized program and may actually contribute toward a further erosion of the 'sense of community in contemporary society and may intensify the individualistic ethic of our time' (p. 288).

Lack of information is another critical pitfall associated with the market mechanism. The market is often criticized for its inability to keep the consumer well informed regarding the costs and benefits of higher education. This inability is especially important, since the cost of private higher education is likely to be much higher than that of public education (Tilak, 1991). Adequate information on the quality and price of goods and services is one of the foundations of market conditions. Massy (2004) argues that 'markets cannot discipline price without meaningful information about quality' (p. 31). Universities usually release a large amount of quantitative data on things such as enrolment rate and academic programs offered, just to mention a couple. However, what is missing is 'systematic data on what actually happens to students between matriculation and graduation' (Massy, 2004, p. 29). Degefa (2011) points out that these quantitative measures tend to 'blind' us to the scarcity of information on the quality of higher education provided in the market. He adds, 'if information is missing in relation to what knowledge and skills are acquired by graduates; what graduates can do after graduation, it will lead to market information asymmetry which at best benefits the sellers' (p.31). This issue is even more complicated with regard to higher education, since it is a so-called 'experience good', where consumers can determine the quality only through consumption (Teixeira et al. 2004, p. 6). As cited in Mengistu and Hail- Mariam (1989), 'the former George Washington University Vice President for Medical Affairs stated "social goods, I've come to the conclusion, don't lend themselves to the free market"' (p. 48). Nonetheless, privatization has found increasing acceptance.

Expansion and Diversity

Both growth and expansion in private higher education has been witnessed over the last two to three decades. It has emerged in both developed and developing countries. The growth of private higher education is widespread across large and small countries, across large and small higher education systems, and across education systems both old and new. Although this growth is almost universal, there is both regional and national diversity in the expansion trends and in the types of institutions created. There are varied regional settings – Asia, Latin America, Eastern and Western Europe, Africa, as well as the United States and the cross- border settings (i.e., the exportation of higher education, mostly from the global north to the global south). In addition to the diversity of settings, there is also national and regional diversity in the forms and types of privatization being practised. This diversity is shaped by both the types and the functions of private higher education institutions, which range from wholly for-profit to wholly not-for-profit institutions. Privatization has also involved the privatization of public institutions. The manifested diversity has also resulted from the implementation of privatization in different cultures, traditions, needs, and political systems. Many scholars, such as Tilak and Altbach, have identified the diversity of the phenomenon. Since there is a considerable diversity among private higher education institutions, classifying their forms is extremely complicated. In this section, I will provide a possible conceptual schema of the different typologies presented in the literature.

In practice privatization occurs in various forms and arrangements. Savas (2000, 2005) presents a simple 'classification taxonomy' that encompasses three broad methods that result in privatizing government-run services and functions and government-owned enterprises and assets: *delegation*, *divestment*, and *displacement*. *Delegation*, in which government retains responsibility and oversight but uses the private sector for service delivery, is sometimes called partial privatization because it requires a continuing active involvement by government. It is often conducted by contracts, franchise, grant, voucher, and mandate.

Divestment, in which government relinquishes responsibility, means shedding an enterprise, function, or asset. Like delegation it requires a direct, positive act by government, but unlike delegation it is generally a one-time

Tab. 1 Three forms of privatization and their components.

Form	Components
Delegation	Contract Public-private competition Franchise Public-private partnership Grant, loan, favoured tax status, and so on Voucher Mandate
Divestment	Sale Free transfer Liquidation
Displacement	Default Withdrawal (load shedding) Voluntary action (voluntarism) Deregulation

(Source: Savas, 2000, p. 127)

affair, often conducted by sale, free transfer, and liquidation. *Displacement* is a form of privatization in which the private sector grows and displaces a government activity. In contrast to the first two methods, which require positive acts by government, displacement is a more passive or indirect process that leads to government being displaced more or less gradually by the private sector-a withering away of the state, so to speak, as markets develop to satisfy people's needs. It is also called privatization by attrition, or pejoratively, privatization by stealth. It either occurs *by default*, *by withdrawal*, or *by deregulation*. Each of these forms incorporates several specific approaches, which are presented in the table below (see Tab. 1).

More specific to higher education are the many classifications and categorizations found in the higher education literature. Bray (2002), for example, provides three forms that can be undertaken in the privatization of education. These forms are: transferring ownership of public institutions; shifting sectoral balance without redesigning existing institutions; and increasing government funding and support for private institutions. Rizvi (2006) adds to these forms a fourth one – contracting out functions and services – as he believes that 'contracting out and enterprise sales may perhaps be the most influential modalities of privatization in the contemporary public sector' (p. 68).

Levy (2010), on the other hand, proposes a typology of private higher education that is largely based on roles and motives, modified however by concomitant facts about ownership and management. His categories are: elite and semi-elite; religious and cultural; non-elite and demand-absorbing; and some cross-cutting consideration of for-profit and PPP (public- private partnership) forms as well. He noted that it is possible for all categories of higher education to function within countries, and that there is no perfect

Tab. 2 Private/total higher educational enrolment: a few examples.

	0-10%	>10<35%	>35<60%	>35<60%
Developing countries	Cuba, South Africa	Egypt, Kenya	India, Malaysia	Brazil, Indonesia
Developed countries	Germany, New Zealand	Hungary, United States	(none)	Japan, Republic of Korea

(Source: A New Dynamic: Private Sector Education, UNESCO, 2009, p. 8)

typology for private higher education where all institutions fit neatly into one classification system, reinforcing the reality of the sector's heterogeneity. In fact, elsewhere, Levy (2008), distinguishes a US model and classifies the private sector as divided between the US model and the global (non-US) model. Geiger's (1986) typology also refers to the US difference, as he classifies private higher education in Japan and the Philippines as a mass private model, while the United States model of higher education is a 'prototype' of its own. Geiger's (1987) typology bases itself on the size: massive private sector, parallel private sector, peripheral private sector, and finally a special case because it does not fit any other category 'the American private sector' (as cited in Tan, 2002).

There has been remarkable growth in privatization during the last two to three decades in the various countries of the world. The number of private colleges and universities has increased, and enrolments in private institutions have increased at a much faster rate than enrolments in public institutions. In many countries, enrolments in private institutions have increased by several times that of public institutions. For example, in Colombia enrolment in private institutions increased by 1.7 times the rate of increase in enrolment at public institutions while the rate of private enrolment at private institutions in Peru jumped 2.03 times from the mid-1960s to the mid-1970s (Brodersohn, 1978, p. 176). In a good number of countries, over half of the enrolments are in private institutions and over half of all educational institutions are private (Tilak, 1991, p.227). In general, most of the literature shows a predominance of private higher education that is greater in developing countries than in developed ones. In a global typology (UNESCO, 2009), for example, Levy found no clearly developed countries in the 35 to 60 percent private enrolment range and most are still fewer than 10 percent. In contrast, few developing countries remain under 10 percent and many are over 60 percent.

Asia, for example, contains the largest concentration of countries with the proportionally largest private sectors. Asia's share of private higher education is 36 percent (Levy, 2010). Indonesia, Japan, the Philippines, and the Republic of Korea are over 70 percent private (UNESCO, 2009, p.9).

Malaysia is around 50 percent with a noticeable growth beginning in the 1990s (Tan, 2002). Meanwhile, India's 30 percent (Gupta, Levy, & Powar 2008) gives it the second highest private headcount in the world – right behind the United States (as cited in UNESCO, 2009). In much of Southeast Asia, the share is below 15 percent (Cambodia, China, Thailand, and Viet Nam) (UNESCO, 2009). However, in these countries participation in higher education as a percentage of the total population is generally much lower than in East Asia (UNESCO, 2009).

Latin America shares the private higher education summit with Asia, whether we look at private shares or private absolute enrolment. Latin America has a longer widespread history than Asia of dual-sector development. By the late 1970s, Latin America was already approaching 34 percent private (Levy, 1986) and current data indicates that it is more like 49 percent today (Levy, 2010). Countries such as Brazil, Chile, Costa Rica, El Salvador, and Peru have private shares over 50 percent (UNESCO, 2009).

In the United States, while many of the most famous American universities are private, more than 80 percent of the students in the United States attend public institutions (Altbach, 1999b). Central and Eastern Europe, on the other hand, have witnessed a dramatic expansion in private higher education (Slantcheva & Levy, 2007). In Eastern Europe, private higher education was basically non-existent under Communism. The collapse of Communism generally unleashed a demand for higher education. A UNESCO report (2009) noted that the growth from zero to substantial in the first half of the 1990s is the most dramatically concentrated spurt ever seen in any region. Between 1990 and 1997 the Czech Republic, Hungary, Poland, and Romania, for example, saw average annual growth rates of nearly 60 percent each year (Giesecke H., 1999; as cited in UNESCO, 2009). The UNESCO report also noted that in these countries, total private sector enrolments have expanded from less than 12,000 students in 1990 to more than 320,000 in 1997. Yet, only a few countries have ever crossed the 30 percent private higher education level (Estonia, Georgia, Latvia, and Poland, with Estonia being close). A few former communist countries have even seen a decline in private higher education shares (Pachuashvili, 2008), while others have never become more than a few percent private (Lithuania and Slovakia) (UNESCO, 2009, p. 11).

In Western Europe, on the other hand, privatization in higher education has mostly been about changes in the finance and management of public institutions. Thus, for example, 'entrepreneurial universities' are basically public universities undertaking major reforms (Clark, 1998). Many of the private higher education sectors have long been largely peripheral (Geiger, 1986). Belgium and especially the Netherlands have had large private higher education shares. However, their private higher education institutions operate under a strong 'publicness' in rules and finance. So much so that they are sometimes reported as only minimally private (Holzhacker, D., Chornoivan, O., Yazilitas, D., Dayan-Ochir, K., & Institute for Higher Education Policy, 2009). The United Kingdom as well fits into the category of small private sectors (UNESCO, 2009) and what has been occurring there is a marketization of the UK public higher education (Brown & Carasso, 2013).

Sub-Saharan Africa has been late to modern private higher education, but the growth is notable (Varghese, 2006). Breakthroughs came in the 1980s and 1990s and then continued into the new century. Nevertheless, African private enrolment shares remain comparatively small. Kenya, having ascended to one-fifth private, shows slippage as public universities take in 'private', paying students (Jamshidi et al., 2012; Otieno, 2004). A recent UNESCO report (2009) noted that, overall, the African data on private higher education are less reliable, scarcer, and more scattered than in other regions. More certain is the fact that there are often more private institutions than public institutions. Most of the private institutions remain peripheral, although there are notable exceptions in Kenya (Oanda, Chege & Wesonga, 2008). With continued low enrolment rates in public institutions and with proportionally high growth rates in demand for education, the future of African higher education may accelerate its present privatizing tendencies (UNESCO, 2009, pp. 12–13).

In the Arab Middle East, the emergence of private higher education is a recent phenomenon that was mostly initiated in the 1990s – largely by the government. Levy (2009) reported that:

> The Arab Middle East stands out as the region in which [private higher education] emergence is mostly planned and promoted by government, often in partnership with European and United States universities as well as with occasional World Bank support. Also notable is that the emergence has become widespread so rapidly, covering the great majority of countries (Bahrain, Iraq, and Saudi Arabia, to name but a few). (p. 14)

Although the expansion of the private sector in those countries is noticeable, it is difficult to differentiate between public and private sectors, as the private sector is highly subsidized by government. And the issue of data reliability and scarcity is experienced here as well, as has been noted in the Arab Human Development report (UNDP, 2003).

The Twenty-Fourth Report of the Investment Climate in Arab Countries (2008) has, for the first time, devoted a section on the development of higher education, acknowledging the emerging importance of education for the Arab World. The report reveals the increase in the number of universities in Arab countries from 233 in 2003 to 385 in 2008, including 115 private universities (about 4.4 times the figure for 1993) (as cited in Sabry, 2009). Sabry (2009) also noted that:

Tab. 3 Geographical shares of private/total higher education enrolment (although there is significant variation inside most regions).

High	Medium	Low
East Asia	United States	Western Europe
Latin America	Central/Eastern Europe	Commonwealth countries
	Anglophone Africa	Francophone Africa
		Arab countries

(Source: UNESCO, 2009, p. 14)

> Although the number of private universities has grown to equal that of the public universities [as reported in 24th Report of the Investment Climate in Arab Countries 2008], this does not reflect their capacity; most of the private universities have smaller capacities. However, the report infers that if we add the enrollment in the successful private higher education institutions, it is likely that the percentage of students enrolled in private higher education has approached its counterpart in public universities. (p. 11)

A geographical classification of the shares of the private/total higher education enrolment between high, medium and low, acknowledges significant regional variations (see Tab. 3, UNESCO, 2009, p. 14).

Therefore, the growth and the expansion of the private higher education sectors are illustrated across the world's regions, with higher rates in developing countries in contrast to the developed world. Levy in a global typology of the private higher education concludes that:

> Yet so strong is the private higher education proportional growth in so many countries, even as public growth often remains strong in absolute numbers, that perhaps 30 percent of global higher education enrolment is now private (Guruz, 2008). Moreover, no region stands apart from private higher education growth. A quarter century ago, many countries had no private higher education; today very few (Bhutan, Cuba, the Democratic People's Republic of Korea; Greece shows that de facto private higher education is possible even without state recognition). No large country is without private higher education. Many countries have the majority of their higher education enrolments in the private sector. (UNESCO, 2009, p. 8)

Globalization of the Ideology of Privatization

As has been argued above, the concept of privatization is not new to economics. However, the introduction of privatization as a broad policy choice for higher education systems worldwide is a recent phenomenon. Two to three decades ago higher education was mostly provided by the government as a public service, which was the norm back then. However, the international trend that shifted the balance towards the market provision of former government services included higher education as well as other sectors of the state.

Nowadays many governments promote privatization policies for their higher education systems. However, the degree of dominance achieved by the private sector is varied. Scholars have examined the phenomenon both in the context of specific countries and regions and also in the worldwide context in an attempt to track the expansion of the private higher education. Levy (2010), Tilak (1991), Altbach (1991, 1999b, 1999c), and Altbach and Levy (2005) are among the scholars who provide an overarching global investigation to the growing phenomenon. For example, Altbach and Levy (2005) have written a book, *Private higher education: A global revolution*, that puts a global perspective on higher education, including essays that investigate the revolution of the private higher education in all continents: Africa, Asia, Europe, Latin America, Middle East, and the United States. However, the investigation of privatization in both the Middle East and the United States lacks the required depth.

Privatization has assumed greater significance in policy strategy for the development of education in recent times, mostly, but not wholly, due to the stagnating – and in some countries declining – public budgets for education on the one hand and, on the other, the increasing social demand for higher education, as manifested by slogans such as 'higher education for all' (Roderick & Stephens, 2011). Many governments have promoted privatization policies for their higher education sector, following different strategies and mechanisms. These governments are motivated by different reasons in their pursuit of privatization. However, the most striking reasons are the unprecedented demand for access to higher education and the inability or unwillingness of governments to provide the necessary support to provide higher education publicly (Tilak, 1991).

The nature of the impact of privatization in addressing higher education crises is uncertain and highly contested. Nevertheless, privatization as an ideology has recently made numerous appearances in higher education sectors. Caillods (2002) noted that privatization has occupied a large place in the education policy debate, but that the debate is loaded with ideological considerations and that little evidence is available on its impact in addressing educational problems so far (as cited in Belfield, & Levin, 2002). In addressing higher education crises, particularly in developing countries, privatization as a political ideology has offered two different but interrelated solutions. The first is the privatization of public institutions by applying market principles to either their funding (corporatization) or educational provision, or both. The second is the promotion of the non-state higher education sector, as it involves not-for-profit and for-profit providers of higher education (Belfield & Levin, 2002).

Despite all of the controversy about the concept of privatization in higher education, it is still expanding rapidly around the world. It has been increasingly implemented in almost all regions, in developing countries particularly. In spite of all the significant arguments raised against the privatization of higher education and the implementation of market principles as discussed above, the education sector has been significantly invaded by the market forces promoted by the neoliberal policies. Since higher education has traditionally been regarded as a public good, 'why [is] the conventional wisdom changing?'(Tilak, 2008). Many scholars have attempted to investigate the phenomenon at both global and national levels, aiming to provide an explanation of the rapid trends in the privatization of higher education and the increasing predominance of the private sector around the world. This section explores the factors that contribute to the spread of the privatization ideology among the world's countries.

Many scholars have investigated the phenomenon of the growth of privatization in higher education (e.g., Altbach, 1999b; Donn & Al Manthri, 2010; Tilak, 1991; Levy, 2010), searching for the main factors that influence privatization policies in higher education globally. Most studies point to the excess public demand for higher education along with declining government expenditure in the sector as essential contributing factors to the rapid expansion. Tilak (2008) noticed that the cut-off in public budgets is not restricted to poor governments, as many developed countries are involved as well in the cutting back in their expenditure on higher education. He figured that:

> ... the decline is not confined to the developing countries, though a larger number of developing countries experienced the decline than the number of high-income countries; there has been a very significant fall even in advanced countries such as the United Kingdom, Australia and New Zealand, and in the group of the high-income countries as a whole. (Tilak, 2008, p. 456)

This involvement of both rich and poor governments in pursuing privatization policies undermines the economic arguments that attributed its popularity to financial restrictions. Other economic arguments attributed the hegemonic expansion of private higher education to the changing perception of the nature of higher education as a good. While traditionally treated as a public good, due to neoliberalism it has been converted into a private good on the ground that its participants gain individual benefits. Although these arguments seem convincing at first glance, Tilak (2008) argues that they are 'too naïve' to explain the rapid expansion and the increasing spread of the privatization phenomenon. Accordingly, he refers to the introduction of the international organizations such as the World Trade Organisation (WTO) and the General Agreement on Trade and services (GATS) as providing a possible explanation. He argues that these organizations have played a significant role in changing the conventional wisdom of higher education. He wrote:

> Even in the earlier decades, while there were some who questioned the concept of higher education as a public good, the heralding of the neo-liberal and globalization policies, and later the advent of international trade in educational services accentuated such thinking. Public good and similar principles are viewed as too naive to be relevant in the rapidly changing, increasingly privatised and liberalised modern context. The conventional wisdom is becoming rapidly invaded by the strong, powerful forces of national and international mercantilists, represented in the World Trade Organization (WTO) and the General Agreement on Trade and Services (GATS), the institutions that were set up outside the United Nations system. Higher education is seen primarily as a private good, as a tradable commodity that can be subjected to the vagaries of national and international markets. (Tilak, 2008, p. 450)

In another study focused on the Asian region, Tilak (2009b) also noted that 'weak government mechanisms and the absence of clear public policies' are other factors that have contributed to the rapid growth (p. 72).

More convincing, however, is Rizvi's (2006) explanation of the processes by which the privatization of higher education became dominant globally. He argues:

> If ...we take political agency seriously, then the global acceptance of the ideology of privatization needs to be understood in terms of a set of historically specific processes articulated through various power configurations. These processes are inherently political and work in various locally contingent and historically specific ways. (p. 72)

He suggested four sets of these processes, the four 'global drivers' of privatization that could be summarized as follows. The first set of processes, Rizvi suggests, is occurring as a result of developments in transportation, information, and communication technologies that facilitate people's international mobility. These developments create a fresh environment for scholars and politicians in which the global circulation of ideas and policies has been enabled. This circulation between countries, he argues, has asymmetrical power configurations, as the superiority is mostly associated with the ideas that spring from the West, even if those ideas are ostensibly about 'self-governance' (p.73). Thus, a new 'policy space' has emerged, often sponsored by inter-governmental organization such as the OECD and UNESCO, with a hidden commitment to neoliberal policies.

The second set of processes that explain the acceptance of privatization ideology relates to 'international conventions embodying consensus between parties' (Rizvi, 2006, p.75). In those conventions, Rizvi argues, there is often a great deal of pressure on countries to conform to particular ideologies, even though their participation is assumed to be voluntary, as 'many of these conventions involve formal agreements and commitments that have exposed the domestic policy practices of nation-states to external scrutiny, thus reducing their autonomy' (Rizvi, 2006, p. 75). As a result, international conventions play a significant role in imposing ideologies among nations.

The third set of processes that drives privatization relates to the 'coercive strategies' that underlie financial settlements. It can be perceived through two types of practices. The first is practices such as those represented by Structural Adjustment programs (SAP). These strategies developed as a 'golden opportunity' of practising power by international organizations such as the World Bank and the International Monetary Fund (IMF) on those countries that need to reschedule payments on their debts, due to their financial disability. In their role as lending agencies, the need for rescheduling the debts allows them to impose their ideologies on the debtor countries. The second set of coercive practices is carried out by the Transnational Cooperation (TNCs) that offer investment opportunities and similar adjustments. These negotiations may involve educational reforms and, as has been noted by Rizvi (2006), 'some of this bargaining involves the demand by TNCs that education be restructured along market lines, with policies conducive to the creation of [a] human resource pool to better meet their labour needs' (p. 76).

Finally, the fourth set of processes that advance privatization involves cooperation among nations in the form of a consensus between countries established to meet similar objectives. Rizvi (2006) argues that these consensuses often mask a number of assumptions. As an example he provides the Bologna Declaration. He argues that:

> Despite its insistence on the principles of diversity and national autonomy, it nonetheless assumes the importance of Europe-wide commitment to neoliberal reforms in higher education, weakening national control and unlinking education from powerful political sentiments in the field of national culture, language, and social emancipation. But more importantly, the Bologna process barely hides its more fundamental economic rationale: its preference for the marketization of higher education. While it does not completely support liberalization and deregulation of higher education, its main objectives are informed by a market logic – the need for the European system to become a more effective and efficient player in the highly competitive global market in higher education. The course of the Bologna process is thus heavily influenced by dominant neoliberal readings of globalization, issues of trade in higher education, and more specifically the World Trade Organization's General Agreement on Trade in services (GATS) negotiations (Roberston & Dale 2004). (p. 77)

Rizvi has argued, though, that his suggested set of processes does not completely determine governments' behaviour. Thus, he stresses the importance of local specificities in shaping imported international ideologies and policies, as he argues that:

> ... these global processes represent pressures that governments have to negotiate, against their own particular histories and political conditions. Each of these processes thus involves a different pattern of political activity and power play and has varied consequences for particular educational systems as they attempt to interpret, negotiate, and translate into practice external global pressures driving the ideology of privatization in higher education. (p. 78)

He emphasizes,

> ... that the circulation of educational ideologies is not a function of globalization per se but involves actual historical processes, human agents, organizations, and governments-with capacity to accept, resist, or reject them. Acceptance of ideas and ideologies is thus a consequence of political processes located within particular configurations of power and hegemonic relations. (p. 74)

In this sense, he is referring to the role of the local historical, cultural, and political atmospheres in shaping the emerged ideologies and policies. Ball (2004), on the other hand, argues that it is not the privatization process itself that should be the focus of policies. Rather, privatization is but one aspect of a larger 'revolution' that is occurring in all educational processes, and not only because of the private sector contribution. In Ball's view, educational processes are being transformed as a result of a larger transformation in social relations. Based on traditional Marxist concepts, he attempts to describe how education has become a commodity that has economic and social exchange-values.

The hegemony of the privatization policies in higher education, then, has been mostly attributed in the literature to the increased demand, financial limitations, poor public provision, weak government strategies, the absence of clear public policies, and more significantly, the global emergence of neo-liberal thinking circulated through Rizvi's suggested sets of process that spread privatization ideology globally – namely, globalization, international conventions, and coercive strategies practised by international agencies as lenders and the TNCs as investors. These mechanisms, to some extent, offer a logical clarification of the phenomenon under the study. In short and according to Tilak (2008), 'Commitment to higher education' has given way to 'commitment of higher education' as envisioned by the WTO under GATS (p. 462).

Conclusion

In conclusion, this chapter has provided a framework and conceptualization for understanding privatization and its introduction to higher education across countries worldwide. It has tracked the intellectual foundations of the concept and has attempted to provide an overarching conceptualization of the phenomenon, discussing its theories, forms, and global practices. It has summarized the global debate surrounding the introduction of privatization into higher education systems and has evaluated its advantages and disadvantages.

It can be concluded that the trend towards the market in higher education provision is, to a great extent, driven by financial factors or pressures. Even expansion of the demand for higher education that has happened in different regions leads to privatization mainly because of the increased financial pressure on governments. However, this understanding of the causes of privatization leads to a paradox in the case of Kuwait. Kuwait is a country that is regarded as one of the richest countries in the world, with a small population that barely exceeds one million citizens. Despite this wealth and resulting absence of financial pressure, privatization has nonetheless found its way to its higher education system. Given these facts, what are the causes of privatization of higher education in Kuwait? Certainly financial pressure does not seem like a plausible answer. And if the noted role of international agencies on the promotion of privatization policies is mostly related to financial influence, then what influence might that have on the introduction of privatization in Kuwait?

Having reviewed the literature of privatization generally and its introduction to higher education in particular, it is appropriate to shift the focus to the context of this study. We must now relate all these global processes of higher education to our context of study – Kuwait, as they mostly 'represent pressures that governments have to negotiate, against their own particular histories and political conditions' (Rizvi, 2006). In the following chapter, I will present Kuwait as a context of the study, focusing on higher education. Since the study concerns the processes of policy production, it will also be significant to discuss the state's formation and its political system. Thus, the focus of the following chapter will be mostly on the historical formation of the modern state of Kuwait as, I will argue, it plays a great role in framing the current policy processes in the country.

Chapter Three: Policy Processes in Kuwait

In the previous chapter, I reviewed recent literature on privatization generally, with a particular focus on its application in higher education. In this chapter, I move to the context of this study – the State of Kuwait. Since this book is investigating the processes of the policy production of higher education privatization in Kuwait, this chapter not only seeks to provide an overview of the higher education system in the state of Kuwait, but also focuses in particular on the processes by which policy is made regarding that system. Beginning with the assumption that policy-making processes in Kuwait may not follow the same systems and procedures that are commonly known in the West, this chapter explores the dynamics of more than just Kuwaiti higher education and its governance, but also seeks to locate them within the state of Kuwait's overall policy processes. Understanding how higher education policies are produced requires a broader understanding of how policy is created in Kuwait in general.

It is important to note, to begin with, that higher education privatization policy is a point in a continuum of public policy reforms in Kuwait, as indeed they are elsewhere. To understand the development of higher education privatization policy in Kuwait, thus, it is of great significance to understand and conceptualize policy practices in the country, investigating historical features that have played a great role in shaping the State's current political representation. In his work 'The Subject and Power' Foucault points to the significance of the historical awareness of present circumstances before forming any conceptualization of the object at the present. He argues that:

> ... the conceptualization should not be founded on a theory of the object-the conceptualized object is not the single criterion of a good conceptualization. We have to know the historical conditions that motivate our conceptualization. We need a historical awareness of our present circumstance. [In addition to] the type of reality with which we are dealing. (Faubion, 2000, p. 327)

Though Foucault's focus is power in relation to the formation of the subject, he has broadly influenced the structure of my analysis in a way that has shifted me back to history, causing me to be historically aware of the circumstances that created the present reality of the public policy processes generally in the State of Kuwait, particularly higher education privatization policies. Rizvi and Lingard (2010) also call for a '*historical orientation* to [educational] policy analysis' in globalized contexts (p. 69). They have argued that '... a critical approach to policy analysis needs to determine how the problem is historically constituted' (p. 69).

Accordingly, this chapter provides an overview of historical factors that have shaped the political orientation of the modern State of Kuwait. It also offers a conceptualization of both 'power relations' and the dynamics of power in both its national and foreign policies. In addition, it gives an illustration of the nature of the dynamics of Kuwaiti governance over time, more specifically before and after the oil exploration. It also provides a historical analysis of the impact this economic shift had on the country's socio-economic and political formations, identifying the most significant determining factors that constitute the roots of the present day political powers and consequently the processes of public policy production. This chapter also describes the relationships between the state and the different social groups of Kuwaiti society and on what basis they have been formulated. The conceptualization of these relations will provide a basis for understanding the nature of the local political practices in the State of Kuwait. This understanding is important, as there are prevailing traditional forms of identity, which are deeply rooted in the political system due to the underdevelopment of the state's democratic institutions since its early formative years. It is worth mentioning here that the main purpose of this chapter is mostly to set the foundation for the forthcoming policy analysis but the entire political, socio-economic and historical evolution of the modern state of Kuwait is more complex and far beyond the scope of this book. Given also the current globalized context of education policy formation, for the purpose of analysis the chapter will discuss the role of the oil wealth on the Kuwait global position – what Marginson (2008) refers to as its 'global agency' – by identifying the nature of most of its international relations that might have potentially influenced its policy processes. It will conclude with providing a conceptualization of higher education in Kuwait, its structure and governance.

Kuwait

The modern Kuwait in brief is a small constitutional emirate located in the Middle East region, the Asian division, situated in the north-east part of the Arabian Peninsula. It is one of the Arab Gulf States and a member of the Gulf Cooperation Council (GCC), a regional organization that is constituted by the United Arab Emirates, Bahrain, Qatar, Oman, Saudi Arabia and Kuwait. It covers a geographical area of 17,820 square kilometres (CIA, 2018), and has a population of about 4,575,620 in 2014 (PACI, 2018). Kuwait has an extremely unusual demographic makeup, as citizens constitute only one third of the population (1,382,825 total Kuwaitis). The remaining population consists of 3,192,795 non-Kuwaitis (expatriates, constituting almost 70 percent of the total population), as is the case in most Arab Gulf States (PACI, 2018). Donn and Al Manthri (2010) attribute this imbalance in ratio of expatriates to nationals to the young population of the nationals and the flexible labour policies in the state concerning expatriate employment. Like other Arab Gulf States, Kuwait is an oil-exporting country, having an estimated 10 percent of total world reserves. As a result, it has budget surpluses and high levels of personal and state savings (Donn & Al Manthri, 2010, p. 47). On the economic level, it is mainly an oil-exporting country with huge international investments; on the other hand, almost all of the society's needs are imported from abroad, except for some small developed industries that have a negligible exporting activity.

The modern State of Kuwait is a constitutional semi-monarchy with a parliamentary system of government. The Amir is the head of the State. He is chosen from the ruling Al Sabah family and must be confirmed by the National Assembly. This parliament, known locally as the *Majlis Al-Umma*, has a four-year political cycle and is composed of fifty members elected by the public. The hierarchy of authority with regard to decision-making in the State is as follows: the Amir, the Cabinet chaired by the Prime minister (representing the Government), and, finally, the National Assembly (the Parliament or *Majlis Al-Umma*, that is composed of 50 elected members, representing the public). Any law, in order to be implemented, must pass all of these three political organizing bodies.

The above briefly describes the modern state of Kuwait and its political system. Yet the State has undergone several transitional phases to become the country it is today. It is indisputable that the oil discovery, in the early 1930s, played a crucial role in the establishment of the modern State of Kuwait. Even though the oil wealth has been central to the development of the modern state, Kuwait has a history that dates back to the eighteenth century, many decades prior to both its independence in 1961 and the first commercial oil shipment in the late 1940s that so shaped the current features of the country's political system. The exact date of the founding of Kuwait is not an established historical fact due to the lack of any reliable historical sources on the matter. In history, the credibility of information presented or claimed by historians is an issue, especially when it comes to the time and place under investigation. In the early years of the formation of the state of Kuwait, there were no records that one can rely on. Most historians based their accounts of this period on local oral narratives, which indicate that the founding of Kuwait was in the late seventeenth and early eighteenth centuries. Moreover, the dates mentioned are sometimes contradictory and controversial. The Kuwaiti historian, Al-Rashid (1995), believes that Kuwait was founded toward the end of the seventeenth century without specifying a date. On the other hand, Sheikh Yusuf al Qana'i (1987) states that Kuwait was settled in 1688. Others, such as the Bahraini historian al Nabhani and the Iraqi historian Ibn Sanad, specify other dates.

The Bahraini claims it was settled in 1611 while the Iraqi reports that it was in 1800 (Abu-Hakima, 1965). Therefore, no final date has yet been agreed upon by all historians, as noted by Al-Rashid (1995). Although there is controversy about the history of Kuwait, for the purposes of applying historical factors to this research, I argue that local narratives to some extent are a sufficient source of information for two reasons. The first is the relatively small geographical space of the area, which leads to the second reason, the strong connections and the social relations that bind most inhabitants of the area, who originally migrated to Kuwait from the surrounding region.

The formation and development of the state of Kuwait and the migration of its people – their origins and the time of their settlement in the area – to a great extent produced the socio- economic and political structures present in the State now. The following will explain the emergence of the different social groups in the State of Kuwait and the associated influences of this development on the country's policy processes.

According to Qal'aji (1970), the development of Kuwait from the second half of the eighteenth century until its independence from the British protectorate in 1961 has been determined by three main factors. These are: the settlement of the area by the *'Utub*, a group of families that are known to be derived from the *'Aniza in Najd* in central Saudi Arabia; the emergence of the merchant community as the most influential economic social group; and the extension of the British protectorate over the area. These factors to a great extent have shaped both the political representation and the socio-economic patterns of the modern State of Kuwait. Ghabra (2011) in his book *Kuwait: a study of the dynamics of state and society* describes the social life of the old Kuwait City prior to the oil discovery as being a simple existence lived in a harsh desert environment and constituted by people who had migrated from different origins – the Arabian Peninsula, Iraq, and Persia. The Kuwaitis were clustered in four main neighbourhoods: *Wasat*, *Qeblah*, *Shargh*, and *Al Murghab*, based mainly on their professions and backgrounds, in integration and harmony (Ghabra, 2011). The city was surrounded by a mud wall that had four main gates that separated the city from the desert for protection from the threats of the desert, mainly the Bedouin, a group of tribes that mostly lived in the desert surrounding the city. Despite the threat they posed to the city-dwellers of Kuwait, the Bedouin were known for their loyalty to Kuwait's rulers. The marginal status and lack of influence of the Bedouin has had significant consequences on the political and the socio-economic dynamics of the state of Kuwait, as has been stressed by many scholars (Ghabra, 2011, 1997; Al-Rashid, 1995; & Al hajri, 2004). Al hajri (2004) describes their existence as follows:

> Prior to the introduction of the representative system in Kuwait, the badu [Bedouin] had limited political influence and were marginal to the political system, although their loyalty and service has been extremely valuable to Al Sabah [the ruling family]. The reasons for that, as delineated by Baz, relate to their lack of a social base or economic power and their migratory mode of living, in addition to being far from urban centres. As a group they are more dependent on the ruling family than urban Kuwaitis, since they were less educated and occupied low working positions and earn low salaries, have settled more recently and their naturalization [providing them the citizenship], on a large scale, only began in the sixties. (p. 143)

As we have seen, the Bedouin were separated from the urban city-dwellers physically by the mud wall that surrounded the city for protection from the desert's threats. This separation, by the wall, of the Bedouin and the *hadhar* (city-dwellers) has had a great influence on both the current socio-economic divisions of the State and, consequently, its policy processes. Several actions have been undertaken by the rulers concerning the political status and representation of the Bedouin. The most important of these actions is the mass naturalization of the Bedouin, a process that provided them with Kuwaiti citizenship and that only started in the 1960s (between 1965 and 1970) (Ghabra, 1997). Later in this chapter, I will further discuss this naturalization of the Bedouin and the corresponding political challenges caused by it, especially as the Bedouin have been utilized by the rulers of Kuwait as a counter-force to the merchants. The initial measure taken by the government on this account not only concerned their naturalization, but also gave them the right to vote in the 1960s and 1970s, by which their documents had to cover up the fact that they were new immigrants in order to change the electoral balance of power to the disadvantage of the urban commercial elite, the merchants (Ghabra, 1997).

The building of a mud wall around the old town of Kuwait under the authority of Shaikh Sabah in the 1760s, in order to protect it from the outside attacks (Shuhaiber, 1981, p. 8), became a watershed in the debate over citizenship by formalizing the settlers/Bedouin division and producing a prototype for the currently existing socio-economic divisions. Those outside the wall were primarily the Bedouin of the area, who have traditionally been seen by those who lived within the boundary of the wall as being outsiders, and not entitled to full Kuwaiti citizenship. Adding to this problem is the attribution of the name of the original town of Kuwait to the state of Kuwait. This attribution increases the feeling of the alienation among the Bedouin, since they are unable to identify with that name. At the same time, giving the name of the city of Kuwait to the entire country aggravates the possessiveness of the urban Kuwaitis towards what they consider their own city/nation and justifies their active exclusion of the Bedouin. The fact that the Al Sabah have used the Bedouin as a counter- force to the merchant community who emerged from the *'Utub*, who were the first settlers of the area, further fuelled the antagonism of urban Kuwaitis towards the idea of the Bedouin being incorporated into the political system of Kuwait and treated as full-fledged Kuwaitis – their mass naturalization. Their extreme loyalty has been criticized by the other social groups as distorting the process of policy-making and preventing it from representing the real public interests of the modern State of Kuwait (Ghabra, 2011).

Forming a conceptualization and understanding of these social divisions is crucial to understanding the structure of the Kuwaiti political system and its political dynamics. These prevailing traditional forms of identity are still deeply rooted in the political system due to the underdevelopment of the State's democratic institutions in its early formation.

Early Governance

Until the 1950s, the Merchant community of Kuwait was dominated by about thirty or so of the *'Utub* families and their descendants (Crystal, 1990). These merchants are a homogenous group. They are urban, Sunni (by religious identification), and consider themselves the *Assil*, the original settlers of Kuwait (Crystal, 1990, p. 37). They intermarry among themselves and sometimes intermarry with the ruling Al Sabah family. Most importantly, they see themselves as being on an 'equal footing' with the Al Sabah. The growth of the merchant community is attributed to several factors. Most important among them is Kuwait's strategic geographic position on a commercial caravan route between the Gulf, the Arabian Peninsula, and the city of Aleppo on the Mediterranean (Crystal, 1990). The flourishing of maritime industries has also contributed significantly to the enrichment of the merchant community (Baz, 1981, p. 97). In the pre-oil era these merchants were essential to the Al Sabah family, since they provided them with an income in the form of taxes and custom duties, and provided employment for the other social groups (Baz, 1981, p. 98). This dependence increased the power of the merchants, who were and are the main source of opposition to the dominance of the ruling Al Sabah family.

The dependence of the Al Sabah family on the merchant's financial resources mainly started after the two other main divisions of the *'Utub – Al Khalifa* and *Al Jalahima* – migrated from the area (Kuwait) to settle independently (in what are now recognized as Bahrain and Qatar) and established their own settlements alongside the Al Sabah. Initially, the three main divisions of the *'Utub* agreed to distribute the responsibilities for administering the new settlement as follows: the Al Sabah were given the functions of governance, the Al Khalifa the responsibility for commercial affairs, and the Al Jalahima the control of maritime affairs (Baz, 1981). This division reflected the strengths of each family and facilitated the growth of the area. The Al Sabah are believed to have had good relations with the tribes of the area and were known for their skills in negotiation and mediation, essential ingredients for the building up of their new settlement. Thus, it was expedient for the *'Utub* families to choose Sabah bin Jabir, the leader of the Al Sabah family, as the Sheikh of the new settlement. As aptly put by Ismael (1982):

> Irrespective of the personal qualities attributed to him, however, the importance of relations with the tribes in the area must be considered as primary in the light of the eclipsing role of the Bani Khalid [in Saudi Arabia]. The very survival of Kuwait depended upon relations with the tribes. First, the community depended upon the tribesmen for the production of basic necessities, second, Kuwait required protection against perennial tribal raiding. No longer protected by Bani Khalid power, Kuwait required a sheikh both respected and feared for the number of tribesmen he could call into arms in an emergency. Third, the labour for pearling, fishing, and commerce was supplied by the tribes. Apparently, unlike many of the *'Utubi* families whose interests turned toward the sea [and whose ties with the Bedouins consequently diminished], the Al Sabah family remained oriented toward the desert, apparently based on their interest in the active caravan trade between Aleppo and the Gulf. They continued an active relationship with the Bedouin tribes, camping out with them regularly and marrying from among them. (p. 27)

Accordingly, the financial reliance of the Al Sabah on the merchant community rose after the Al Khalifa and the Al Jalahima sent out settlers to colonize Bahrain and Qatar. This increased the scope of operations of the merchants and increased their prosperity, enabling them to make a greater contribution to the government. The merchants, in turn, benefited from the Al Sabah family's relations with the tribes of the interior. These relations created a bridge of negotiations that secured the rest of the area. Alan Rush (1987, p. 2), perhaps the most tenacious investigator of the history of Kuwait's ruling family, says merely that '[the Al Sabah] are said to have acquired the right to rule through a voluntary division of responsibilities between themselves and the other leaders of the community' (as cited in Tétreault, 1995, p. 31).

From the early days, the Merchants were differentiated from other social groups in Kuwait, specifically the Shi'ite and the Bedouin, both of whom were electorally excluded. However, the Bedouin were closer to the rulers, as they were often recruited as labourers by the leading families and as men-at-arms by Al Sabah. In fact, they were the core of the Kuwaiti security force (Crystal, 1990, pp. 40–41). The Shi'ite group, on the other hand, had no direct contact with the rulers, having access only through his secretary (Crystal, 1990). The current social divisions in the State of Kuwait are embedded in these early stages of its formation. Al Hajri (2004) argues that 'the historical roots and the shaping of present day societal divisions and tensions can be clearly seen as early as the 1920s' (p. 38), although the socio-economic status of the less advantaged groups, the Bedouin and the Shi'ite, has changed significantly over time in terms of social, economic, and subsequently political status.

At the time of the early formation of Kuwait, political arrangements and decision-making were exclusively confined to the two most influential groups, the merchants and the rulers. The relationship between the ruling Al Sabah and the merchant community, which developed long before the discovery of the oil, formed the basis for the political structure and practices in the State. This agreement on the distribution of responsibilities between the most influential social groups – the Al Sabah and the Merchants – determined the significance each had on developmental processes in the State of Kuwait. The merchants were responsible for providing the funds for the government and Al Sabah family were responsible for ensuring the stability and security of the area (Qalʿajī, 1970). The consensus between these groups can be mainly attributed to the facts that both the ruling family and the wealthy influential merchants were Sunni, were of *'Utubi* lineage, and were dependent on each other. Despite having formal power as sheiks, it was nonetheless essential for Al Sabah to keep on good terms with the merchants, since acceptance by the *'Utubi* families was the basis of their legitimacy. The acceptance by the merchants of the Ruler's *'Ahd* (promise) to rule justly and in accordance with the Islamic principle of *Shura* (consultation) was the foundation of a sheik's right to rule. *'Ahd* and *Shura* thus became the two essential elements of rule in Kuwait. Al-Rashid (1995) described the way of governance in Kuwait at that time:

> From the day of Sabah the First until the time of Mubarak al Sabah, al-hukm [the rule] continued to be one of shura [consultation]. The ruler consults the notables on the important issues at hand particularly on how to safeguard the country against unexpected outside attacks, and has no choice but to accept their decisions since real authority rested with them and not with the ruler whom they only allowed to be their chief out of courtesy. (p. 90)

Al-Qana'i (1987) described the way of governance as follows: the Sheikh based his decisions on both *'Ourf* (customary rules), and Sharia (Islamic law), as well as seeking advice from the *qadi* (judge). Accessibility and public open discussion were carried out through the daily holding of the *majilis* (council). This political organization was a reflection of the tribal organization prevalent at that time. In this type of organization, the tribal Sheikh was the head of the tribe and was chosen due to certain necessary characteristics and qualities such as bravery, leadership, good mediation skills, and being regarded as a 'fatherly' figure to the whole tribe. However, the tribal Sheikh could not rule without consultation with the older and more experienced tribesmen. The same applied to Al Sabah ruler. The difference was that the ruler, in this instance, needed to consult primarily the merchant community, which provided him with essential funds, while he in turn provided them with the stability and security necessary to conduct their economic affairs. Hassan Ali al-Ebraheem said that the selection of the first Amir, Sabah I, was made by his peers, that is, through consensus reached by an oligarchy (Al-Ebraheem, 1975, p. 25; as cited in Tétreault, 1995, p. 31).

The Oil and the Modern State

From the above discussion of the early formation of Kuwait, it appears that the relationship between the rulers and the people were of a basic simple kind, with face-to-face interactions. The early era shaped the current State-society relations, aligning with other factors that strengthen the social structure and deepen the divisions between different social groups. Since the discovery of oil and the resulting increase in wealth, the country has undergone massive transformations at both the socio-economic and political levels. The subsequent political and social transformations cannot be investigated in isolation from the impact of this wealth. Ghabra (2011) argues that, since the discovery of oil in 1938 and the first commercial shipment of it in 1946, it has become impossible to separate the State's socio-economic development from oil wealth and its impact. In another publication, in an attempt to provide a conceptualization of the sudden wealth and the rapid change the country's undergone, Ghabra (1997) sums up:

> Since oil began to be exported from the Burqan oil fields in Kuwait in 1946, Kuwait's socio-economic and political developments have been intricately linked to its oil industry. By means of its oil wealth, Kuwait developed from a tribal entity into a state, moving from subsistence to state-sponsored welfare, and from a nation of little importance to one of significant power in regional and international affairs. Oil lifted Kuwaiti society out of its traditional economic environment of hunting, pearl-diving and limited trade. The entire way of life of Kuwaitis changed in a very brief period of time. While in 1946 Kuwait's income from oil did not exceed $760,000, by 1971 it had risen to $963 million and by 1977 to $8.9 billion. (p. 359)

Even over a shorter period, it revenues increased from 16.8 million dollars in 1951 to 168 million dollars in the following year and by 1961 it reached 467.4 million dollars (Shuhaiber, 1981, p. 70). It is within this context of rapid economic development that new social forces emerged in Kuwait. The sheer size of the increase within such a short period of time reveals the vast extent of the changes that such an increase in the funds available to the state can induce in a society. The 1950s and early 1960s saw a rapid and unprecedented transformation of Kuwait and its people. One example is when it became the 111th full member of the UN on the 7th of May 1963, guaranteeing its place in the international system and inaugurating a new phase in the development of the modern state of Kuwait (Al hajri, 2004, p. 60). Kuwait's joining the Arab League and the United Nations as a sovereign state were also significant developments signalling the start of a new phase of its political development.

The centrality of oil to the State of Kuwait is indisputable, but it is necessary to look into the specifics of the situation and examine its impact on the dynamics of the relationship between the state and the society. The most substantial and to some extent predictable change is what this wealth has brought to the rulers, Al Sabah. In early Kuwait, the Al Sabah rulers were financially dependent on the merchants, a fact which gave the merchants an upper hand in their dealings with the rulers. The new oil wealth, flowing directly as it did into the Al Sabah coffers, liberated them from financial dependence on the merchants, thereby almost diminishing merchant power and influence. In early Kuwait, and even into the 1950s and 1960s, the merchants could claim to be financially necessary to the state as its primary funding source. As such, the merchant class had a moral and practical foundation for pressuring the government into concessions, which is represented in their attempts at establishing the consultative councils of 1921 and 1938 (Shuhaiber, 1981) (for more information see appendix 1). It was during this time that democratic reforms had their greatest chance of success. However, due to intervention by the British, formal autocracy was retained and the Al Sabah monopoly on formal power survived this dangerous period (see Abu-Hakima, 1983; Crystal, 1990). Now, fortified by oil money, the Al Sabah autocracy could not be feasibly challenged by the merchants. Thus, the new oil production substantially changed the situation of Al Sabah by giving them a strong economic basis for their political power.

While the new oil wealth has augmented Al Sabah political power and ended their financial dependence on the merchant community, it has also created a new division between the ruling family and the rest of the society. The sheer size of wealth and power that the new oil revenues gave Al Sabah has not only changed the dynamics of the relationship between Al Sabah and the merchant community, but also changed the entire dynamics of Kuwaiti society. The prosperity created by oil attracted a huge influx of Arab and foreign migrants, creating a minority status for native Kuwaitis within their own country, making identity and citizenship matters of controversy and ambiguity. The new divisions played right into the Al Sabah strategies to maintain their absolute power. As one might guess, exploiting these new divisions is central to the maintenance of Al Sabah rule, by which policy processes have been negatively affected.

Up to the present day, the presence of migrants in Kuwait has been mostly based on work contracts. The new wealth in addition to the lack of a skilled national workforce necessary for development had attracted migrants from different countries to come and work in Kuwait, as well as all countries of the Arab Gulf. Their increase in number, in the private sector in particular, in the face of the country's small and young population created imbalances between nationals and expatriates in the labour market, raising the alarm of national unemployment. In all six Arab Gulf countries, but especially in Kuwait (IMF, 2008) and Saudi Arabia, flexible labour policies have increased these countries' dependence upon foreign workers, with 81 percent in Kuwait (PACI, 2018), and 53.12 percent in Saudi Arabia being expatriate (Donn & Al Manthri, 2010, p.53) that has been surprisingly reduced to 5.38 percent according to their Ministry of Civil Service (MCS, 2018). Despite their large numbers, they have no political representation. Therefore, they almost have no direct official role in the policy processes in Kuwait.

Practising their new power, Al Sabah family reshaped and reframed the new political representation of the modern state of Kuwait. Under the British protectorate (1899–1961), especially after the oil discovery, the British were in favour of political reforms and the creation of a representative government, as long it did not undermine their own power (Abu-Hakima, 1983). Due to the raised demands, mostly by the merchant community, for greater political participation there were political unrests that threatened the power and the interests of the British in the country (Shuhaiber, 1981). Therefore, the British played a role in convincing the Sheikh to be flexible and accepting public demands, since they were in favour of political reforms and the creation of a representative government, as long it did not undermine their own power (Abu-Hakima, 1983). Alongside the pressure of Iraqi claim of Kuwait, this convinced the ruling family to allow political participation by the public merchants in particular, particularly by the end of the British protectorate (Tétreault, 1991; Yetiv, 2002). Iraqi threats were a major factor in forcing Al Sabah to grant partial democracy, since greater political participation would help ensure the continued existence of Kuwait under their rule. Tétreault (1991) reported that the first main initiative by the rulers was to placate the merchants by means of

> … the establishment of the National Bank of Kuwait, whose success he [Sheik Abdullah Al Salim] underwrote with an interest-free deposit of one million pounds. The second was the implementation of the Land Acquisition Policy, little more than a thin disguise for the distribution of large sums to selected individuals. Both initiatives strengthened the merchants as a class and persuaded them that their economic opportunities would increase once the protectorate had ended and sectors of the economy then dominated by British nationals would be available to them to exploit. (pp. 579–580)

The Al Sabah strategy of using their oil wealth to conciliate the merchants was rewarded by the agreement with the merchants that produced the Constitution in 1961, which preserved the rights of citizens but reserved absolute power for the ruler. Concurrent with the use of Al Sabah oil money to woo the merchants were measures that confirmed the merchant class in their position of dominance over the remaining Kuwaitis, while simultaneously using the new oil wealth to appeal to a broader segment of society. Tétreault (1991) states:

> In 1960, the shape of this future exploitation was indicated by the passage of the Law of Commercial Companies, which required that 51 percent of all companies in Kuwait be owned by Kuwaitis. A large sector of the population was wooed by the construction of a welfare state whose benefits included free housing, utilities, education, and medical care. (pp. 579–580)

Oil revenues not only changed the dynamics of the relationship between Al Sabah and the merchant community. It also changed the whole dynamic of Kuwaiti society by creating new socio-economic divisions. Ghabra (2011), examining the socio-economic dynamics of the state, pointed to a new social division, 'the New Money', defined with reference to the previously existing 'Old Money' – that is, the old merchant class. This 'New Money' segment of society emerged from the government strategy of distributing wealth among citizens in the early years after independence.

However, despite the expansion of available wealth, members of the old merchant class still had a significant advantage over others. Education, for example, played a role in determining who could find and utilize the new opportunities offered by the government. Since most higher education was obtained abroad, it was available mainly for wealthy families, as moderate Kuwaiti families lacked both the necessary financial resources and cultural capital. As a result, the educated merchant class had an advantage over others, both in obtaining an education and in obtaining access to the new government supplied wealth and opportunities. This is not to mention their illustrated early political consciousness as a group, represented in their early demands for greater political participation.

The Constitution

Since the promulgation of the Constitution, formal participation by the public in policy decisions has been guaranteed through the establishment of the parliament. This body consists of fifty members, elected by the general public. The ruler, however, reserves the right to veto its acts. He also retains the right of dissolution – the right to suspend and terminate the Parliament. These rights have raised doubts by many scholars about the efficacy of the parliament and the genuineness of the democracy being practiced in Kuwait (Al-hajri, 2004). The existence of the parliament, however, has nonetheless reduced the power of the ruler and ensures that Kuwait is a semi-monarchy rather than an absolute monarchy.

It can be argued that the Amir's rights of veto and dissolution over parliament devalues public political participation and negatively affects the processes of public policy production. This devaluation can be illustrated by the many dissolutions of the Parliament since the formation of the modern state, including the recent frequent dissolutions (five to seven since 2005), when Sheikh Sabah assumed the throne (Shultziner & Tétreault, 2012, p. 289). The most recent spate of dissolutions has created a political unrest that negatively affects the processes of public policy production and, consequently, the general development process of the state. These dissolutions have also brought many developmental projects to halt, including higher education projects. Article six from the Constitution states that 'The system of Government in Kuwait shall be democratic, under which sovereignty resides in the people, the source of all powers', which sounds democratic enough. Unfortunately, it also says that 'Sovereignty shall be exercised in the manner specified in this Constitution', which given the ruler's rights of veto and dissolution, effectively nullifies the democratic sovereignty suggested earlier.

In addition to the above-mentioned powers granted to the Amir by the Constitution, Al Sabah has adopted several specific strategies that limit any challenges to its authority, which consequently undermine the democratic nature of the State of Kuwait and affect the efficiency of the processes of public policy production. Al hajri (2004), in his thesis, analysed some of these strategies, such as:

- **The control of the legal frame of political participation through citizenship and election laws.** The citizenship law separates some segments of the population of Kuwait and grants them full political rights, while the election law fragments the population along traditional lines of differing affiliations and identities. The combined effect of these two laws is the particular model of parliamentary democracy that developed in Kuwait; highly fractured and ineffective in curtailing executive power.
- **The use and emphasis of traditional forms of affiliations and loyalties as being the primary source of identity,** drastically reduces the importance of having a general atmosphere and a 'universal' feeling of citizenship, as well as the different class status.
- **The ban on the formation of political parties,** which acts as an obstacle on the elaboration of political agendas and programs which would be based on policies that transcend the segmental interests of the different groups.
- **The skilful use of the National Assembly to contain, curb and exploit differences among the various groups in society,** in order to enhance the relevance of the ruling family as the only possible unifying force for the society.

- **Combining the two roles of ruling and governing provides Al Sabah with a huge leverage over the Society** by the mere virtue of controlling the state revenues and the key ministries of Information, Foreign Affairs, Defence and Interior. In addition to this, Al Sabah combines the two posts of Prime Minister and Crown Prince. (pp. 4–5)

All of the above provides an illustration of the rulers' efforts to protect their dominance, regardless of the destructive impact these strategies might have on the overall political system and on the democratic nature of the State. The top two strategies clearly illustrate how they have reinforced the traditional forms of identity, discussed early in this chapter, that have prevailed since the formative years of Kuwait. Al Sabah have embraced the traditional social divisions and played the different social groups against each other. A major incident in this context is the unplanned decision taken by the ruler with regard to mass naturalization of the Bedouin, the 'wholesale' granting of citizenship to them in the late 1960s and the 1970s. The purpose of this act was mainly to give them the right to vote. The altering of the electorate enabled Al Sabah to establish a counter force against the merchants in the elections. It was a short-sighted decision that has had a long-term impact on many different social, economic, political and demographic levels. Ghabra (1997) argues, commenting on this incident, that 'Ironically, the government became a victim of its own strategy regarding [those] bedouins' (p. 366). Instead of the attempted urbanization, the government achieved the phenomenon of '*Desertization*', the transfer of the desert's customs, traditions, beliefs, dress codes, and mentality into the city (Ghabra, 1997). This phenomenon has important implications for political processes, especially as the Bedouin currently constitute more than 60 percent of the total citizens. Among other things, the inclusion of the Bedouin among the voting citizens disrupts the proper functioning of democracy, since the primacy of tribal loyalty and a blind loyalty to Al Sabah effectively destroy the nature of work relations and process productivity in public institutions. This strategy, although useful for consolidating the power of Al Sabah, has killed the formation of a modern, systematic, coherent, civil society in Kuwait. Instead, it has brought the tribal way of governance into the modern political system of the State.

The Kuwaiti system of governance has many systematic limitations and political instabilities. However, I would argue that it is the ban on the formation of political parties that has most affected the nature of the processes of public policy production. Regarding the impact it has had on the effectiveness and the consistency of the processes of public policy production, I strongly agree with Al hajri (2004). He argues that this ban acts as an obstacle to the elaboration of political agendas and programs that transcend the segmented interests of the different groups. The impact of the absence of formal political parties on policy practices in the State of Kuwait can be better understood in the light of the theory of assemblages as applied to public policy. Rizvi and Lingard (2011) use the idea of assemblage to underline the performative character of policy in their paper 'Social equity and the assemblage of values in Australian higher education' (p. 11). Analysing the Bradley report (2008), they demonstrate the tensions between different values and public policies in education. They show that 'public policies are always about trade-offs, compromises and of course, politics, sometimes informed by narrow personal or sectional interests, but more often by ideological differences'. This is true even in Australia, a relatively simple democratic system that has only two political divisions, the Left and the Right, framing the political debate. Rizvi and Lingard (2011) argue that the debate between these two political divisions 'are more accurately characterised as being located within a discursive struggle over competing assemblages, as each side seeks to rearticulate and realign differently the meaning and significance of key values associated with public policies' (p. 11).

Now keeping in mind the traditional cultural divisions discussed earlier, we can see that the situation in Kuwait is so complex that categorization is almost impossible even for purposes of analysis. Imagine the impact of these trade-offs, compromise, and sectional interests on the politics of a nation-state like Kuwait that lacks any official sectarian political representation. Instead of two great political groupings mediating the diversity of social interests and building alliances at the grass roots prior to elections, there is a multiplicity of social, economic, religious, ideological, and family backgrounds directly represented in parliament, each with its own different perspectives, beliefs, and interests. Even more, these perspectives have no continuing institutional existence across different political cycles. My interview data clearly supports this argument, as almost all participants refer in one way or another to the chaos of policy processes in the country. A previous minister of education and a current president of private a university said:

> Unfortunately the production of public policies, generally, is whether being produced in a rush under urgent conditions lacking any study or continuous line of discussion across political cycles; or being delayed and taking very long time to the point when they reach the final production stage there will be outdated decisions that do not match or keep up with the actual needs, either [necessarily or unnecessarily] deceleration or acceleration of the production of public policies. She related it to the arbitrariness of the legislator in a way does not relate to the main purpose of the policy. (M.H., 18 March 2013)

This randomness results from the exclusive dependence on informal political groupings, which are subject to frequent shifts in beliefs, interests, and approaches to public matters. Shultziner and Tétreault (2012) report that, in an attempt to categorize the dimensions of political debates in Kuwait,

> Formal political parties are not allowed in Kuwait although organised political groups frequently sponsor, support or ally themselves with parliamentary candidates (Te´treault & al-Ghanim 2009). The majority of Kuwaiti citizens are Muslim, about 70% Sunni and about 30% Shi'i. The main social and political divisions among Kuwaitis occur between social conservatives (including Islamists) versus liberals, badu [Bedouin]or tribal persons versus hadhar or city people, and Sunni versus Shi'i Muslims. These dimensions are not mutually exclusive. (pp. 281–282)

Even though these political groupings are informal, they are still strongly represented in the parliament and, consequently, in policy decisions, determining the type of democracy being practised in the state of Kuwait. These groupings have the power to steer the processes of policy production. However, their lack of stability across political cycles is a matter of concern and devalues their long-term efficacy. Consistency is crucial, particularly when compromises in policy-making are not only about the ways in which values are prioritized, but also a matter of satisfying the various power groups. Without stability in the power groups to be satisfied, no stable and long-lasting policy can be forged. Even in a normal political environment, 'policies are allocated, represented and promoted, within the shifting terrain of contingent political concerns and the role the state is expected to play in their assemblages' of values (Rizvi & Lingard, 2011, p. 11). However, when not only political concerns are contingent and shifting, but also the power-grouping that must be satisfied, no stable alliances or policy are possible. Understanding these socio-political divisions is useful in analysing the emergence of any public policy in Kuwait, especially the emergence of higher education privatization policies. In fact, understanding the policy creation processes of higher education privatization cannot be understood without the historical context that explains the major divisions of Kuwaiti culture and politics.

Exacerbating these social divisions is the fact that urban settlement in Kuwait followed a distinct pattern of segregating society according to social and economic background, creating relatively autonomous social communities. This segregation reinforced the elite status of the Sunni merchant community, who had more wealth and power than the general public. It also strengthened religious conflict over the power of representation in the parliament, since the Shiite's are excluded from the merchant elite. This religious identity conflict undermines the effectiveness of the parliament and the type of democracy practiced in Kuwait. Instead of emphasizing the political debate over the production of necessary public policies, the debate focuses on issues of identity between different Islamic groups. This condition seriously affects the State's policy production processes and, consequently, the overall development of the country. Most participants agree that the focus of political debate on the issues of identity and citizenship results in the neglect of producing public policies that would contribute to the development of the State.

International Relations

As education policies are now being formed in a globalized context (Rizvi & Lingard, 2010), for the purpose of analysis, a conceptualization needs to be formed of Kuwait international relations and their nature. Given Kuwait's financial independence from other powers of the world, what is important at this point is what type of external powers influence national policy processes in Kuwait.

Kuwait's strategic vulnerability is a major factor shaping its foreign policies and the nature of its international relations both in history and up to the present day. Kuwait is a tiny state situated in the north-east of the Arabian Peninsula (on the north-western edge of the Arabian Gulf), located between great regional powers that create both security and economic threats (Iraq, Iran, and Saudi Arabia). Historian Hassan Ali Al-Ebraheem has described Kuwait as a 'small state living in a bad neighbourhood'; it will always face the strategic limitations imposed by its small national population and tiny territory in its efforts to keep that population and territory free from outside 'encroachment' (Tétreault, 1991, p. 590).

Historically and even before the oil discovery, Kuwait had a significant strategic location as a centre of trade and commerce. It served as a hub of trade between India, the horn of Africa, the western Middle East and the Eastern Mediterranean rim countries. Additionally, up until the advent of Japanese pearl farming, Kuwait had one of the largest sea fleets in the Gulf region and a flourishing pearling industry, with trade consisted mainly of pearls, wood, spices and dates. Its strategic location attracted regional powers to take over its land. Even before the oil discovery, Kuwait's strategic location as a port of trade attracted regional powers, including the Turks in Iraq, Persians, and Bani-Khalid tribes in Saudi Arabia, to take over its land demanding its annexation.

At the end of the nineteenth century, the hegemonic power of Bani Khaled in the Arabian Peninsula declined. As a result, survival has been a major concern for both the government and the population of Kuwait. Alongside security, autonomy has been a goal equally valued by Kuwaiti rulers of the twentieth century. 'Their choice of security strategies has been shaped by the desire to maximize their independence from domestic social groups as well as from external allies' (Tétreault, 1991, p. 566). Those security strategies, to a great extent, formed the type of external influences impacting the state's domestic policy decision up to the present day. However, the context has varied.

The first creative decision undertaken by the Kuwaiti government in order to survive regional threats that surrounded the country at that time was the appeal for British protection and signing of the agreement between the two countries in 1899. This agreement made Kuwait a British protectorate, and provided Britain with significant power over Kuwait's foreign policies in particular. Although the country lost its autonomy concerning its foreign policy decisions at that time, it was a creative measure for the state's survival. This measure, to a great extent, constitutes the first step that shaped the Kuwaiti foreign policies and the nature of its international relations. Tétreault (1991) argues that 'the internal and external components of the Kuwaiti government's strategy for maintaining autonomy and security were conditioned by Kuwait's experience as a British client' (p. 566).

Tétreault (1991) argued that 'international cliency' is the appropriate theoretical framework to describe the Kuwait initial strategy to maintain security against external threats. Cliency is a strategic relationship between a strong state and a weak state. According to Mark Gasiorowski (1991), who developed the theoretical concept of the international cliency to describe the US forging policy in building a client state in Iran, cliency is characterized by

> ...a reciprocal exchange of goods and services between the patron and client governments that serve[s] to enhance the security of the two countries and cannot easily be obtained by them from other sources. The importance of the goods and services to the security of the patron and the client . . . bind[s] the two governments together in a cooperative, mutually beneficial relationship. (as cited in Tétreault, 1991, p. 567)

The primary motivation for the relationship is the desire of each partner to obtain goods and services or 'cliency instruments'. Patron motivation may also involve what could be called 'defensive cliency'; the acquisition of a client to keep it out of other hands. Tétreault (1991) summarizes the cliency relationship as follows:

> ... goods and services provided by each side in any particular case of cliency are unique, but the types of goods and services provided by patrons to clients or by clients to patrons are generic to each side. Patrons receive strategic goods and services that advance their power and international position, particularly within the region of the client. They include basing rights, port access, and influence or even control over important segments of the client's foreign policy. Clients receive strategic goods and services that advance their regional security interests. They range from military equipment and personnel training to direct intervention against a regional rival or a potential regional hegemon. Many cliency instruments can be used to advance the power of the client state and its regime with respect to domestic social groups. (p. 567)

Initially Kuwait was exchanging its strategic position services for British protection. Eventually, and after the discovery of the oil, it was substituted with their (British) protection. However, that external component of security under imperialism left Kuwait with only 'half- a-loaf', the government, and increasingly Kuwaiti society as well, sought a post cliency strategy that would ensure substantial external autonomy for the state (Tétreault, 1991). As a result, the state's independence in 1961 coincided with the ending of the protection agreement with the British. However, for the state to be able to stand independent at that time there was a need to make its independence and autonomy valuable to other regional nations. Just before its independence from the British cliency relationship, the Kuwaiti government sent official delegations to other not so wealthy Arab states in order to determine the best way to participate in their economic development (Tétreault, 1991). Abdullah Al Salem was the first ruler to seek outside support for an independent Kuwait through foreign aid. As a result, many Arab countries were convinced, once Kuwait became officially independent, that an independent Kuwait could be economically beneficial to them.

The role of the oil wealth has been clear in giving a small nation like Kuwait relative autonomy in deciding its own interests. Oil exports, thus, since 1946 have provided Kuwait with a source of instrumental resources, largely controlled by the government, which even enabled Kuwait to remain nonaligned during the Cold War and supported an active regional foreign policy (Tétreault, 1991).

Since then, the Kuwaiti government has changed its strategy in seeking external international support to secure its autonomy. Forging international alliances has accordingly been a major factor in shaping the state's international relations and defining the type of external factors that influence its national policy decision. Oil then has been substituted for cliency. Tétreault (1991) noted that, if the primary domestic goal of cliency was to acquire instruments enabling the government to meet domestic demands with a minimal loss of autonomy, oil was even more useful than cliency for obtaining such instruments' (p. 579). Oil revenues not only enabled the ruler to buy off domestic elites quite openly and to retain his independence from domestic society as the source of state income, but they also expanded his resources so astronomically that he could create a huge constituency supporting the regime by making the whole population of Kuwait dependent on the state. In the external realm, the shift from cliency to oil was trickier, but the same strategy was applied. Oil revenues were used to buy off the most dangerous of the state's external enemies, also quite openly. In addition, they were used to mobilize an international constituency of supporters of Kuwait by creating foreign aid dependencies.

Through foreign aid policies and direct foreign investment, the Kuwaiti government put a great effort on strengthening the state's international position, heavily relying on supporting countries with material incentives by which the importance of the existence of Kuwait as an independent body has been supported. Merely six months after, the country became the first developing country to establish a fund to provide economic assistance to fellow developing countries. In a visionary announcement on the occasion of launching of the Kuwait Fund for Arab Economic Development (since commonly known as the Kuwait Fund) on December 31, 1961, His Highness Sheikh Jaber Al-Ahmed Al-Jaber Al-Sabah, the late Amir of Kuwait declared that: 'Here we are embarking on the tides of change, but we will not forget our friends in need' (WTO, 2012, p. 5). Mr. Robert McNamara, who served as President of the World Bank from 1968 to 1981, also hailed the country's gesture in the following words:

> When first established in 1961, the Kuwait Fund was without precedent. Here was Kuwait, a tiny country, until recently among the poorest places on earth, establishing a development fund in the year of its political independence. While welcoming its new-found prosperity it was declaring a willingness to share its future wealth with its Arab neighbours. (WTO, 2012, p. 5)

Direct foreign investment started initially with neighbouring countries and eventually spread worldwide. The decision of shifting investment from the so-called Third World was mainly due to the problem encountered by investors in those countries, such as corruption, poor infrastructure and the resentment of the local population. Such obstacles resulted in poor investments and, subsequently, poor returns made the Kuwaiti government gradually sell these holdings to place RFFG's (Reserve fund For Future Generation) funds in developed countries, actions that may in turn reduce the support of Kuwait in neighbouring countries (Tétreault, 1991, p. 584). In addition to poor investment in those countries, the experience proved to Kuwait that the dependence on regional support was fruitless in protecting the sovereignty of the state, even after the establishment of the Gulf Cooperation Council (GCC) as attempt to create a regional power. This is a reason that made the Kuwaiti government opt to depend on the more powerful Western countries that have strategic interests in the region. Kuwait's resources and its tiny size, both in population and land, clearly contributed to the external support that it has received from the world's powers to protect its sovereignty and independence. Interestingly, Draper (1987) noted that, if Kuwait were just a place with 'the population of Houston and an area two-thirds that of Vermont' and not also 'a gigantic oil well', interest in its survival would have been unlikely to have commanded the extent of the assistance its patrons eventually provided (pp. 40–48).

Kuwait's strategic vulnerability, to a great extent, has shaped its foreign relations. Apparently, those strategies to forge international alliances (international cliency, foreign aid policies, and direct foreign investment), which Kuwait has followed in order to secure both its security and autonomy have influenced its national policy decision, either directly or indirectly. Globalization has produced another international power represented by international or transnational organizations such as the World Bank, IMF, and the OECD, which play a major role in steering policies around the world. Arguably, those organizations constitute the modern form of power in a globalized world. Accordingly, following the same approach, Kuwait strategy of forging international alliances has incorporated establishing strong relationships with those organizations. Those relationships are illustrated either in funding their projects, or requesting their consultancy for the state's national policy matters. Tétreault (1991, p. 582) argues that the state works with and channels much of its foreign aid through international organization such as the United Nations and the Organization of the Petroleum Exporting Countries (OPEC), reflecting its dependence on widespread acceptance of the norm of sovereignty upon which these organizations are based. Thus, the state of Kuwait's foreign policies have never been a matter of choice, but were crucial in order to secure its independence, security, and autonomy. Added to that, Kuwait started to use its financial resources to build 'First World constituencies', both by increasing its investment and visibility in the International Monetary Fund (IMF), and by encouraging the active engagement of its national oil company (KPC) in the international oil industry and the engagement of its overseas investment arm (KIO) in financial markets in the City of London (Tétreault, 1991, p. 583). Adopting a modern international cliency, the state became a member of the IMF on September 13, 1962 and the World Bank in 1962, signed on to the General Agreement on Tariffs and Trade (GATT) in 1963, and subsequently the General Agreement on Trade in Services (GATS) agreement in 1995, and becoming an original member of WTO since then. This modern approach of seeking international acceptance explains the potential external influence on the country's policy processes, which will be the focus of Chapter Six. Despite its financial prosperity, Kuwait's economy is largely dependent on its oil wealth. Without owning the technology, its economy then is highly dependent on the global economy.

Higher Education

As the higher education sector is the scope of this study, this section will provide a brief overview of this sector in the state. In the preceding discussion of the history of Kuwait prior to independence, you may have noticed that there was no mention of the role of higher education or universities. As was the case in many former colonies, higher education only came into being after independence. Higher education in Kuwait only dates back to 1966, five years after independence establishing the first university in the Arabian Gulf region. Prior to this, students could only pursue higher education studies by going abroad to countries such as Egypt. Before 2000, higher education in the State of Kuwait was mainly owned and funded by the government and was under the control of the Ministry of Higher Education. Locally, it was represented by only two large institutions: Kuwait University (KU) and the Public Authority for Applied Education and Training (PAAET). It was provided as public service, free of charge, to all eligible citizens.

Currently, the higher education sector consists of four main divisions. The first two divisions are the public institutions – KU and PAAET. The third division is the Ministry of Higher Education (MOHE), which in addition to overseeing the entire higher education sector, has a scholarships department that is responsible for external scholarships, which sponsors a respective segment of higher education enrolments. The fourth and final division is the recently emerging private higher education sector. This sector is the newest, coming into existence following the passing of the private universities law (PUL 34/2000).

KU was the first public higher education institution in the country, being established in 1966, only a few years following independence. It is still the only public university in the country. In the academic year 2017/2018, it accommodated around 36,124 students enrolled in 15 different colleges (Kuwait University, 2018). It primarily offers four-year Bachelor's degrees. Some colleges – engineering, medicine, and most of the allied health colleges – require five years of study. In addition, KU offers a few postgraduate courses, mainly comprising Master's programs. The university supports research and offers various research opportunities for it faculty.

The second public education institution is the Public Authority for Applied Education and Training (PAAET). The PAAET was established in 1982 and consolidated the pre-existing vocational education and training programmes that dated back to the 1950s (Al-Atiqi & Alharbi, 2009). It was established by Amiri Decree law No.63 of 1982 in order to overcome shortages in qualified technical workers (UNESCO & IBE, 2011). PAAET oversees a number of work-oriented programmes conducted in different colleges and institutions. These include the basic teacher training college, the technical institute, the communication institute, the business institute, the health institute, the industrial training institute and the institute for electricity and water training (PAAET, 2018). These programs award diplomas to secondary school graduates after two years of successful completion. In addition, the basic teacher training college offers a four-year Bachelor's degree (UNESCO & IBE, 2011). In the 2017/2018 academic year, the PAAET had more than 58,000 students enrolled among its colleges and institutes.

The Ministry of Higher Education's External Scholarships Department supplements the local higher education institutions by sponsoring students to study abroad. It offers undergraduate scholarships for eligible participants to study in internationally recognized universities. These study-abroad students constitute the third largest publicly funded student cohort. The sponsored students are supervised and overseen by cultural offices established and run by the Ministry of Higher Education in those countries where the quantity of Kuwaiti students is high. Currently, there are eleven cultural offices operating in the following countries: the United States, the United Kingdom, Australia, France, Ireland, Egypt, Bahrain, United Arab Emirates, Saudi Arabia, Lebanon, and Jordan. Each office is responsible for managing all of the students' academic and financial issues, not only for the country that the office is located in, but also in the surrounding countries if there are no offices in them. In addition to their role in sponsoring students, these offices are responsible for strengthening international interaction between Kuwait and their host countries (cultural exposition). In fact, they are often attached to Kuwaiti embassies.

The most recent division in the Kuwait's higher education system is the private universities sector. This sector was effectively established by the production of the Private Universities Law in 2000, which allowed for the local provision of higher education services by the private sector for the first time in Kuwaiti history. Subsequently, many private institutions have commenced their activities. Since privatization policies and the private higher education sector are the focus of this study, further in-depth discussion of the sector will be the focus of the following chapters.

In short, the Kuwaiti public higher education system has only two local institutions, Kuwait University and the PAAET. The remaining Kuwaiti students must either complete their higher education internationally abroad or commence their studies at one of the local private universities. The students that attend local private institutions may either be funded by the government's internal scholarship program or by paying their own educational expenses.

Higher education is governed differently in different countries, with different political systems defining how it is ruled, funded, and organized. Since Kuwait is governed constitutionally, higher education is not exclusive. Articles seven, eight, and 13 of the Kuwaiti constitution call for the promotion of higher education and guarantee equal educational opportunities to Kuwaiti citizens.

Article 7: Justice, liberty and equity are the pillars of society; co-operation and mutual help are the firmest bonds between citizens.
Article 8: The State safeguards the pillars of society and ensures security, tranquillity and equal opportunities for citizens.
Article 13: Education is a fundamental requisite for the progress of society, assured and promoted by the State.

Consequently, higher education considered to be a right for each citizen and the government is responsible to provide it free for all qualified seekers. Enrolment is mainly based on students' academic achievements.

Higher Education Governance

Both public institutions, the KU and the PAAET, are independent bodies with an autonomy promoting and regulating their own rules and policies. Each has an administrative board of directors chaired by the Minister of higher education representing the government. The Ministry of Higher Education established in 1988 by the Amiri Decree No. 164 oversees tertiary education in Kuwait after transferring the sectoral managements of both KU and PAAET to it by the Amiri decrees no. 140 and 141 respectively. Only in 1992 the MOE and MOHE became under one Minister. Before that there was a Minister of Education and a Minister of Higher Education. The private sector however has been placed under the authority of the PUC formed in May 2001. The council set out immediately after the passage of the law (PUL 34/2000) to control and regulate the establishment of the private higher education sector in Kuwait. The PUC is given the superior authority over private institutions from the initial licencing approvals and accreditation of certificates to recruitments and enrolments. The private sector is greatly subsidized by the state, starting from offering free lands up to guaranteed student enrolments funded by the government through the program of Internal scholarship initiated in 2006 (PUC, 2018). Nonetheless all private universities are for-profit corporation generating enormous revenues from the state.

There are six main laws organizing Kuwaiti public higher education. They are:

- The Amiri Decree Law No. 29 of 1966, concerning organizing higher education.
- The Amiri Decree Law No. 63 of 1982, concerning the establishment of the Public Authority for Applied Education and Training (PAAET).
- The Ministerial Decree No. 54121 of 3-07-1966, for the financial regulations of the higher education.
- The Amiri Decree No. 140 of 1988, transferring the sectoral management of the Kuwait University to the Ministry of Higher Education.

- The Amiri Decree No. 141 of 1988, transferring the sectoral management of the Public Authority for Applied Education and Training to the Ministry of Higher Education.
- The Amiri Decree No. 164 of 1988, regarding the establishment of the Ministry of Higher Education.

The structure of Kuwaiti higher education and its relationship to the state is illustrated in Fig. 2 below. Note that different governing bodies are responsible for supervising public and private institutions. The organizational structure can be simply explained as follows. As can be seen from Fig. 2, the Minister of Higher Education is the highest authority on higher education sector in the state. Under him are the two main administrative divisions that respectively govern the public and private sectors. The first is the Supreme Council for Higher Education, which oversees the two major public higher education institutions – (KU and the PAAET). The second is the Private Universities Councils (PUC), which oversees the local private colleges and universities. There is also the External Scholarships Department that is responsible for the many students that study abroad. This department is supervised directly by the Ministry of Higher Education (MOHE).

Although the two public institutions are overseen by the Supreme Council for Higher Education, each institution has its own administrative board and has a considerable degree of autonomy in the administration and organization of operations. Nonetheless, government interference is still common, as the institutions are publicly owned. Their sectoral management was transferred to the Ministry of Higher Education in 1988 when the Ministry of Higher Education was established, although previously they were operated as separate bodies.

According to Law 29/1966, article 13, the Supreme Council for Higher Education consists of the following members:

- The Higher Education Chancellor
- The Secretary General of Higher Education
- The Undersecretary of the Ministry of Education and one of his assistants
- The Undersecretary of the Ministry of Finance and Oil
- General Director of Planning
- The Deans of the colleges
- Three of the heads of the scientific departments according to their seniority
- Three members from the private sector as chosen by the minister for two-year duration, with possible renewal

The Supreme Council has various authorities attached to it by law concerning higher education generally and public universities in particular. Curiously, the members of the Supreme Council also serve as board

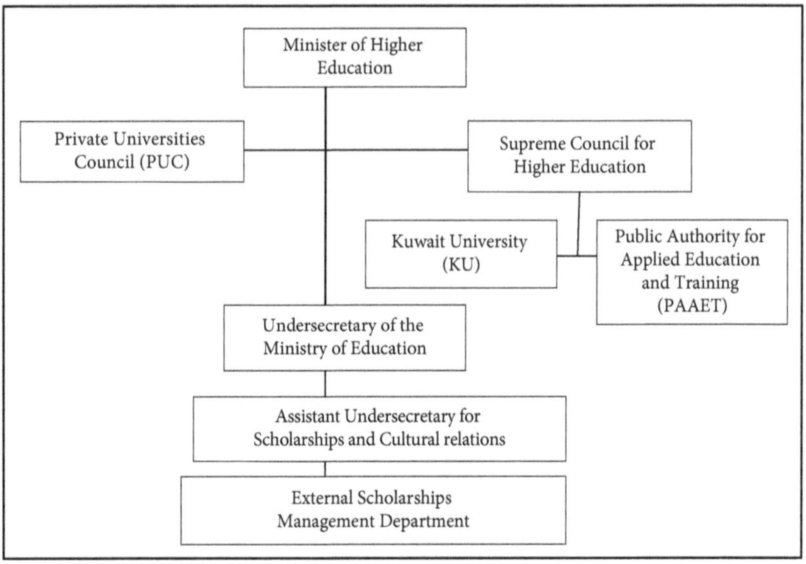

Fig. 2: The organizational structure of the higher education sector in the State of Kuwait. (Source: This flow diagram has been cropped from original chart quoted from MOHE 2012)

of directors for Kuwait University. Although the two assemblies are institutionally distinct, their members are the same. The practical effect of this identity of membership between the Supreme Council and the KU Board of Directors has been to increase the influence of Kuwait University in setting policies for public universities in Kuwait. It is worth mentioning here at this point that the role of the Supreme Council today is vague, inactive and superficial.

PAAET, however, does have its own board of directors, chaired by the Minister of Higher Education, and has a significant degree of autonomy in administrating PAAET's institutional operations. PAAET's board of directors consists of the following members, as stated in the Law of its establishment:

- General Director Manager
- Deputy Director Manager
- Undersecretary of Ministry of Planning
- Undersecretary of Ministry of Education
- Undersecretary of Labour and Social Affairs
- Civil Service Bureau representative
- Secretary General of Kuwait University
- Representative from the Chamber of Commerce and industry
- Representative from the General labour union

- Representative from the Oil sector, allocated by the oil minister
- Two experienced citizens allocated by the Council of Ministers for four years

Regarding funding mechanisms, the state's higher education is fully funded by the government's annual budget. However, each public institution has its own independent budget, distinct from the main budget, with a degree of autonomy given to their administration boards in managing their own finances. It is worth mentioning here that contracting out services is generally popular among government institutions, but not for full-time faculty positions.

Conclusion

In a global environment, it is increasingly important for research to begin with the state perspective, so as to enable the examination of the role of other influencing and interacting forces in shaping the governance of a society (Tan, 2002). It is equally important to consider the differences of local context, the history, politics, and culture that will have an impact on a nation's policies (Taylor, Rizvi, Lingard, & Henry, 1997). Bearing these considerations in mind, this chapter has provided a historical, cultural, and political understanding of the Kuwaiti context in order to provide a basis for the policy analysis in the following chapters. The historical overview of the development of policy formation in Kuwait has focused on describing the periods before and after the discovery of oil, regarding this discovery as the critical transformation point in Kuwait's development.

Oil wealth was essential in shaping the modern composition of political power in the country. Al Sabah family, the merchants, the Bedouin, the old money and the new money are Kuwaiti socio-economic divisions that must be understood prior to any policy analysis. Beginning with the old city of Kuwait and progressing to the development of the modern state, this chapter has provided a description of the origins and the socio-economic status of the various divisions of modern Kuwaiti society and a discussion of their role in the policy-making process. The roles of both oil and the Constitution on policy processes have been discussed, as well as the changing dynamics of socio-political power, in addition to the discussion of the role the oil played in fortifying the existence of the state and its international recognition. The development of higher education has been discussed, beginning with its foundation six years after independence. It has been represented as a public service provided by the government to citizens for free, at least as far as local public institutions are concerned. It has been governed, controlled, and funded by the government in a way similar to many other public services that are guaranteed by the welfare system of the State.

The recent production of higher education privatization policy raises questions of why and how it was developed. The research reported and discussed in this study relates to the factors which led to the development of the privatization policies in Kuwait. Therefore, it is important to examine the dynamics of the policy processes of decision-making in Kuwait that created the Private Universities Law (34/2000). It is important to note, however, that this book does not claim to provide an account of the implementation of the policy, nor its multiple and contingent outcomes, even if at times reference to these cannot be avoided. Nor does it seek to make any specific judgements about the merits or limitations of the policy. Rather, the focus of the research is on the processes of production of the privatization policy: why and how the state of Kuwait with its abundant wealth considered it necessary to pursue privatization of higher education. And how did it develop this policy, drawing upon technical and ideological resources from global sources, but locating them within the context of local national priorities? Given these research aims, in the following chapter, I discuss the methods I used for data collection and analysis.

Chapter Four: Research Methodology

In the previous chapter I provided a background to the context where the policy under analysis was developed. As noted in the first chapter, the principal aim of this research has been to analyse and explain the adoption of higher education privatization policies in Kuwait. As a result of the absence of similar financial pressures attributed to its introduction in most emerging systems, this book aims to analyse some of the key reasons for Kuwait to pursue a privatization policy in its higher education. More broadly, the project seeks to examine how global processes have influenced the production of national policies of higher education in Kuwait. In this chapter I will describe the methods used in this study to answer the previously noted research questions. I will also specify the sources of data used. Details of data collection and analysis are also specified in this chapter.

To research these questions, I have followed a 'continuum qualitative approach', a mixed methods approach proposed by Laura L. Ellingson (2011), which encourages the utilization of multiple tools and methods to add depth, richness, and complexity to an understanding of the phenomenon under investigation. The inspiration for this approach may be found in Denzin and Lincoln (2011), who argue that:

> The combination of multiple methodological practices, empirical materials, perspectives, and observers in a single study is best understood ... as a strategy that adds rigor, breadth complexity, richness, and depth to any inquiry. (p. 5)

Clark, Creswell, Green, and Shope (2008) define mixed methods research 'as a design for collecting, analysing, and mixing both quantitative and qualitative data in a study in order to understand a research problem' (as cited in Denzin & Lincoln, 2011, p. 7). According to Howe (2004), qualitative methods may be 'employed either singly or in combination with quantitative methods, including the use of randomized experimental designs' (as cited in Denzin & Lincoln, 2011, p. 7).

Ellingson, on the other hand, proposes the continuum qualitative approach in order to loosen some of the unproductive methodological constraints highlighted by K. I. Miller (2000):

> [Researchers] do jump across traditions, we do straddle metatheoretical camps, and (unfortunately) we do let pragmatic 'definitions' constrain our work. ... [I want to] allow for comfortable jumps and straddles and to loosen some of these constraints. (as cited in Ellingson, 2011, p. 595)

Ellingson encourages qualitative researchers to consider jumping and straddling multiple points across the field of qualitative methods – consciously, actively, and creatively. She urges researchers to navigate the possibilities for analysis and interpretation in a fluid and diverse way (p. 601). 'A continuum approach to mapping the field of qualitative methodology constructs a nuanced range – broad spectrum – of possibilities to describe what traditionally have been socially constructed as dichotomies such as art/science, hard/soft, and qualitative/quantitative' (Ellingson, 2011, p. 596). Qualitative research is 'multiparadigmatic' in focus. It is a set of complex interpretive practices.

According to Van Maanen (1979) qualitative research is 'an umbrella term covering an array of interpretive techniques which seek to describe, decode, translate, and otherwise come to terms with the meaning, not the frequency, of certain more or less naturally occurring phenomenon in the social world' (as cited in Merriam, 2009, p. 13). Therefore, Denzin and Lincoln (2011) encourage qualitative researchers to,

> ... learn to think outside the box ... [they] must apply [their] critical imaginations to the meaning of such terms as randomized design, casual model, policy studies, and public science (Cannella & Lincoln, 2004; Weinstein, 2004). At a deeper level, we must resist conservative attempts to discredit qualitative inquiry by placing it back inside the box of positivism. (p. 7)

It is in terms of this line of thinking that my research approach has been framed. It recognizes the importance of qualitative methods in order to open up the black box of the processes of policy production, especially in a still-developmental state, such as Kuwait, with complex traditions of ruling.

Investigating policy processes in the state of Kuwait is thus not an easy task, even for a native researcher who was brought up and educated in Kuwait and has extensive social networks there. In Kuwait, there is an inherent lack of public documentation to rely on for investigation, excluding few recent reports that have been done by external bodies on education. Much of the policy decisions takes place through private face-to-face interactions. In the modern state of Kuwait most political activities and reform movements furthermore are pursued through voluntary organizations and associations that are broadly based and include more of the public than just the merchant families as viewed by Smith (1999). Most important of these associations is the institution of *Diwaniyya* or reception hall. Most associations are not independent from the government control. However, the *Diwaniyya* was an autonomous social space, where the government traditionally had no right to interfere. As Norton (1993) argued, it was (and is) the essential element of the Kuwait civil society:

> Arguably, the essential element in Kuwaiti civil society is the diwaniyya, the 'meeting places which have historically been behind many political events. The diwaniya is traditionally a male gathering, but [in recent years some women have started their

> own diwaniyat]. It is well understood that no candidate could win election if he did not visit most, if not all, of the diwaniyat of his district. When the law of gatherings prevented the holding of any meeting without prior permission from the authorities, the diwaniya was excluded.' As Ghanim al-Naijar notes, Kuwait's pro-democracy movement started in a diwaniyya. (p. 210)

Therefore, it can be argued that great deal of political debate in Kuwait is occurring in *Diwaniyya(s)* as unofficial political units, at a micro level of planning. This fact valued data gathered from individuals and their personal experiences concerning the making of policy in Kuwait.

This fact, among others, makes a mixed methods approach, or 'continuum qualitative approach', the best methodological approach for my research. This approach provided me with more of an open space in which to include significant data sources, such as interview data that allowed me to investigate how private face-to-face interactions began the policy-making process. Another significant factor is a simplicity common to the texts of Kuwaiti laws that reveal almost none of the prior processes of policy production. That is another reason why interview data was necessary to supplement more formal written sources such as the reports of international organizations and official reports. Only interviews can provide insights that are impossible to find elsewhere, insights that significantly help the investigation of the policies under examination. Concerning the validity of the data from interviews, I have not used the term triangulation. '[T]he use of multiple methods, or triangulation, reflects an attempt to secure an in-depth understanding of the phenomenon in question, [however] objective reality can never be captured' (Denzin & Lincoln, 2011, p. 5) – we know a thing only through its representations (Denzin & Lincoln, 2011). Triangulation is not a tool or a strategy of validation but an alternative to validation (Flick, 2002; as cited in Denzin & Lincoln, 2011).

However, I found Ellingson's (2011) postmodern term 'crystallization' more appropriate than 'triangulation', because my methodology mixes more than three sources of data, namely interviews, policy documents, reports, and student surveys. Ellingson disputes the narrow conception of 'triangulation' and, instead, endorses a postmodern form, which she calls 'crystallization'. On this model, the central image for qualitative inquiry is the crystal – multiple lenses – not the triangle. She sees crystallization as embodying an energizing, unruly discourse, drawing raw energy from artful science and scientific artwork (p. 605). Ellingson (2009) explains:

> Crystallization combines multiple forms of analysis and multiple genres of representation into a coherent text or series of related texts, building a rich and openly partial account of phenomenon that problematizes its own construction, highlights researchers' vulnerabilities and positionality, makes claims about socially

> constructed meanings, and reveals the indeterminacy of knowledge claims even as it makes them. (p.4)

Drawing on Ellingson's model, I have attempted to ensure the crystallization of both data collection and its ongoing analysis. This chapter describes the methods used in this study to investigate the introduction of higher education privatization policies in the state of Kuwait. It also specifies the sources of data used. These sources include interview data from interviewing policy-making figures and prominent actors – both public and private – in the field of higher education, policy documents, official reports from international organizations such as the IMF, and survey data from higher education students. Details of data collection and analysis are also specified in this chapter. Issues of research limitations and challenges of data collection will also be addressed.

Research Question(s)

The 'choice of research practices depends upon the questions that are asked, and the questions depend on their context' (Nelson et al., 1992; as cited in Denzin & Lincoln, 2011, p.4). It is, therefore, important to make explicit the questions that guided my research. The data was collected and analysed according to the following research question(s):

1. **How might we explain Kuwait's adoption of a privatization policy in higher education in year 2000?**
2. **Why was this policy developed in Kuwait; who were the main policy players; and what interests does the policy serve?**
3. **What were some of the local and global pressures that led to the production of a privatization of higher education policy in Kuwait?**
4. **How does this case study of Kuwait illustrate the ways in which global processes influence the production of national policies in higher education?**

As noted in the Chapter One, the principal aim of this research is to explain the State of Kuwait's adoption of higher education privatization policies, mainly because arguments based on financial necessity do not apply, since Kuwait is one of the richest countries in the world and, in fact, often has an annual budget surplus, or has had at least over the last decade. The specific focus is on the processes of policy production that resulted in the Private Universities Law (34/2000). It was this law that, beginning in 2000, permitted the establishment of private higher education institutions in Kuwait for the first time in its existence. The main sources of data used for this study are interviews with key policy actors and official policy documents. The data from these interviews is then aligned with official reports and a student survey. The purpose of conducting the survey was mainly to obtain a general impression of how the students view the privatization of higher education policies in Kuwait. This enabled me to investigate policy from below and gain some insights into how it affected their higher education experience (access, quality, employment, etc.). In what follows, further details concerning the methods of data collection and analysis will be provided.

Data Collection

Flick (2002, pp. 226–227; 2007) stresses that 'qualitative research is inherently multimethod in focus' (as cited in Denzin & Lincoln, 2011, p. 5). Therefore, for the purposes of this study, four major data resources were used:

1. Primary interviews conducted with thirty key policy actors in both the public and private higher education sectors, including former and current education ministers and parliament members (note: both general and higher education are controlled by the same Minister in Kuwait).
2. Primary policy documents were collected through the Private Universities Council (PUC) or directly from the Official Gazette of Kuwait, *Al-Kuwait Al- Yawm*, first issued in December 1954, through which all new laws in addition to their explanatory by-laws must be published publicly.
3. Official reports and publications from international organizations (such as IMF, WTO and World Bank).
4. A student survey conducted in both public and private higher education institutions.

Each of these is described below.

Interviews

Critics of qualitative approach of research 'presume a stable, unchanging reality that can be studied with the empirical methods of objective social science' (Denzin & Lincoln, 2011, p. 2). 'The province of qualitative research [however] … is the world of lived experience, for this is where individual belief and action intersect with culture' (Denzin & Lincoln, 2011, p. 2). In the previous chapter, I argued that policy processes in Kuwait are highly connected with individual policy actors and their own interaction with the surrounded environments. Therefore, interviewing those policy actors will be out of the greatest benefit to enrich data collected to examine policy processes in the Kuwaiti context.

Data collected from interviews, thus, constitute a primary source for my research study. This study concerns incidents that took place almost two decades ago. This fact, combined with the private and non-official nature of policy production processes in Kuwait, necessitates the use of interviews. It is only by interviewing people who have been involved in those processes that we can grasp how these policy processes function. Moreover, since this sort of policy production still affects policy creation in the country, this method also illuminates current practices. Fraenkel and Wallen (2006) argue that interviews reveal those things about people that we cannot directly observe, like their behaviour at a previous point in time, or what is on their mind – their ways of thinking or feeling about something.

Gall, Gall and Borg (2003) highlight four main advantages of interviews: (1) They collect data about unobservable phenomena like beliefs, feelings, opinions, and attitudes; (2) They collect the unique data of the participants' own words; (3) They adapt and clarify vague statements with open-ended exploration of the topic; and (4) They build trust and rapport with the participants for in-depth information. All of the above applied to my interviewing experience. More specifically, the design of semi-structured interviews allowed for open-ended questions and, sometimes, on-the-spot alterations to track the flow of information given by participants based on their specific personal experience with regard to the phenomenon under examination. Semi-structured interviews allowed for a degree of flexibility while conducting the interview. As Kvale and Brinkmann (2009) note, openness of interviews allows for many of 'on-the-spot decision[s]' (p. 3).

Kvale and Brinkmann (2009) also note that different forms of interviews serve different purposes. For example, research interviews have the purpose of producing knowledge. But there are many types of research interviews. The proper form and design of the research interview is related to the sample and the purpose of the study. In the case of this study, taking into account the research questions mentioned earlier and the nature of the information required, semi-structured interviews were most appropriate in order to realize this study's objectives. Even more specifically, semi-structured life world interviews were the best tool for use in this study. Kvale and Brinkmann (2009) define a semi-structured life world interview as 'an interview with the purpose of obtaining descriptions of the life world of the interviewee in order to interpret the meaning of the described phenomena' (p. 3). They suggest seven practical stages of interviewing. In a linear progression these are: (1) thematising an interview project, (2) designing, (3) interviewing, (4) transcribing, (5) analysing, (6) verifying, and (7) reporting. Accordingly, my interview questions have been thematised in the following way based on the research questions:

- Historical investigation of privatization of higher education in the State of Kuwait [Who? and Why?]
- Decision-making or Policy processes [procedures & obstacles]

- Current Debate [pros and cons]
- General processes of public policies production in Kuwait
- The nature of external influences
- Future expectations based on current practices

The interview questions were generally organized from the more general to the more specific. There were many types of interview questions, each with its purpose in directing the path of the conversation. Accordingly, each section includes more than one of the following types of questions: introductory questions, follow-up questions, probing questions, specifying questions, direct questions, indirect questions, structuring questions, silence, and interpreting questions (Kvale & Brinkmann, 2009). Thus, the 'openness' and the 'on-the-spot decision' features allowed through the semi-structured interviews gave the researcher the space to improve the interview by moving between the different types of questions. In general, questions asked in the interviews progressed from general to specific. The more general questions asked were derived from research questions, while the more specific questions asked were initiated by the momentum of the interviews in the search for relevant findings.

The Conduct of Interviews

The above discussion addressed the design of the interviews and the framework of the questions. The following discussion concerns the approaches followed in conducting the interviews and in the allocation of participants. Targeted participants were mainly from the following higher education bodies in the country as illustrated in Fig. 3 below. Since the policy under investigation was produced in 2000 and the processes under investigation occurred prior to its production, former education ministers and parliament members were interviewed. The selection of former policymakers was mainly due to their lived experience in the political field during the production of the Private Universities Law (34/2000).

The use of former rather than current office-holders also made access to participants easier than it would have been if they still held their positions, especially as many of these interviewees had held high status positions such as ministers. As will be noted in the following chapter, the frequent suspensions and changes in both government and parliament required the researcher to locate participants from different political cycles. There were also some overlaps in the positions of participants, a fact that was considered an advantage with regard to data collection. This kind of varied experience enriches the knowledge of participant with regard to the phenomenon under investigation and consequently increases the quality of data gathered.

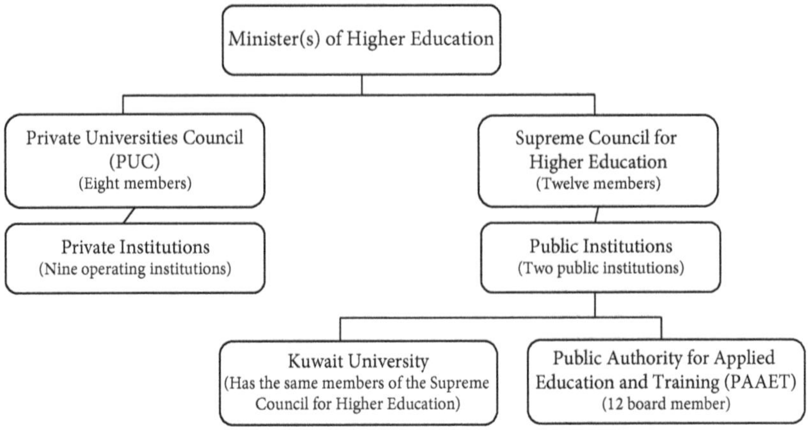

Fig. 3: Targeted sample.

The interviewees' disciplinary specializations range over both the humanities and the natural and applied sciences. More specifically, the fields of the interviewees are as follows:

- Computer engineering (1)
- Political science (2)
- Law (1)
- Medicine (1)
- Business administration (7)
- Accountancy (4)
- Marketing (2)
- General Science (1)
- History and Geography (1)
- Civil Engineering (1)
- Biological Science (1)
- Social Science (1)
- Engineering (3)
- Computer Science (1)
- Management Information System (1)
- Information Technology (1)
- Chemical Engineering (1)

There are several points to note about the approaches adopted for the interviews. To begin with is the allocation of the sample. Merriam (2009) argued that:

> The most appropriate sampling strategy is non-probabilistic – the most common form of which is called purposive (Chein, 1981) or purposeful (Patton, 2002).

> Purposeful sampling is based on the assumption that the investigator wants to discover, understand, and gain insight and therefore must select a sample from which the most can be learned. (p. 77)

Patton (2002) adds that:

> The logic and power of purposeful sampling lie in selecting *information-rich* cases for study in depth. Information-rich cases are those from which one can learn a great deal about issues of central importance to the purpose of the inquiry, thus the term purposeful sampling. (p. 230, emphasis in original)

Merriam (2009) further noted that '[s]nowball, chain, or network sampling is perhaps the most common form of purposeful sampling' (p. 79). It is a strategy that involves locating a few key participants who easily meet the criteria you have established for participation in the study. Through interviewing those early participants, each one has been asked to refer to other participants. Accordingly, '[by] asking a number of people who else to talk with, the snowball gets bigger and bigger as you accumulate new information-rich cases' (Patton, 2002, p. 237). Morgan (2008), on the other hand, argues that:

> Snowball sampling is a useful way to pursue the goals of purposive sampling in many situations where there are no lists or other obvious sources for locating members of the population of interest, [however] it does require that the participants are likely to know others who share the characteristics that make them eligible for inclusion in the study. (p. 3)

Although I targeted particular institutions, there were no such lists that I could use as a guide for the allocation of participants. Therefore, the most practical way of allocating participants was by using 'snowball sampling', a method that relies on tracking participants through other participants' connections. 'The name reflects an analogy to a snowball increasing in size as it rolls downhill' (Morgan, 2008, p. 3). Accordingly, I targeted a small pool of initial informants to nominate other participants who met the eligibility criteria for a study.

Appointments for interviews were made either by phone calls or in person. Where requested, interview questions were sent through email or attached to the official invitations. These official invitations included the plain language statement and consent form, and were handed to the interviewee either personally or through their secretaries in advance of the interviews. It was tough process that consumed a great deal of the study time frame; there were long waiting periods as well as rejections to be dealt with.

Is worth noting here is that, in this case study, snowballing was more about access to participants than about the size of the sample, since many of the desired interviewees are from highly ranked positions and were often hard to reach. Therefore, some of the researcher's social connections were used as well in order to allocate participants for the study.

It was possible for the researcher to attempt to organize the field interviews in terms of a strict set themes or categories and to follow a prearranged sequence in conducting the interviews. However, this approach could have problems. To name but one, many of the participants have had interwoven roles between both public and private institutions in addition to their political positions as executive officers and policymakers. For example, there were former Ministers of Education who are now running private higher education institutions, and there were deans and faculty members who were Parliament members at the period under investigation. This complexity of roles rendered any attempt at a pre-set interview formula useless, as each interview subject has a unique set of potentialities as a source of information.

It was therefore deemed more advantageous to conduct the interviews using a random approach based on who came available first. This technique allowed the interviewer to move between different sectors and different policy levels, an ability that enhanced the 'crystallization' of data. The more flexible approach to interviewing also allowed the researcher to probe for unnoticed themes, as well as sought clarification of facts and interpretations of policy from participants. The multifaceted data acquired by this approach enabled more appropriate interpretations to be made of Kuwaiti policy processes and higher education operations.

In addition to interviewing high-ranking education officials and policymakers, the researcher also chose to interview random students from both public and private institutions, as well as graduates who were in the workforce during the conduct of the research, some of whom were employers. These people were interviewed in order to obtain a general impression of how the students view the privatization of higher education policies in Kuwait. This enabled me to investigate the policy from below and gain some insights into how it affected their higher education experience (access, quality, employment … etc.). Students were selected for interview via a question on the student survey concerning their willingness to be interviewed.

Documentary data was sought in the midst of interviews or when the interviews were done. All interviews were audio recorded with participants' permission and consent, as recording 'frees the interviewer to concentrate on the topic and the dynamics of the interview' (Kvale & Brinkmann, 2009, p. 179). Interview data was transcribed and translated within the shortest time possible in order to preserve the original intention of data recorded in a way that allows for the retrieval of most of the actual expressions made by participants, which in most cases validate information given and revealed participants' state of mind about specific incidents or practices, in each interview.

Documents

Data collection is usually guided by research questions as well as emerging findings. Merriam (2009) suggested that 'the researcher must keep an open mind when it comes to discovering useful documents' (p. 150). Documents can include so many things – records, letters, newspaper accounts, poems, songs, etc. (Merriam, 2009). In the current study all forms of data not gathered through interviews or observations are considered documents, in accord with the Merriam's (2009) definition of documents. Documents were gathered by the researcher for the purpose of triangulating or the unrestricted 'crystallization' of data gathered from interviews. They also served as a source of stimulus for interview themes and questions, and provided direction for the conduct of interviews.

The main documents used in this study included primary local policy documents, official reports and publications from international organizations such as the International Monetary Fund (IMF) and the World Bank, and the General Agreement for Trade in Services (GATS). Statistical data was obtained from governmental databases and higher education institutions both public and private. The policy under investigation, the Private Universities Law (34/2000), has a very simple policy text that does not reveal much about the processes of its production. Although the subsequent 'policy bylaws' further explain its primary articles, they only cover technical issues concerning the implementation of the law rather than casting light on how the law was produced. All laws collected for this study were either from the PUC web page, or directly from the Official Gazette of Kuwait, *Al-Kuwait Al-Yawm*.

Student Survey

The student survey was performed during the final stage of data collection as a significant measure to obtain a general impression of how the students view the privatization of higher education policies in Kuwait. It enabled me to investigate the policy from below and gain some insights into how it affected their higher education experience. As most interviewees refer to excess student demand as a major influence on the policy production, I wanted to investigate the effect of the introduction of the private universities on the higher education experiences and opportunities of some affected students.

The survey was conducted electronically, utilizing the Survey Monkey online tool, which allows for the electronic distribution of the survey among large number of participants. In addition, the Survey Monkey offered helpful tools for collecting data and analysing results through charts and diagrams that provided a better understanding of the results. The survey has been distributed across two private universities out of nine (GUST and ACK).

These two were chosen because they had the greatest enrolments among private higher education institutions, having around 4,000 students combined. They were also among the first private institutions established in Kuwait. In the public sector, the link to the survey was distributed by faculty members during lectures at Kuwait University and PAAET. It was distributed this way due to the lack of an effective email system in public universities that connect students to their lecturers.

Analysis of Data

> Data collection and data analysis are tightly interwoven processes, and must occur alternately because the analysis directs the sampling of data … (Strauss & Corbin; as cited in Tan, 2002, p. 61)

Accordingly, my analysis was started directly after the transcribing of the first interview, and has been continued in accordance. 'Policy analysis depends on the site of production of the policy as well as on the nature of the policy in question' (Rizvi & Lingard, 2010, p. 45). Data gathered was analysed using thematic analysis. According to Braun and Clarke (2006), thematic analysis 'represents some level of patterned response or meaning within the data set' (p. 82). Consideration of a theme was not dependent on quality but rather on the ability to capture important points related to the research aim (Braun & Clarke, 2006), which in this case was the process of the production of the Private Universities Law (34/2000). In the analysis, the real names of participants have been retained because of their high status positions and as it was stipulated in the consent. Furthermore, it is worth mentioning that some of the documents and most of the interviews transcripts were in Arabic, hence the translations are those of the author.

As noted above, policy documents and interviews were the main sources of data for this study. The survey served as a complementary support method to enhance understanding of the policy under investigation. It also provided valuable data that added further material for analysis. The study data was primarily qualitative; therefore, data analysis was based on coding. The coding was then classified and categorized into main themes. In doing this, I used the analysis software Atlas.ti that I found more user friendly than Nvivo. The software was helpful in organizing the coding process, and the following classification and categorization was managed in a systematic way that allows easy access to the original data. The themes that emerged from the classification process were then interpreted and cross- examined at the macro level with official statistical data and the historical background of policy processes obtained from the historical literature of Kuwait. Trends identified from data analysis were also verified with some of the key informants in the field in order to seek justification for judgments made. This approach to data analysis was used both for policy documents (policy texts and reports) and interview data (i.e., data collected from open-ended survey questions and the following optional student interviews).

Crystallization is an important approach used in this study in order to justify the analysis and the conclusions drawn concerning the factors that influenced the production of higher education privatization polices in Kuwait. Crystallization also allowed the researcher to overcome the scarcity of written literature on this phenomenon by applying multiple levels of analysis. This technique allowed the researcher to look at data through multiple lenses and compare the Kuwaiti perspective with that of higher education privatization practices in the rest of the world by applying the 'glonacal agency heuristic' (Marginson & Rhoades, 2002).

The glonacal heuristic, mentioned earlier, emphasizes the simultaneous significance of global, national and local dimensions and forces in shaping any phenomenon in an era of globalization. Globalization has triggered new theoretical and methodological approaches to educational research. Marginson and Rhoades (2002) argue that, rather than being constrained to local or national boundaries, education is increasingly shaped simultaneously in global, national and local dimensions of action. They propose a glonacal heuristic for comparative research in education that accounts for the multifaceted impact of globalization in all dimensions. Rizvi and Lingard (2010) also call for a 'historical orientation to [educational] policy analysis' (p. 69, italics in original) in globalized contexts.

In the specific circumstance of Kuwait, the national dimension of the glonacal agency heuristic has been substituted with a regional dimension concerning the nature and the size of the state. 'Regional' here refers to the position of Kuwait in both the Arabian Gulf as a member of the (GCC), and in the broader Middle East and North African countries (MENA). Marginson and Rhoades (2002) argue for the glonacal agency heuristic as a remedy for the incomplete conceptualizations and the shortcomings of the prevailing framework of cross- national higher education research that ignores the existence and the significance of the three dimensions and their simultaneous intersections. Accordingly, the data analysis framework for this study has been framed with the glonacal agency heuristic in mind, as illustrated in Fig. 4 below.

Limitations and Challenges

The focus of this study is to investigate and understand the forces that shape and influence the processes of policy production and, specifically, policy production for higher education.

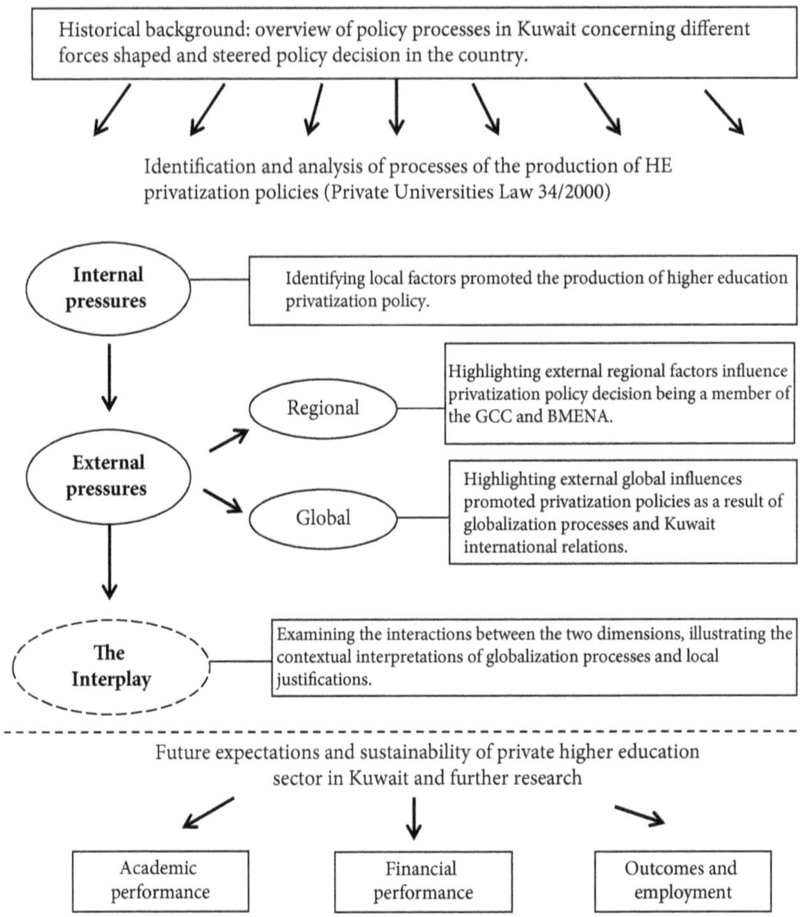

Fig. 4: Analytical framework.

Although some sections reflect on the implementation of the privatization policy and its implications for higher education experience, the study is not an evaluation of the policy or an analysis of its implementation. Investigating the influence of the policy from below is only for the justification and triangulation or the previously argued 'crystallization' of judgments made that rely on the primary data collected for the study. Evaluation of the performance of the private higher education sector in Kuwait should be accomplished in a separate future study.

It is natural for any research to face different difficulties or obstacles that hinder the processes of its conduct. Concerning this research study there were several difficulties faced by the researcher that can be summarized as follows. The first and the most significant among them is the general lack of research culture in Kuwait. In a Kuwaiti study, Dr. Ahmad Bsharah pointed out the obstacles facing scientific research in Kuwait as follows (Al douahees, 2006, pp. 21–22):

- Pluralism of research institutions.
- Pluralism in institutions concerned funding research.
- The absence of active relationships between research activities.
- The absence of coordination between institutions in their research efforts.
- Scattering research effort on different scientific fields.
- Weak connections with the beneficiaries of the research.
- Lack of mechanism to transfer research outcomes into applied techniques.
- Lack of localization of knowledge and skills resulted from research.
- The absence of correlation between the state development plan and research.
- Weak scientific culture and the enthusiasm of the community for research.

The reality of research in Kuwait can be understood through viewing the obstacles that hinder scientific research as summarized above. Accordingly, there is a lack of national literature and data available for further study. Even when literature does exist, there is a clear lack of effective knowledge dissemination. In order to tackle this problem, the researcher has had to personally track necessary data in the originating organizations, an activity that consumed much time and energy.

Another major obstacle is the extreme brevity of policy texts in most Kuwaiti laws. The text of the policy under analysis consists of only eight articles and can be fitted onto a single page. This brevity of policy text means that there is little or no written guidance as to how the law is to be applied. The actual implementation of the law is therefore frequently undocumented altogether. Even when there are written sources for the law's implementation, they are often spread out among the administration and not easily accessible. These facts increase the value of the data collected from the interviews and other documents. The new data collected in this study helped to overcome the lack of clarity provided in the law text and provided an understanding of how these laws have worked out in practice.

Researcher 'positionality' is significant factor that has a large impact on directing the focus and subsequently the outcomes of the study. It can also create an obstacle for the researcher if he/she lacks the required institutional positionality that provides both accesses and connections. The importance of positional access to the data and information required for this research is due to the absence of effective knowledge dissemination in Kuwait. Being connected or knowing people is extremely important in a society such as Kuwait. If the researcher lacks the connections necessary to reach the people required for the research, it will hinder the process of participant allocation significantly. And, even if those connections exist, there is another obstacle that confronts female researchers in particular – that is, the difficulty that women face in gaining access to participants, especially male participants, in informal settings. This difficulty created a challenge for me as a female researcher. The plain fact is that approaching participants would have been easier if the researcher were male. A male researcher would have had much easier access to the many participants from different socio-economic backgrounds and would have had greater access to their social gathering places, especially the politically crucial *Diwaniyya*.

Rizvi and Lingard (2010) have pointed out issues related to the positionality of the policy researcher and to the significance of such positionality to policy analysis, (as well as access to data). They indicate four different meanings of this positionality. The first meaning relates to actual location of the policy researcher with respect to the focus of the analysis and how such positioning frames the type and conduct of policy analysis. The second meaning of positionality relates to the researcher's methodological and political backgrounds. This type of positionality will have intellectual implications on the resources considered for the analysis, theory, and methodology. The third meaning of positionality is relationship of the researcher with respect to globalization. This type of positionality refers to the 'spatial location' of the researcher, more specifically the researcher's national location and the positioning of that nation with respect to global geopolitics. And finally, Rizvi and Lingard (2010, p. 46) have noted that 'positionality' should also be recognized as the national location of the researcher that has implications for the nature of the analysis done and the availability of the theoretical and methodological options; pointing to some 'quick and dirty' research done by some international agencies in the countries of the global south reflecting 'positionality' and the purpose of the research. All of the above highlighted dimensions of positionality could have, by some means, influenced the conduct of this study.

Concurring with Rizvi and Lingard's (2010) views of 'positionality', I have expanded the focus of my study to incorporate the awareness of the general and historical policy processes in Kuwait, in order to construct better judgments of the phenomenon under investigation. With regards to the pointed 'spatial location', I have experienced reasonable interactions with global contexts. For instance, as a Kuwaiti researcher located in Australia to complete her further studies, in addition to several experiences in countries around Europe and Asia, I have built a broader sense of globalization and its implications. Due to my loyalty to my country, I have been motivated by the hope that my study might lead to future improvements in Kuwaiti higher education.

Last but not least, however, I must address the potential bias of some participants, more in the private sector, as they were naturally concerned about their reputation. Both the purpose and the scope of the study were explained in the Plain Language Statement in both English and Arabic languages. Nevertheless, it was very difficult to eliminate the feeling of some participants, in the private sector in particular, of being examined or evaluated. As a result, there was some bias from participants in an effort to protect the reputation of their own sector. While it is impossible to entirely eliminate bias, as a researcher, I feel I was able to identify and take into account its expressions by juxtaposing particular claims against claims of others, derived from multiple sources.

Chapter Five: Local Pressures

This book is concerned with an attempt to understand the production of privatization policies of higher education in Kuwait. The purpose of this study is to investigate major pressures, both local and global, which led to the production of privatization policies, examining in particular the interplay between the two. In this sense, the study seeks to explain how pressures of globalization intersected with policy-making processes within the local context. The focus of this research is in particular on the policy processes of the production of the Private Universities Law (PUL 34/2000). However, the broader scope of the study lies in its attempts to understand the general dynamics of policy-making processes in Kuwait through an investigation of the multiple forces promoting the introduction of privatization policies. As a case study, this research should be seen as an illustrative example, which is largely underrepresented in the literature, of how the forces of globalization have been mediated locally in Kuwait, which has a different history, political system, and, most importantly, economy than most other countries in the world, where privatization has become a widespread phenomenon.

Rizvi and Lingard (2010) stress the importance of 'globalization from below', local factors, in shaping educational public policies and reforms, even though they might have been imposed by external global powers. Privatization is becoming a common policy priority in higher education reforms around the world. However, the variations illustrated in the different local forms of private higher education (see Chapter Two) support Rizvi and Lingard's (2010) argument that local factors play a crucial role in mediating global influences and shaping the form of privatization policies adopted. Relying on the data collected for this study, this chapter highlights some of the local realities in the state of Kuwait by which privatization policies have been promoted internally to meet demands of higher education.

The findings show that major local arguments and pressures in favour of privatization can be classified into six broad categories: growing demand, inconsistent policies, inefficiency, poor quality, socio-cultural challenges, and imperatives of economic reforms. In what follows, each of these categories will be discussed, though it should be pointed out that these arguments are often interconnected. In this discussion, the presentation of the data collected is presented alongside its analysis, using relevant literatures on both Kuwaiti higher education as well as general theories of higher education privatization.

Growing Demand

Statistics produced both by the Kuwaiti government and international organizations show that Kuwait has a young population with a school-age population that is greater than 60 percent of the society (Al-Atiqi & Alharbi, 2009; PACI, 2018), and with an annual population growth rate of 2.9 percent (UNESCO, 2011). It reached a 6 percent annual increase in high school graduates in the 1990s, an increase that was followed by further expansion thereafter due to the increasing size of school enrolment and the increasing numbers of schools being built each year across the country (Al-Atiqi & Alharbi, 2009). Given the availability of universal secondary education, this growth has led to a 15.6 percent average annual growth rate of enrolment in tertiary level of education (King & Hill, 1993, p.123). Meanwhile, the public higher education sector has been static for a long time, with no significant increase in either school capacities or number of institutions. These realties were further devastated by the Iraqi invasion in (August, 1990 – February,1991), by which almost the entire infrastructure of the country was demolished, including higher education sector (Abd-El Bary, 1993). As a result, the increase in the demand has overwhelmed the already existed limited capacity of the public institutions and most financial resources were spent on the reconstruction of the damaged higher education institutions at the period of time followed the liberation from the Iraqi invasion.

Despite the fact that the reconstruction was a huge financial burden on the state, the blame for higher education problems cannot to be placed exclusively on the invasion. The higher education sector was already troubled even before the Iraqi invasion, said Tim Thornborough (1990). In the American journal *The Chronicle of Higher Education* he reported that, 'Whatever may happen in the crisis, the academic system and job market were already in trouble – in part, ironically, because of Kuwait's extraordinary wealth' (p. A27). He noted that the trouble is largely because of the virtually assured jobs offered by the government for its citizens that resulted in reducing their incentives to study hard. He said, 'Efforts to combat declining standards at Kuwait University have included a tightening of admissions requirements, but that has caused a big drop in enrolments in the past year – to 12,600 from 19,000' (Thornborough, 1990, p. A29). Attempts to open a private university were begun early in the 1990s, even before the invasion. In a final statement in Thornborough's article there was a reference to such attempts with regard to academic concerns, which had not been clearly presented by the study participants referring to the period prior to the invasion. Thornborough (1990) reported:

> In recent months, concern over academic standards has been growing as plans for a new private university-backed by many leading Kuwaiti academics-have neared

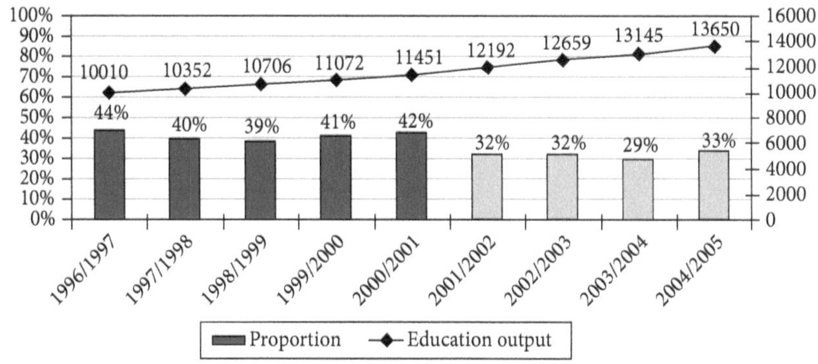

Fig. 5: Comparison between high school output and university input. (Source: Al-Atiqi, Al-Rashed, & Al-Ali, 2010, p. 113)

> completion. The new institution had been scheduled to open next month in temporary facilities. (pp. A27, A29)

Kuwait University is and always has been the only public university operating in the country. The PAAET vocational colleges and institutes have also significantly increased in number. In order to accommodate increased demand, these public institutions have been stuffed with students in a way that exceeds their actual capacity. Statistics shown in the chart in Fig. 5 illustrate the widening of the gap between public demand and the admission rates into Kuwait University between 1996 and 2005, in order to provide an example. Kuwait University, in order to avoid the political pressure to increase its enrolment rates, has had to raise its admission requirements. This decision to cut 10 percent from its annual enrolment rate in the 2001/2002 academic year, as shown in Fig. 5 and 6. This decision by the university put the government in a critical position to deal with the growing numbers of secondary school graduates demanding places in institutions of higher education as similarly pointed to by a participant (H.J., 13 February 2013).

Fig. 5 also illustrates the growing demand in the years preceding the production of the PUL (34/2000), which has been used to pressure the government to produce the higher education privatization policy by both academics and the private sector. As similarly noted by Al-Atiqi, Alharbi, and Al-Ali (n.d.):

> The evolution of private higher education in Kuwait began with interest from the private sector which formalized at least three groups that demanded licensure prior to the government action. Intellectual efforts that contributed to the awareness of society needs were also taking place in Kuwait University. The project titled 'Establishments of Community Colleges in Kuwait' provided evidence of demand exceeding supply and suggested governance options using feasibilities study and Delphi type surveys. (p. 2)

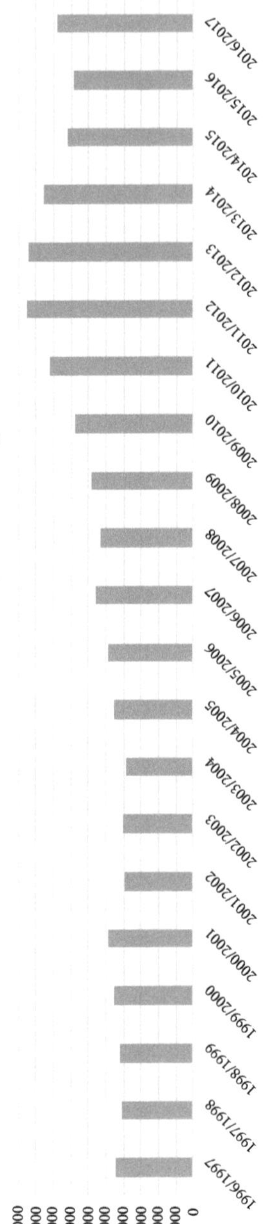

Fig. 6: Numbers of students admitted to the University of Kuwait. (Source: Kuwait University Admission Centre)

It should be noted that Al-Atiqi is the first Secretary General of the PUC and has been an active policy actor in the production of the PUL (34/2000) and the subsequent HE privatization policies. Al-Ali used to be his and the current deputy secretary general, and Al-harbi used to be the president of Arab Open University (first private university). Al-Atiqi at the present is the president of a private institution. This provides an example of the intersection of roles experienced among participants during the data collection processes for this research. The demand has continued to increase constantly in the following years (see Fig. 6).

The action taken by KU to reduce its enrolments came directly after the production of the PUL (34/2000). It can be seen as intended to further add pressure on the government to enhance the role of the established private institutions in accommodating the growing demand, which has eventually produced the program of internal scholarships in the academic year (2006/2007) that is feeding private institutions with publicly funded students. Law (34/2000) stipulates in its second article: 'The aims of private universities are to contribute to the fulfilment of Higher Education and the applied education goals, in order to realize the coordination between these objectives and the evolving needs of society.' The law's explanatory note stated that the law was passed to address the issue of the limited number of places at the University of Kuwait which was therefore unable to accommodate the growing numbers of high school graduates who wished to pursue their university studies (see appendix 4). Accordingly, the Private Universities Council took advantage of the competence given to by articles 3 and 6 of the Law's executive regulations related to the establishment of rules and procedures for students' admission to private educational institutions, tuition fees, and the scholarships system (see appendix 4). The PUC argued that the law's provisions and its executive regulations filled the legislative gap in the MOH's decree, which limits its authority to scholarships outside Kuwait only (Al-Atiqi, Al-Rashed, & Al-Ali, 2010). Accordingly, the Council issued its decision concerning the local scholarships policy in March, 2006 in order to respond to the growing social demands (Al-Atiqi, Al-Rashed, & Al- Ali, 2010, p. 119). The policy will be further discussed in Chapter Seven.

Growing demand as a major factor in the expansion of the provision of higher education in the country is also supported by the data collected specifically for this study. Participants repeatedly stated excess demand as a major factor in promoting the need for expanding the provision of higher education in the country. According to a former member of a ministerial committee that had been assigned to improve the national higher education in the 1990s:

> *The major demand was for offering more places in higher education, since the student numbers are rapidly increasing the pressure on existing public higher education institutions.*[1] (W.R., 17 March 2013)

The following statement by a dean at KU illustrates the pressure on the university. He said:

> *If the decision is left to the university, we will choose not to admit students for the next semester.* (R.A., 13 March 2013)

All participants shared the view that increased public demand for higher education was a major factor leading to the introduction of private higher education. A few also pointed to the urgency of the situation, an urgency that was almost the core of the policy debate at the time. The government's main reason for expanding the presence of private universities was the consequence of an overflow of high school graduates who could not enter the existing public higher education institutions. A former parliament member, who was also a member of the educational committee in the parliament that produced the PUL (34/2000) (1996 and 1999 parliaments) confirmed that[1]:

> *The major policy debate back then was concerned with the increased number of students and the lack of higher education places offered by public institutions. Moreover, the main demand was to find an immediate solution to address the dilemma of the excess numbers of qualified high school graduates who had failed to be admitted into higher education institutions back then.* (H.J., 13 February 2013)

He emphasized that:

> *The main demand was to find the best and fastest solution to secure higher education places for all eligible seekers.* (H.J., 13 February 2013)

As a consequence of what can be recalled as a crisis in higher education availability, the idea of private higher education was seriously considered, even though earlier attempts had been previously rejected. A prominent professor at Kuwait University, who held several important positions in the state's higher education sector reported:

> *In January 1997, an assembly of Kuwait University (KU) faculty members chaired by a former president of KU and current president of private university was formed with the intention to discuss the feasibility of establishing a private university. The discussion produced a conceptual framework for a private university system that would contribute to higher education in Kuwait in the face of the rapidly growing social demand and the shrinking capacity of Kuwait University, the one and only public university.* (J.A., 25 April 2013)

---

1 Italic has been used to differentiate between quotes I obtained from data collected directly from participants for this research and other quotes from the literature.

Another participant summed-up the then-existing higher education problem in the following statement:

> *The existence of KU as the only university operating in the country for a long period of time, along with the increased number of high school graduates in a way that exceeds the actual capacity of the existing public higher education institutions led the government to search for urgent possible solutions to accommodate the excess number of applicants.* (F.A., 11 December 2012)

Therefore, the non-responsiveness of the public higher education sector to the state's demographic changes resulted in the oversaturation of most public higher education institutions. The government issued random ad-hoc decisions due to pressure from the parliament to absorb the excess demand by increasing enrolment rates, neglecting the actual capacity of those institutions. A faculty member described the resulting situation at KU:

> *Kuwait University has the same capacity as it had years ago, but it now admits double the number of students, causing sometimes a hundred students to be fitted in a small lecture theatre.* (A.F., 18 March 2013)

Another faculty member shared similar views, commenting:

> *There is only one public university in the country, which is unable to accommodate the increasing numbers of high school graduates. It might have been adequate in the past but not recently. This is what raised the need for other universities either public or private.* (R.A., 13 March 2013)

The Arab Human Development Report (UNDP, 2002) also identified similar demographic changes occurring in the entire Arab world. The growing youth population is mainly due to the high fertility rates experienced in the region, in contrast to most developed countries, where falling birth rates are expected to continue to lead to an aging population. The Gulf region's population has risen from just over 28 million in 1998 to an estimated 39 million in 2008 (The Economist Intelligence Unit, 2009). It is expected to remain an unusually young part of the world, with two-thirds of the population under 25 years old (Dakhli & El Zohairy, 2013, p. 46). Romani (2009, p.3) also argues that these demographics certainly play an important role in the future of higher education in the region, as half of the population of the Arab world is below the age of 18. Given the availability of universal secondary education, this fact dramatically increases the prospects of significant college enrolment in the future. Along with the new trends in adult education, the youth population creates a huge pressure on those countries to expand their higher education sectors.

A former minister of higher education endorsed the role of the private sector in accommodating the excess in the public demand. She stated:

> *Currently, private universities have come out of the nursery phase into the growth and progress phase. Now there are more universities – nearly nine. Imagine if there were no private universities until now in the country! How would it handle or deal with the rapid increase in high school graduates, given that public institutions are already accommodating great numbers of students and still student pressure is an issue? This year the public sector had to accept roughly 8000 in KU, 6000 in the PAEET, and 2,500 have been sent abroad by the external scholarships programs. Thus, private universities are playing a great role in accommodating the excess demand for higher education places.* (M.H., 18 March 2013)

However, the establishment of private institutions has not completely addressed the problem of excess demand. Rapid demographic changes continue to create pressure on both public and private institutions. A PUC official reported that:

> *The number of students and the limited capacity of higher education places are still an issue. Because of the demographic changes and the rapid increase in student numbers, all nine working private institutions have reached their maximum capacity based on their current available buildings.* (F.A., 11 December 2012)

If the choice were left to the private sector, it wouldn't hesitate to admit more students for its financial benefit, as has been noted by the president of a private university. However, strict policies by the PUC prevent them from doing so as a governmental measure to control their quality, performance, and operations. This private university president stated:

> *We are working for the expansion our university and are happy to accommodate more students, but the PUC regulations are slowing our expansion. When we are establishing a new program, the PUC treats us as new applicant and we have to start from the beginning in our licensing applications to them.* (S.S., 5 December 2012)

A former Parliament member noted that:

> *The increase in students seeking higher education is still considered as a pressure. The existence of the private universities reduces the pressure of student numbers; however it does not accommodate all of the excess. In other words, it does not address the whole problem.* (H.A., 11 December 2012)

A surplus that exceeds the capacity of public institutions continues to appear, even after the establishment of the private institutions (see Tab. 4). If financial pressure is not the issue in Kuwait, then what is the problem of public policies that were created from the projected growing demand and pressure on the government to introduce privatization policies to accommodate this demand.

Consistency Across Public Policies

The debate went on for years about the need to expand the provision of higher education in the country, whether public or private, as has been illustrated in the above discussion.

Tab. 4 Student numbers exceeding the University of Kuwait absorption capacity for three years.

University year	High school graduates expected to graduates*	KU absorption capacity (according to the Plan)	Surplus (exceeding absorption capacity)	Surplus ratio
2008/2009	7,635	4,910	2,725	55%
2009/2010	7,912	5,005	2,907	58%
2010/2011	8.322	5,100	3,222	63%

*fulfilling University of Kuwait condition for admission

(Source: Al-Atiqi, Al-Rashed, & Al-Ali, 2010, p. 112)

However, political instability, due to the frequent conflicts between the government and the Parliament for years, prevented any development projects from being processed or completed either publicly or privately. The political situation shifted policy decision away from development generally and more towards conflict over power and resources. As an example a participant recalled:

> *Three years ago, I was a member of the committee created for establishing three new public universities. The project was ready to be commenced; yet nothing has been done concerning this project up to this date, as political conflict between the government and the parliament hindered and delayed most of the development processes in the country, mostly benefiting the private sector.* (A.F., 18 March 2013)

Even before the crisis, statistics presented by Ghabra (1997, p. 361) projected the increase in demand for higher education as early as the census of 1980 and 1985, which showed more than 60 percent of Kuwaitis were below the age of 19, while one-third was below the age of nine. These numbers foreshadowed the growing need for the government to expand its higher education provision, especially when it is considered a right for all citizens. Unfortunately, public higher education has not grown in proportion to the increased public demand. Even as late as the year 2000, Kuwait University was the only public university other than the PAAET vocational colleges. As a result, the government had to send thousands of students to continue their university education abroad, a situation that continues to this day, despite the establishment of the private higher education.

Students are the victims of the growing demand pressure and the government's random policies to accommodate this excess demand. Apart from the difficulty they face in securing an opportunity to complete their higher education, their future career is determined by pressures based on wrong standards. Centralized admission processes have been followed by public institutions, according to which students are sorted into universities and fields of study based almost exclusively on secondary school examinations. This sorting system creates a rank-order of academic concentrations with clear minimum scores for admission. However, it neglects students' interests in determining their specific majors and, ultimately, their future employment. Students' experience shows that this demand pressure has negatively affected their opportunity to continue their higher education. Based on his personal experience, one student explained:

> *I graduated from high school with a moderate GPA, which limits my chances of completing my higher education, due to the high competitiveness for the limited spaces offered locally. I had to apply for all available opportunities offered by the ministry and waited for any offer, regardless of the major.* (S.9, 3 April 2013)

A dean at Kuwait University noted that there are many students changing their majors and colleges after enrolment. He said:

> *As a result of student pressure on colleges of Humanities, we decided to steer students into the scientific fields and other colleges, but unfortunately many have been able to change their majors or colleges after the first or second year of their enrolment.* (H.A., 11 December 2012)

To resolve the excess demand pressure, the Kuwaiti government opted to shift the pressure to other vocational colleges under the PAAET. An official from Kuwait University stated that:

> *The government followed the strategy of shifting the student load to vocational colleges; however those institutions are facing similar pressures.* (J.M., 28 November 2012)

The above statement reflects the random and instantaneous policy decisions that characterize most policy processes in the country. This strategy, he pointed out, is also a part of the general centralized admissions system that has negatively affected both the reputation and performance of vocational colleges in Kuwait.

Buckner (2013) noted that those centralized admission processes are common practices in most Arabic countries. By examining the impact of such admission processes on Arabic society, she noticed that many Arab students have been steered into majors that they have little interest in or understanding of. A rank-order of majors in terms of prestige has been internalized by ordinary students and families. As a result, students are pressured by families and socialized by peers into pursuing only the most prestigious fields, even if they enjoy social sciences or humanities. Buckner argues that centralized admission has dual negative impacts. On the societal level, this centralized admissions means that the best students are heavily steered into medical fields, engineering, and some natural sciences. This distortion turns the fields of social sciences and humanities into a dumping ground for students who are not academically motivated, leaving Arab countries without leaders educated in disciplines focused on writing and analysis, for instance. On another level, the centralization of the admission process also deprives universities of autonomy, as they often have been forced to accept more students than they can actually educate. The impact of such processes has effects that go beyond higher education and affect employment and the country's economic performance generally, effects that will be discussed later in this chapter.

The already limited capacity of public higher education has been further aggravated by the production of the gender segregation law (24/1996), which provides another example of the in consistency in public policies. The gender segregation bill was passed in 1996, ending three decades of coeducation at Kuwait University. This policy, applicable to public postsecondary schools, was enacted in 1996 and became effective in 2001 for Kuwait University, the only public university (Al Mughni, 2010). Gender segregation is a policy that passed when the Islamists obtained the majority of the seats in the parliament, and has been subsequently extended to include private higher education. Its production illustrates the chaos and randomness of public policy production processes in Kuwait. It shows how the individuality of policy decisions affects the consistency of public policies. A former parliament member commented:

> *Generally speaking, the main obstacle facing the production of any law in the state of Kuwait is the unstable political situation and the continuous struggle between the parliament and the government that leads to the decision to terminate the parliament and call for another election. Because of this scenario, from the '90s until now only one national assembly has completed its full four-year cycle. Such political crises play a great role in deferring and suspending very important development plans, as well as producing random unplanned policies.* (H.J., 13 February 2013)

The production of the gender segregation law was not preceded by any studies about the applicability of its implementation or accompanied by any plans that took into account the required physical space, faculty members, or time framework. Rather, it was produced just to pacify political powers that demanded the separation of the sexes in accordance with Islamic Sharia laws. As explained by Bush (2003, p. 97), 'Ultimately the success or failure of interests groups in promoting their objectives depends on the resources of power which they are able to mobilize'.

The production of the gender segregation law neglected the difference between the number of male and female enrolments. In fact, it further exacerbates the issue of inadequate facilities for the higher education student population due to the ratio of male to female enrolment rates. In Kuwaiti public higher education, female enrolment often exceeds male enrolment. Since the establishment of Kuwait University in 1966, as shown in Tab. 5,

Tab. 5 Gross Enrolment Rates at tertiary level.

Year	Tertiary enrolment	
	Male	Female
1969	0.9%	2.5%
1975	7.1%	11.2%
1987	11.9%	21%
2004	15%	31%

(Percentage of relevant population) (Adapted from King & Hill, 1993, p. 122; UNESCO, 2012)

the gross enrolment rate of females at tertiary level has often been double the male enrolment rate. According to more recent statistics in 2009, total enrolment in public tertiary education was 61,920 students. Of this number, female enrolments accounted for 41,495 students, or about two-thirds of the total (UNESCO, 2013).

Al Mughni (2010) attributed this phenomenon to the fact that men often choose to pursue their degrees abroad. There are a number of cultural issues that discourage most females from pursuing their studies abroad. However, these differences in enrolment numbers, to a great extent, reflect the ratio of men to women in the countries' total population. Otherwise, it might be attributed to the fact that males can pursue different paths after completing their secondary education, which used to be restricted to them. Such roles included those in the military and police forces, which were not opened to girls until recently, when some police collages opened access to female enrolments. Therefore, the separation required more staffing and physical space and, since public higher education institutions are already stuffed with more students than they can accommodate, the law produced a new challenge that aligned with the excess in the number of applicants to be accommodated.

The processes of the production of the PUL 34/2000 had not encountered the gender segregation law as a policy obstacle in the final stages of its production, when it had been proposed to the Parliament in 1999 to be voted on. Subsequently, private universities also faced the policy of gender segregation. This policy requires substantial financial resources in order to provide two separate campuses for each program (one for each gender), with more staff and faculty members. It was one reason for opposition to the law by the private sector. Another issue was the contradiction between the gender segregation policy on the one hand and the nature and objectives of their educational approaches on the other. Since the programs of most private institutions have been imported or borrowed from the West, coeducation and the interaction between the two genders is considered as being a significant matter. Ultimately, all private institutions have been obliged to implement the policy in one way or another, since their licence is at stake. The fieldwork showed that the implementation of the law mostly consists of offering 50 percent of the classes to males and 50 percent to females. However, some institutions, such as the Australian Box Hill College of Kuwait, opted to turn into an all-girls school. Public institutions showed more power in this matter, as resistance to the implementation of the law lasted for more than four years. Even now, some colleges at KU have escaped the implementation on the law because of practical considerations that require interaction between the genders such as medicine and health sciences.

Interview data revealed that, in the early years of gender segregation, some private institutions were assisted by the PUC in avoiding the law's implementation. A former president of a private university viewed the law as unnecessarily disturbing the educational process. He explained:

> *...the law only separates the students in the lecture room, but not in the corridors or any other space in the campus. Thus the interaction is remaining outside lecture rooms. I was assisted by an official from the PUC in avoiding 100 percent implementation of the law in my university as we both shared similar beliefs concerning the shallow concept of the law.* (S.G., 5 December 2012)

In this matter, the survey result reflected this reality, as more than 70 percent agreed that public universities are more committed to Kuwaiti cultural tradition than private universities, and almost 50 percent agreed that private universities are not serious about implementing the segregation law.

In short, the excess demand resulting from rapid demographic changes had already challenged the limited capacity of public institutions. In addition, this challenge has been further aggravated by the production of inconsistent unplanned policies and the gender segregation law is a good example representing the spontaneous and understudied policy decisions. Since financial factors have not been an issue the only possible explanation is inefficient policy processes.

Making the System Efficient

Given that the early statistics discussed above predicted the increase in student demand for higher education and demonstrated the need for its expansion, the total lack of readiness of the state to accommodate these rapidly growing demands raises the question of efficiency. Kuwait's rich financial resources exclude financial deficiencies as a factor in preventing the development of its higher education sector. There is no credible way that the government can claim that financial shortages were an obstacle to providing higher education opportunities for all qualified citizens. Participants denied the possibility of such a claim, pointing to the fact that Kuwait's state-supported charities build universities in other countries as clear evidence that the state has more than enough resources to develop universities in Kuwait. The following statement reflects participants' views about the country's financial capability by rhetorically asking the following question:

> *Kuwait has built a number of universities in other countries, why it is incapable of improving its own public higher education?* (R.A., 13 March 2013)

Even the financial challenges that have been invoked by the government to rationalize the need for a private sector were not referring to financial shortages. Rather, the government was demanding more efficiency in utilizing public resources and in cutting out unnecessary spending on the higher education sector. According to Al-Atiqi et al. (2009, p. 11), one of the challenges the government had to overcome was that financial backing by the government for an educational system that unnecessarily burdened the country's resources. Thus, the state is not suffering from shortages in the resources available for higher education; it is only viewing the increase in higher education expenditure as an unnecessary burden on the state budget.

The Twenty-Fourth Report of the Investment Climate in Arab Countries (2008) in its higher education development section ranked Kuwait as one of the countries spending the most on its higher education (Sabry, 2009). It is reported to have the highest expenditure on higher education as a percentage of the total public expenditure on education (32.6 percent), followed by the UAE (27.6 percent) and Tunisia (24 percent). It also has the highest per student expenditure as a percentage of the per capita gross domestic product (80 percent of income per capita). Nevertheless, Kuwait's high expenditure on its higher education is not reflected in its performance and outcomes. Its higher education system has not met the country's economic and labour market needs, as is shown by Kuwait's continuing reliance on a foreign workforce. Foreign workers form a majority of the total workforce in Kuwait, and make up more than 90 percent of the workforce in the private sector (Donn & Al Manthri, 2010). Therefore, apparently the problem of an excess in the demand for higher education is not a consequence of lacking financial resources. It is a problem of financial inefficiency rather than financial deficiency.

From different point of view, Al-Atiqi et al. (2010) compared government expenditure on higher education to the increase in the national budget. They noted that the Kuwaiti national budget has more than doubled during the last five years, while the number of seats available for the students at KU and in the PAAET has increased by only 25 percent (p. 119). Further anomalies can be illustrated by examining both local and foreign studies on Kuwaiti public expenditures on higher education. One foreign study compares the percentage of the budget spent on higher education in Kuwait to other countries with similar considerations (UNDP, 2002). Thus, high expenditure does not always mean high quality higher education.

Efficiency adopted in allocating those resources is a crucial factor in determining the performance of the sector. However, it is the local studies that enable a deeper analysis. The local studies compare the state higher education budget to the overall increase in the state budget. Thus, they can focus on the processes of budget and efficiency in public spending. It is these studies that cast light on the failure of Kuwait's high expenditures on higher education to produce the development and expansion needed. This study aims to reveal such inefficiency noted in policy processes in Kuwait.

Kuwait's high expenditure is a fact and none of the study participants denied this reality. However, inefficiency in allocating monies and outright corruption were both noted as local factors that caused problems in effectively expanding public education. Several participants pointed out that students at public schools cost the government much more than they do at private schools. A participant who works in both the public and private higher education sectors commented that:

> *Private universities are offering higher education services that benefit them financially and at the same time benefit the government by reducing the burden of student cost. In a way, the government chose to open private institutions in order to seek cost efficiency. An individual student costs the government much more in a public university than it does in a private institution. It is a service or an aid to the government in reducing the pressure of student demand for higher education, because unfortunately the government neglects to plan for the possibility of facing the problem of the growing demand.* (R.H., 10 March 2013)

Eid Al douahees (2011, 2012, 2013), a Kuwaiti professor, has several publications that describe the absence of appropriate planning in Kuwaiti public institutions, pointing out that most public development projects in Kuwait lack efficient planning or there is a general misconception of the purpose of planning. It is this lack of efficient planning, he argues, that explains most failures in Kuwaiti public development. Another participant claims that the establishment of the private institutions:

> *Saves the government funds by providing a partial substitute of external scholarships, as locally-offered programs by private universities cost less.* (S.S., 5 December 2012)

His argument refers to an internal scholarship program introduced by the PUC that was enacted in the 2006/2007 academic year (Al-Atiqi, Al-Rashed & Al-Ali, 2010). A study presented by the PUC argued that the internal scholarships program allows the state to save 50 percent each year as compared to the alternatives of funding additional governmental educational institutions or foreign scholarships (Al-Atiqi, Al-Rashed & Al-Ali, 2010,

p. 119). In light of the delay in the opening of KU's new headquarters in *Al-Shadadiyah*, planned for 2014, the study suggested that the scholarships program seems to be the only available cost-effective solution for absorbing high school graduates. The sources agree then that subsidizing students at local private universities is cheaper than sending them to foreign universities or establishing a new government university. Since this subsidized program allows students to choose between public or private education, it refutes the idea that private education is monopolized by affluent students because of its high cost.

Public projects to expand higher education provision locally were planned and, to some degree, commenced more than three decades ago. However, nothing has been successfully completed. For example, the new buildings for Kuwait University *Al-Shadadiyah* were planned in the 1970s, with budget and land allocated. The work started more than two decades ago. However, the project has not been completed yet. Thus, over thirty years have passed and the new public university is still under construction. Even back in 1982, the national TV news was reporting that the Parliament was discussing the budget of Kuwait University and the planning and building the new university *Al-Shadadiyah* (https://www.youtube.com/watch?v=DDw-bkq-nSc&list=WL&index=6). Why has this project taken so long to finish? More generally, why is the project to expand public provision of higher education taking forever to be completed?

Interview data reveals two major reasons for the delay in many development projects in the country. The first reason is the conflict between the government and the parliament, which has stalled many development projects. The second reason is government's high levels of bureaucracy and the resulting prevalent corruption. Political instability in particular has negatively affected higher education provision. A dean at Kuwait University complained:

> *There is no long-term or future vision taken into account in policy decisions, along with very slow implementation! In 2005 KU submitted a study proposal to the government showing the need to establish three new public universities and until now it is still frozen and no real actions have been seriously taken!* (R.A., 13 March 2013)

He added:

> *The new buildings for KU or* 'Al-Shadadiyah' *were commenced in the late 1970s to accommodate a specific number of students (40,000). This new campus has not been completed yet and the university will reach this number of students next year. So the relocations of all colleges to the new campus 'If finished anytime soon!' will do nothing to address the space problem. If the project had been implemented when proposal was submitted to the cabinet, it might have solved the problem of student pressure years ago.* (R.A., 13 March 2013)

The above statements illustrate the inefficiency in the processes of public policy production and implementation. Policy decisions are driven not by real public needs, but by conflict over authority and personal interests. Delays in policy decisions create more unnecessary financial burdens because of the rapidly changing market, and the changing in the costs of raw materials and labour market services. Regarding calculations of the cost to expand public higher education, a former president of Kuwait University said:

> *The cost of the initial planning of the new KU was 98KD million, now it will cost 1.5- 2KD billion if not more.* (S.S., 5 December 2012)

He added:

> *There was also the project of the new buildings for KU in Al Shewikh city. The project has been stopped since the 1980s because of a problem with a contractor who was caught stealing money from the project. In 1982, PAAET was established and the government was looking for a location for it. Al Shewikh's buildings were offered as a 'temporary' location and, since then, those buildings have been taken by PAAET and will never return back to the University.* (S.S., 5 December 2012)

Some participants viewed the introduction of private higher education as a normal development concerning government bureaucracies. An official from the PUC stated that:

> *The state has been undergoing privatization policies generally and it is the time for private sector participation in providing public services. ... State bureaucracy in the face of the flexible private sector pushed the Government into producing the private universities law in order to solve the problem that they faced of the excess number of graduates without available places in HE sector. In addition to the private sector's willingness to participate, it is considered as being a great investment opportunity, taking into account all the high subsidies offered by the government.* (F.A., 11 December 2012)

Others view it as a clear business opportunity and are driven by profit-making, regardless of whether privatization responds to public demands. Participant from KU claimed that:

> *The idea did not originate in Kuwait University. It was an investment opportunity with a clear profit motive. Profits are guaranteed for two reasons: the first is guaranteed costumers, students sponsored by the government through internal scholarships program. The second is that public institutions are incapable to accommodate the increased number of students.* (J.M., 28 November 2012)

The government was fully aware of the increase in the number of higher education seekers (Al-Atiqi & Alharbi, 2009). However, political instability and excess bureaucracy prevented the development of public higher education, just as they did to other sectors in the country. The development of public higher education has not been responding to the annually increasing numbers of high school graduates. There have been many other projects to improve the public provision of higher education, but these initiatives have been frozen for years. According to one survey participant:

> *Jaber University is a proposed new public university. We have done the report on it and the report has been submitted to the Minister, who should then establish the management board and commence its activity in September of this year. But as far as I know, nothing has commenced yet.* (W.R., 17 March 2013)

One question is – which Minister of education he was talking about? Due to frequent conflicts between the government and the parliament, new governments are often established. As a result, it is rare for any Minister of Education to complete his full term. Dozens of ministers have passed through the Ministry of Education, sometimes more than one or two in the same year. Jaber University is a part of project entitled '*Al Madinah Al Jamee'iah*', or the academic city, that accommodates three new public universities. According to a participant:

> *There is the law which has been passed for the establishment of* 'Al Madinah Al Jamee'iah'*, an academic city that accommodates several universities at the same place. In addition, the state development plan is working on establishing three new public universities, such as Jaber University of Applied Sciences.* (H.J., 13 February 2013)

The president of KU, on a TV report discussing the delays in opening '*Al-Shadadiyah*' the new public university, reported that:

> The new university '*Al-Shadadiyah*', if it becomes ready, could operate as a branch under the supervision of KU. Or it could be a new independent institution … in the end it is a state decision and KU has nothing to say in this regards.

His statement reveals the unsystematic and chaotic nature of the public processes for the development of Kuwaiti public higher education. The project in question has been in existence for thirty years and is currently under construction. It was initially commenced by KU. And yet its administration and processes have still not been planned. The president of KU himself doesn't even know if the new university will become a branch under the supervision of KU or an independent public institution.

None of the public projects to expand the provision of higher education has been completed yet. The private sector, on the other hand, has proven to be more flexible and adaptable when it comes to business and profit-making. It has more autonomy in its decision-making concerning its processes of management and operations. As a result, the scenario was different when it came to the establishment of the private universities. Quick decisions and speedy implementations characterized their establishment, mainly because time means money and profits do matter to the private sector. Accordingly, within only a decade or so after the production of the private universities law, there are now more than ten operating private institutions. An achievement that contrasts sharply with the one public university that has been under construction for more than three decades and is still not complete. A president and a board member of one of the private universities recalled:

> *The government gave us the land with a restrictive six-month time frame to finish the buildings of our private university. We started building on 2002/03 and the relocation to the new buildings took place in the 2005/2006 academic year.* (S.S., 5 December 2012)

Government bureaucracy and lack of systematic processes have created an advantage for some private institutions in providing higher education services to the country. However, troubled policy processes and Government bureaucracy continued to negatively affect other private institutions. A board member at a licensed private institution complained:

> *We got the license from the PUC four years ago. However up to this date we haven't commenced building our universities because of some issues found in the land allocated for the university and also because the ministry of municipality has not approved the land and its borders. Although everything has to be done through the PUC, nothing is going to actually happen without personal intervention using my own connections in the country's different ministries involved. Without* 'wasta' *[connections], nothing is going be finished.* (A.S., 27 March 2013)

The above statements reflect the corruption prevalent in the various public institutions. This corruption is the second explanation revealed by the data that explains the delays and inefficiency experienced in public projects. The '*wasta*' or '*vitamin waw*' (known as vitamin B – *Beziehungen* – in Germany, which means relationship) is a local term used to describe a type of corruption that uses connections and relationships to finish most of the work in the state's different institutions. The prevalence of *wasta* in policy processes has empowered the interference of socio-cultural factors in steering policy decisions. Kinninmont (2012) noted its negative impact on the functioning of the parliament in Kuwait. She reported:

> They are often described as 'service MPs' [MPs: members of the Parliament], whose main function is to obtain economic benefits for their constituents. A focus group on Kuwaiti politics organized by a US NGO, the National Democratic Institute, noted the perception that *wasta* (which roughly translates as connections, social capital, or 'who you know') from an MP was required to get things done in Kuwait and that this service role diverted MPs from their legislative and over-sight functions. (p. 9)

Another example of short-sighted and inefficient public decisions is the government's method of dealing with the growing demand for higher education. To resolve the growing demand pressure, the government simply shifted the balance to the vocational colleges under the PAAET. An official from Kuwait University noted that:

In the past, the government followed the strategy of shifting the student load to vocational colleges. However, those institutions have accordingly been facing similar pressures. (J.M., 28 November 2012)

Being a common second choice has negatively affected the reputation of vocational colleges in Kuwait. The impact of the centralized processes of admission on the country's human capital will be expanded on further in this chapter in the discussion of the needs of the changing labour market.

Thus, excessive bureaucracy characterizes the Kuwaiti government. This factor, along with the political unrest and the conflict between the parliament and the government, has made solving the problem of rapidly growing demand in a way that is both local and reasonably quick almost impossible without the participation of the private sector. Given the state's financial capabilities, the only convincing explanation for the higher-education supply crisis is the fact that unsystematic, random, and inefficient Kuwaiti policy processes have made the establishment of the private institutions the only practical solution to address the growing demand pressure. The situation has been visualized in the caricature in Fig. 7.

The research data also support this argument. One survey participant from KU assured the interviewer that the major purpose of allowing the establishment of the private institutions,

...was only to solve the problem of the excess in public demand. They reduce part of the pressure on public universities, but still not at the required amount. A new public university is still needed. (R.A., 13 March 2013)

Lack of efficiency is not only seen in the management of higher education; it is part of a broader phenomenon that affects all national public policy production. However, concerning higher education, the two cases cited above should demonstrate this inefficiency in producing higher education policies. The production of the disruptive gender segregation law and the failure of the public higher education development projects both demonstrate the failure and inadequacy of the Kuwaiti policy production processes.

The call for the expansion of higher education was general and not assigned to the private sector specifically. However, the failure of the public sector to address the problem for years created an opportunity for the private sector to step in. A former president of KU who is currently a president of one of the private institutions said:

Because of the pressure of student numbers on Kuwait University, there was a great demand for higher education and KU exceeded its normal capacity of student enrolment. [In his exact words] *All of the circumstances were calling for a private university.* (S.S., 5 December 2012)

Inefficiency is also seen within the administration and management of higher education institutions. A student tells of his study experience at KU as follows:

Fig. 7: Caricature describes the challenges of development in Kuwait. (unknown, n.d.)

> *Buildings were in a very bad condition; they were very old in my college. The registration system was not convenient, as there were always closed subjects and we were facing problems due to the lack of available places for most of us. The university created something they called 'registration by force' to overcome this problem at the end of the registration period. This problem was generated by forcing the university politically to admit too many students, more than it could accommodate. This situation did not affect my time of completion, as at the last moment I was enrolled in the subject, but not with my preferred professor and with a very long day at university because the administration had to open late classes to tackle the excess number of students. ... Something needing to be mentioned is the ratio between student and faculty numbers. There were very few faculty members compared to the number of students.* (S.1, 31 March 2013)

She added:

> *There are inequalities in treating students due to the professors' methods of lecturing about a subject, as they have different styles and different grading systems with different levels of difficulty.* (S.1, 31 March 2013)

An inadequate supply of academic faculty was also noted by an official at KU. He reported that:

> *The total number of staff members in Kuwait University counted for only 6,419 members in the face of around 56,000 enrolled students [both graduates and undergraduates].* (A.B., 3 January 2013)

Another participant reaffirmed that:

> *Along with student pressure, public institutions lack sufficient faculty members, space, and classes.* (J.M., 28 November 2012)

This imbalance in the ratio between students and faculty members is caused by two conflicting policies. On the one hand, public institutions maintain a strict recruitment strategy in order to insure the quality of their faculty members. But, on the other hand, there is almost universal student enrolment. The result is too few faculty and too many students.

Another student from a private higher education institution described his experience:

> *Generally, I like it. However, there are pros and cons everywhere. For example, the registration system previously used to be done manually by the supervisor. But now it has been improved so that the students can do it online. This has the disadvantage of creating anonymity as to the faculties teaching the subjects we are choosing. It is a kind of university system to control the process by distributing the students equally among the classes regardless the lecturer. In my opinion, this is unfair and I don't like it. I believe that the student has the right to choose between lecturers.* (S.3, 3 April 2013)

It seems that, due to demand pressures, students at both public and private institutions are facing similar problems. However, generally students at private institutions seemed more satisfied and less affected by inefficient management.

In general, inefficiency in policy processes has ignored significant indicators pointing to the limited capacities of public institutions in the face of the rapid demographic changes. It is this inefficiency, and not financial shortages, that have favoured higher education privatization in Kuwait. Given the presented inefficacy in policy processes, what about the quality of higher education that has been provided under such conditions?

The Pursuit of Quality

Although the development of private higher education in most developing countries has been in response to growing demand pressure (Tilak, 1991), its introduction into the Kuwaiti higher education system is found to be in response to differentiated demands as well. Internal factors indicated by the data discussed later in this chapter can be categorized under differentiated demand pressures. The most obvious differentiated demand pressure is the fact that privatization is promoted in Kuwait because of the need for better quality higher education. The following statement reflects the general feeling regarding existing public higher education:

> *A major demand was for better alternatives to the deteriorating, outdated, and overly saturated public higher education.* (S.S., 5 December 2012)

The participant emphasized the poor outcomes of public higher education that have caused public debate for years. Demand pressure, along with inefficient management and administration, has negatively affected the quality of public higher education, leading to a poor academic environment for students. A student complained about his study experience at KU:

> *Buildings were in a very bad condition; they were very old in my college. The registration system was not convenient, as there were always closed subjects and we were facing problems due to the lack of available places for most of us. The university created something they called 'registration by force' to overcome this problem at the end of the registration period. This problem was generated by forcing the university politically to admit too many students, more than it could accommodate.* (S.1, 31 March 2013)

Another student claimed that the old facilities at public institutions and student pressure contributed to her dropping out from the university. She said:

> *The general environment from old buildings, over forty students in a small lecture room, and the faculty members and how they treated us in an irresponsible way were to a great extent the reasons that caused my dropping out. They [faculty members] want to fail us without any reasons. They are happy with dropouts because of the pressure they are facing, I think. Why they don't bring in more faculty members and expand our buildings?* (S.11, 3 April 2013)

A former student of KU, after completing two degrees in the private sector, claimed that:

> *Kuwait University lacks the simple technology that gives students flexibility in dealing with university system such as online registration, electronic library etc I believe that Kuwait University staff members choose to operate in this way. I argue that the implementation of such technologies would cause faculties to lose the authority they have over students. This is the only reason that can explain the situation, mainly because the university has the required experience, knowledge and the financial capability to implement such systems. It has very poor facilities compared to the least funded private institution in the country. ... [He added] Public institutions lack recent academic resources, as is shown by the outdated libraries.* (S.K., 19 March 2013)

A faculty member also complained:

> *...Why does a country such as Kuwait, which is one of the richest countries in the world, have only one public university, and one that does not even have its own complete campus? ... Kuwait University, for example, still lacks an effective email system that connects all faculty members and students with each other!!* (R.H., 10 March 2013)

The above complaints mirror the general public's feelings about public higher education. Such practices have caused Kuwaiti society to lose faith in its public sector and lead to increased public demand for better education, regardless of whether it is public or private, since the government will be paying its expenses in any case. As a result, there was wide acceptance of private higher education at the beginning, mainly because of the public sector's long-term failures in meeting public expectations. In addition, the introduction of the internal scholarships program through the PUC created new opportunities for students to choose between public and private institutions in continuing their higher education at state expense. According to PUC official:

> *Today, this program is feeding private institutions with 80 percent of their total enrolments.* (F.A., 11 December 2012)

However, despite the apparent popularity of choosing private schools, it must be remembered that for many students, the choice is constrained by the lack of available spaces in public higher education.

In an attempt to address the pressure of poor quality, the privatization policy (PUL 34/2000) opted to implement internationally recognized higher education programs borrowed from foreign universities as stated in the first article of the law:

> It is permissible by a decree issued in response to a request by the Minister of Higher Education to license the foundation of private universities/colleges or higher institutes/branches of foreign universities where the majority of shared capital funds is wholly owned by Kuwaitis. (PUL 34/2000, article 1)

And has further emphasized through the subsequent policies, such as in the law regulating 'Rules and procedures for private educational institutions license application: Branches of foreign educational institutions'. It stated that:

> The (Parent) Educational Institution is qualified in accordance with the adopted Standards and Criteria of the Private Universities Council no. (PUC 16/d 25-02/2006) which stipulates that the institution must be among the best 200 universities listed in the latest appendix of the Times Educational Magazine. Educational Institutions have the capacity to grant Diploma degrees are qualified according to PUC resolution (PUC 4 26-3/2006) which requires the parent educational institution to be distinguished in its domain in conformity with the standards laid down by the licensing committee. (PUC 2/ 30-4/2007)

The policy also strengthens the role of the parent institution in the operations of the local institutions. For example:

> The Educational institution in Kuwait is a branch of the parent educational institution. Graduation certificates are issued by the branch of the parent university/ college in Kuwait. (PUC 2/ 30-4/2007)

And also in the second section from the same law:

> Second: Role of the (Parent) Educational Institution
> The Educational institution in Kuwait is a branch of the parent educational institution. Graduation certificates are issued by the branch of the parent university/ college in Kuwait.

> The parent educational institution is encouraged to become a financial partner with the licensed corporate (body corporate) with a share not exceeding 49% of capital. The parent educational institution nominates academic, financial and technical working teams approved by the General Secretariat to assist the founders in preparing the preliminary application and the detailed statement as well as preparing visual presentations to the specialized committees on demand.
> The parent educational institution is required to appoint the head of the university/college, members of teaching staff, and support staff as well as participation in enhancing scientific research and developing a system of quality control. It should also be committed to accepting transferred students from the branch. (PUC 2/30-4/2007)

Therefore, higher education privatization policies illustrate that the government, in an attempt to control the quality of national higher education, has shifted the responsibility to external, foreign higher education institutions.

The poor performance of Kuwaiti higher education has been also attributed to an unsatisfactory general education. The poor outcomes of general education produced students with low academic capacities to complete their higher education, which as a result affected their performance in university. Schools then need to better qualify their students for a better higher education performance. An official from KU claimed that:

> *The problem of the university's poor academic performance originates in the years of general education. I would suggest standard tests at the end of the general education years to create an equitable basis for all students to get the best opportunity in higher education.* (A.B., 3 January 2013)

He went on to say:

> *The main problem in higher education is the weakness in general education outcomes and there is an urgent need to develop the quality of its provision.* (A.B., 3 January 2013)

The above statement highlights a significant problem in the learning processes used by Kuwait's education system, including its higher education. That problem is the widespread overdependence on rote learning. *The Road Not Travelled* report (The World Bank, 2008) argued that one of the major factors hindering the advancement of the GCC educational systems is the outdated pedagogical methods that they generally incorporate. The KU official quoted above avoided mentioning that, with some exceptions, the rote way of learning is also widely used in public higher education. According to the World Bank, most MENA countries continue to use the traditional model of pedagogy; a method that is far from the inquiry-based learning approaches followed by highly scored countries on the Knowledge Economy Index (KEI). Al-Tarrah (2008) points out that 'the education system in the GCC countries is based mostly, [if not exclusively], on memorization rather than on the development of students' critical thinking and creativity skills' (as cited in Dakhli & El Zohairy, 2013, p. 44). Robert Wallace Baxter, spokesman of Qatar Foundation, argues that 'a system that has so far been reliant on rote-learning has produced a 'brain-drained' society, which lacks skills of analysis, curiosity and creativity' (Gulf States Newsletter, 2007). A president of a private institution confirmed that the graduates of public education are better-qualified academically (higher achievers) than their counterparts from private education. However, public institutions lack the focus on building students' critical thinking skills because they rely on memorization and rote learning. He commented:

> *Education in public schools is much better than it is in private schools. However, the public system does not promote critical thinking by students. Another challenge faced by public school graduates is acquiring fluency in the English language, since they only teach math and science in English! The advantages of private graduates over public graduates are both language and critical thinking.* (S.S., 5 December 2012)

The great reliance on rote learning at the general education level also affects learning the process at public higher education institutions. Since students are already used to the rote- learning system, their expectations of higher education are formulated accordingly. Higher education participants expect all learning materials to be prepared by the lecturer. One student complained:

> *Doctors gave us tests that included external questions that they never mentioned before. Sometimes I feel they did this on purpose in order to fail us.* (S.2, 3 April 2013)

A faculty member viewed the problem from different angle:

> *In Kuwaiti public institutions there is no campus life, as most of the campuses are open buildings and the weather in most of the year in Kuwait is extremely hot. That is why the students are barely attending their lectures. On the other hand, private institutions are designed to be indoor campuses where students can hold all kinds of activities inside the buildings. Private schools, in that sense, are designed in a better way. That is why students can have all of the activities that they want, although there are still some constraints due to the higher education gender segregation law.* (R.H., 10 March 2013)

Thus, he emphasized the significant role that building-structure plays in forming students' perceptions of higher education and their general knowledge experience. According to this faculty member, the problem had been most successfully addressed by the private institutions. In the survey, 50.87 percent of the sample agreed that better education is provided in public institutions. However, survey participants also maintained that better facilities (77 percent), academic resources (52 percent), and greater variety (51 percent) are found in the private sector.

Better quality in higher education is often connected with the use of English language as a medium of instruction. Generally speaking, data from interviews reflect a public preference for English. Most participants were aware of the significant usefulness of acquiring the English language. English is considered useful for various reasons, among which are easier access to employment, the prospect of further studies abroad, social status, and international communication. The use of the English language as a medium of instruction is referred to by many as the most significant advantage of private higher education in Kuwait over public higher education. In the survey, a student commented:

> *Learning all subjects in English is one of the advantages of private universities over public ones.* (160)

Another student pointed to the need of students for English-speaking higher education locally:

> *The existence of private universities gave me the opportunity to continue my education and to complete my higher degree without the need to look for universities outside the country. Kuwait University did not accept my GPA, although they lowered their standards 2 years after I graduated. They would now accept my high school GPA, except that I can't apply after 2 years have passed; it is their policy. I am glad private universities were established, as I have no interest in travelling and leaving my family to get a degree abroad.* (50)

Another commented:

> *Private institutions increase my chances. Most teachers in Kuwait University (the only public university in Kuwait) teach in Arabic and always use Arabic terminologies and ways to explain. However at private universities, all subjects, except Arabic of course, are taught in English. And as I have graduated from a Private school, it obviously helps.* (170)

A former president of a private university refers to the use of the English language at private higher education institutions as an advantage they have over public institutions. He states:

> *Programs offered by private institutions are more developed and updated, and are also conducted in English, which is an advantage.* (S.G., 5 December 2012)

A dean at Kuwait University agreed that the English language as a medium of instruction is an advantage that private universities have over the public sector; however, he argued that it is the only advantage they have. He stated:

> *Using English as a medium of instruction is the only advantage that private institutions have over the public ones, as we have adopted higher quality and internationally recognized programs that are lacking at most privately operated institutions as of yet.* (R.A., 13 March 2013)

Most colleges in Kuwait University have adopted English textbooks and claim to enforce the use of English language as a medium of instruction (excluding social sciences). However, the actual implementation is more flexible, and relies greatly on both the lecturer's preference and discipline. It is not as strict as it should be. A graduate from Kuwait University, commenting on the use of English language in the school of business, explained:

> *All of our textbooks are in English. However, the language of instruction in lectures varies among the different faculty members. It also depends on what agreement they come to with their students about conducting the lecture. For example, some lecturers ask students for their preference, but they insist on using specific terminologies in the English language for the benefit of their students. This is only the case for local lecturers. For English speaking lecturers, everything has to be in English.* (S.1, 31 March 2013)

These conditions explain how it is possible to have graduates that lack sufficient English language skills to qualify them for work in private sector, where English language skills are an essential requirement. That being said, it would be premature to argue that graduates from private sector are necessarily more fluent in English than their counterparts from the public sector. In order to make any generalization, further studies need to be conducted.

The use of English as a medium of instruction is considered to be an advantage for foreign expatriate children, as well as anyone who wants to continue their education in Kuwait, especially when admission to public institutions is extremely limited. Another problem caused by the need for private higher education and the demand for English-speaking higher education will be further discussed in the following section. A survey participant stated:

> *The absorption capacity of the higher education sector in the state of Kuwait continues to be a challenge, to a great extent because private universities are targeted by both citizens and expatriates, for whom they are their only choice.* (S.G., 5 December 2012)

The poor quality of public sector, according to the data, can also be attributed to the absence of competition as a significant influence on both performance and quality. One survey participant commented:

> *Logically, you can't have one public university operating in the country. You need at least to cover different areas for easier access. ... There is also the absence of competition, which is a significant factor in shaping higher education provision. The existence of more than one university is supposed to create the atmosphere for a kind of competition between schools, but this is not the case in Kuwait. This is why I see higher education in Kuwait as only a kind of higher level of high school. Most students come mostly to attend classes and don't bother participating in any other activity.* (R.H., 10 March 2013)

On the other hand, others argued that competition has come into existence with the establishment of the private sector. However, this competition among private institutions is limited to a competition for governmental scholarships. In other words, it is only a competition for enrolments and financial resources. One participant commented:

> *The existence of private institutions in Kuwait relies, to a large extent, on the internal scholarships offered by the government. Some institutions like the International Law School are composed entirely of publicly sponsored students.* (A.F., 18 March 2013)

Because of private institutions' great financial reliance on the government, it places them under an even greater control by the government than is experienced by the long-established public institutions. Bureaucracies and the long existence of public institutions weaken the government control over both the quality and the general administration of public higher education institutions. In contrast, the private sector allows for greater control over their general operations and performance, since their license is always at stake. A former minister and current president of a private institution commented, endorsing higher education privatization in Kuwait:

> *Where there is weak supervision of private institutions by the state, privatization can bring disadvantages. The state of Kuwait however, has great control over its private institutions. Although there are differences in their performances, they are now all subject to the universal standards organized by PUC. The experience in Kuwait is free from small shops selling higher education certificates, in contrast to what can be found in other countries. The main objective of private universities is general development, not commerce or profits. There are inevitably faults in any experience, but if the pros exceed the cons, then this is what we want.* (M.H., 18 March 2013)

A founder of a private institution has a contrasting viewpoint concerning the nature of the private higher education in Kuwait. He endorses privatization policies, but only with precautions concerning the overwhelming profit motive that negatively affects their academic quality. He states:

> *I view private universities as a necessity. However, there is a need to focus on their quality. The problem of quality exists because of the general commercial atmosphere at all private institutions. Education provided by the market needs more supervision. Institutions are too focused on profits. Even with PUC supervision, they know how to get around the rules.* (S.G., 5 December 2012)

Moreover:

> *In the first announcement of the establishing the American University of Kuwait, they were advertising it in the newspaper as a great investment opportunity for investors instead of discussing how it would benefit the society academically or help in developing the country's higher education.* (S.G., 5 December 2012)

About two-thirds of the survey sample agreed that private universities are exploitative and mostly motivated by commercial interests. A law expert, former member of the PUC, and faculty member at KU considers the privatization policy to be pure business opportunity. He claims that:

> *The purpose of Private Universities Law (34/2000) was far from improving higher education academically. The merchants had a great involvement in the production of this law.* (A.F., 18 March 2013)

He added:

> *Personally, after it became obvious to me that the PUC was not serious in improving national higher education and after witnessing the Merchants' power over council decisions, I withdrew from my position on the Council of Private Universities.* (A.F., 18 March 2013)

A visit to GUST, a well-established private university, provides an example that supports his viewpoint. The general atmosphere and socio-economic background of the students raises questions about the type of education being provided. Private institutions are the main target for low achievers. 62 percent of survey sample agreed that the admission requirements of private universities are lower than those of public universities. This is mainly because, given a choice, most Kuwaitis still prefer to study at a public university (46 percent of the survey sample agreed). This data suggests the notion that there is an 'elite demand' for private higher education similar to the recognized phenomenon in Kenya (see Jamshidi et al., 2012, p. 795). That is to say, private universities have emerged in response to the demands of wealthy families with low-achieving children that can't get into KU. Private universities provide these families with a more prestigious alternative to the vocational public institutions, and without the need to send their children abroad.

Thus, suspicions concerning quality affect both public and private institutions. Alongside the pursuit of quality there are other local pressures for different higher education that responds to social and cultural needs.

Socio-Cultural Challenges

The data also highlights some of the social and cultural concerns that have influenced and promoted the establishment of private higher education in Kuwait. Among these concerns are restrictions on women's education abroad, the consequences of the 9/11 terrorist attacks for Muslim international students, and, finally, the demand of expatriates for higher education. These three factors have contributed to the increased demand for different higher education in Kuwait.

Regarding women's education, there are both religious and cultural restrictions on women's education abroad. One survey participant noted that:

> *One of the advantages that private higher education offers is that it solves some of the cultural and religious issues concerning travelling abroad to study, more for girls than boys.* (S.G., 5 December 2012)

Studying abroad is usually a viable option for male students. However, it is not always an option for girls because of cultural and religious restrictions. In addition, the number of female applicants is often double that of male applicants, as shown in the section on demand pressures. Thus, the establishment of new universities, which supposedly implement an international curriculum imported from the West, is seen as a valuable opportunity for girls' families.

The major concern regarding women's education abroad is about women living abroad alone, without male relatives, or *Maharim*, to accompany them, which is a topic that could alone make a PhD research. Both cultural and religious constraints are thereby imposed on women who wish to pursue higher education abroad. These constraints have created a demand for importing international education into Kuwait, so that women can have access to it locally.

This is a major factor promoting the establishment of private higher education in Kuwait. Local private education creates an option for families who refuse to send their daughters abroad. It is also true, however, that some female students prefer to complete their higher education locally rather than by travelling abroad. They think that leaving the country alone to study in foreign country would be a great responsibility, and one that is too hard to be borne by everyone. A student commented:

> *My GPA is very high, which gave me the advantage of being able to choose from among all of the opportunities offered for continuing my higher education. However I didn't apply for a scholarship to study abroad, as I don't think I am able to handle it.* (S.1, 31 March 2013)

Dakhli and El Zohairy (2013, p. 58) similarly noted that women in the GCC countries have especially benefitted from the establishment of private higher education in the region, since they now have the opportunity to further their education with minimal travel and cultural barriers.

The cultural constraints on women affect not only their choice to study locally, but may also influence what type of local institution they attend. For example, Kuwaiti families who choose an American-style university for their daughters may be ambivalent about their choice. They want the prestige and quality of an American education, but wish to limit the social and intellectual impact of the foreign qualities associated with critical thinking, secular attitudes, and coeducational practices (Tolmacheva, 2011, p. 6). As a result, Kuwait has some private institutions that are foreign run but nonetheless all-girl, such as the Australian Box Hill College.

The second social and cultural factor that has helped to promote the establishment of private higher education in Kuwait is also related to the practice of studying abroad. Specifically, it concerns the reduction of the number of students studying in Western countries, especially the United States, as a consequence of the 9/11 attacks. Discussing the causes of the increased demand for higher education in Kuwait, one participant recalled:

> *The 9/11 attacks prevented many students from travelling to study in the US. Even some students, who were already there, had to return and suspend getting their degrees. The changes in visa regulations and other student security concerns resulted in a reduction of the number of students studying abroad, especially in western countries. Political complications resulted in the reduction of external scholarships at that time and thereby promoted the local provision of western models of higher education through the establishment of private institutions.* (S.G., 5 December 2012)

According to the United Nations (2003), the number of Arab students in the United States dropped by about a third between the years 1999 and 2002 (Dakhli & El Zohairy, 2013, p. 47). Romani (2009, p. 4) also noted that 'since the September 11, 2001 attacks, escalating security constraints have impeded Arab students' mobility vis-à-vis the West. Hence, many more of them prefer to study in their home countries.

Finally, there is the social pressure caused by the huge numbers of expatriates living and working in Kuwait. For many of them, Kuwait is a second home. They constitute a large segment of Kuwait's population – about two-thirds (60 percent) of the total (PACI, 2018). A former president of a private university in Kuwait noted that:

> *The existence of large community of expatriates created the need for the private higher education, as it is almost the only opportunity for their children to complete their higher education in Kuwait.* (S.G., 5 December 2012)

Public higher education in Kuwait is only available to citizens, except for very few exceptions. In general, children of expatriates are not permitted to attend public institutions, as they are reserved exclusively for citizens. Accordingly, before the establishment of private higher education, expatriates had to send their children outside of Kuwait in order to complete their higher education. The long-term presence and overwhelming numbers of these expatriates created a need for higher education institutions other than the existing public ones. Dakhli and El Zohairy (2013, p. 47) note that the emergence of private higher education in the GCC countries responds to the demand of the majority of skilled expatriates, who rely heavily on it to educate their children.

Currently, many skilled expatriates are financially capable of paying for their children's education in the private institutions. Romani (2009, p. 4) argues that, aside from the demographic realities of the Gulf region and the overall need of post-oil rentier economies for knowledge-based societies, there are two specific circumstances that underlie the post-2000 academic boom. One of them is the fact that between 25 percent and 75 percent of the population of the various GCC countries are foreign expatriates. Many of these expatriates have the wealth and will to provide their children with higher education in their host countries. The desire of prosperous expatriates to educate their children locally in their host country can be regarded as one contributor to the growing demand pressure that helped create and sustain privatization in Kuwait. One survey participant considered skilled expatriates' reliance on private higher education as a factor that increased demand pressures on private institutions. He stated:

> *The absorption capacity of the higher education sector in the state of Kuwait is still an issue because private universities are being targeted not only by citizens, but also expatriates, for whom it is almost their only choice.* (S.G., 5 December 2012)

Increased financial capability is also witnessed among nationals. Many Kuwaitis are capable and willing to pay for their education, welcoming the establishment of recognized private higher education institutions in their country, despite the existence of the free public higher education. Thus, the demand for private higher education can be regarded as cumulative demand by individuals who fail to get free public higher education for various reasons.

Although education is a free public right for all citizens, many Kuwaiti families opt to send their children to private schools, more so than before. This phenomenon illustrates the increase in the financial capacities of the general public, both Kuwaiti and expatriate. As a result of this increased financial power, many Kuwaitis are financing their own education at private schools; fully 47 percent of the survey participants who were in their fourth year described themselves as self-funded, which means that despite the introduction of the internal scholarships program, almost 50 percent of the survey's participants are paying for their higher education.

Higher education is the entrance to employment. Thus, logically they are connected and each is affected by the other. Since there were major labour market reforms that happened in that period I included questions in my research to investigate possible pressures that labour market reforms might have on the production of higher education privatization policies. The following section discusses pressures emerged from the changing labour market.

Needs of the Changing Labour Market

A survey participant from the private sector claimed that:

> *The outcomes of public higher education are poor and irrelevant to market needs.* (S.S., 5 December 2012)

He also raised the problem of the lack of planning between higher education sector and the market pointing out that:

> *Public Higher education institutions in Kuwait are operating in isolation from the market and the expatriate workforce has filled the gap for decades.* (S.S., 5 December 2012)

This alienation of higher education from the labour market is emphasized by the fact that almost 50 percent of the survey sample was undecided concerning the alignment of higher education curricula and employment.

Lack of connection between public institutions and the market is also noted by high school students complaining about the poor counselling they received concerning future higher education decisions. One student complained:

> *As new graduates, we are suffering from the lack of places in higher education. There is also no connection between high schools and higher education institutions. We as students really need to be counselled and consulted in choosing our paths for completing our higher education throughout our high school years, not leaving us to face the challenge of competing for higher education places only after graduation in a very short period of time.* (S.4, 3 April 2013)

While shortages in the skilled national workforce may require supplementation from expatriates, the government continues to employ nationals even if they lack needed skills. According to the State Constitution (article 41, Right and duty to work section):

> Every Kuwaiti has the right to work and to choose the type of his work. Work is a duty of every citizen necessitated by personal dignity and the public good. The State shall endeavour to make it available to citizens and to make its terms equitable. (The Constitution of Kuwait, 1962)

This almost-guaranteed employment of nationals in the public sector explains the difference between the percentages of nationals and expatriates employed in the public and private sectors. Expatriates constitute about 90 percent of private sector employees, while about the same percentage of nationals work for the government (Dakhli & El Zohairy, 2013, p. 54). On the similar matter of national employment, a former parliament member noted:

> *The state is obliged to provide employment opportunities for all Kuwaiti graduates, even if not in their area of specialization unfortunately. There is no academic preference on students' achievement applied in employment process. ... If the state continues to be the main employer for graduates without implementing any academic performance competition, higher education will only become educational service provided by both public and private sectors.* (H.J., 13 February 2013)

These employment procedures negatively affect the function and perception of higher education in Kuwait. The purpose of higher education as a result is misunderstood, and the motivations and personal interests of students, accordingly, are neglected in choosing their path of higher education. Responses by students mirror their purpose of obtaining higher education. A student stated:

> *Although I have met the admission requirements of Kuwait University, I prefer to study at one of the private universities. It will be easier to finish the degree there because of the type of students they enrol – low achievers – and the easy commercial programs they provide in comparison to the level of difficulty students face at Kuwait University.* (S.1, 31 March 2013)

Another student responded:

> *My GPA didn't allow me to apply for a bachelor degree program after the Ministry raised the GPA required for universities. As a result I applied for a diploma program at one of the private institutions, ACM. ... I applied for the Military as well, and the PAAET for their Diploma programs. But the ACM admission came first and cancelled the PAAET application automatically.* (S.2, 3 April 2013)

Asking about the most preferable course to him, he replied:

> *Honestly, it doesn't make any difference to me. To me, they are both the same (ACM or PAAET). Although I have heard that graduates from public institutions (PAAET & KU) have the priority when it comes to employment.* (S.2, 3 April 2013)

These are some of the negative effects of the centralized admission processes practiced in most Arabic countries noted previously. Buckner's (2013) study points to the impact these processes have on society. She argues that this centralized admission has two primary negative impacts. On the societal level, centralized admissions cause the best and most prestigious students to be heavily skewed to medical fields, engineering, and some natural sciences, a distortion that leaves social sciences and humanities to the remaining students who are not academically motivated. This fact leaves Arab countries without leaders educated in disciplines that focus on writing and analysis. On another level, the centralization of the admissions process also deprives universities of autonomy, as they are often forced to accept more students than they can actually educate. A survey participant from the private sector complained:

> *The government's guaranteed employment policy destroys our students' ambition in both public and private higher education institutions. I believe that only the top 10 percent of them have ambitions in choosing their paths in higher education for their future employment.* (S.S., 5 December 2012)

Kuwait University, in an attempt to reduce the effect of centralized admissions, tried to distribute students across different colleges and disciplines. However, this attempt failed. A dean at Kuwait University stated:

> *Even though we made an effort to create a balance by distributing applicants across different colleges, the end result was often that students transferred from scientific*

> *colleges to the humanities after completing their first or second year of enrolment.* (H.A., 11 December 2012)

The World Bank report, *The Road Not Travelled: Education Reform in the Middle East and North Africa* (2008), identified similar trends towards business education, especially in the broader Arabic region, which tends to attract large numbers of high school graduates.

The same report related the weak relationship between education outcomes and economic growth, possibly due to the high levels of public sector employment and the low numbers of people employed in dynamic and internationally competitive economic sectors. The almost-guaranteed employment of nationals along with Kuwait's slow economic growth has created a burden on the state budget, since most of the excess labour is absorbed into relatively unproductive public sector office work. The common Kuwaiti employment strategy that consists of going to a University and getting a more or less guaranteed public sector job has created demand pressures on public sector employment similar to the excess demands on higher education institutions. As a result, the government has attempted to shift this pressure onto the private sector, producing the policy of *Kuwaitization*, which was enacted in 2002.

This policy reforms the labour market in Kuwait by nationalizing the country's workforce, especially the private sector workforce. It provides incentives for private employers to encourage the employment of Kuwaiti nationals in the private sector. In short, the policy addresses underemployment of Kuwaiti nationals in the private sector that emerged due to an overreliance on expatriates.

Labour market reforms in Kuwait centre on two fronts. One front is *Kuwaitization* – the plan to create employment opportunities for nationals in the private sector. The second front is a plan to generate the required skills and incentives for nationals' employment in the private sector (IMF, 2004, p. 11). The Kuwaitization policy explicitly obliges the private sector to employ specified percentages of Kuwaitis. These percentages are determined by two factors: amount of commercial activity and type of profession. The obligations that Kuwaitization has imposed on the private sector have had the effect of increasing private sector interest in seeing a Kuwaiti higher education that produces outcomes relevant to private sector needs. However, despite the private sector complaint that *Outcomes of public higher education are poor and irrelevant to market needs* (S.S., 5 December 2012), apparently private sector hiring preferences continue to be for public higher education graduates, except for positions requiring English language skills. One employer stated:

> *Honestly, public sector graduates are more disciplined and qualified than their counterparts from the private sector, as I believe that in private institutions students*

are spoiled and are used to having everything prepared for them. While in the public sector, mainly due to students' pressures and poor management, students have to learn how to facilitate all circumstance in order to complete their higher education. Nevertheless, English language skills are often better in private graduates, although that is not always the case. (S.K., 19 March 2013)

The preference for public graduates is influenced by the fact that private institutions are still mostly targeted by students with lower academic achievement. Public institutions, in order to raise their academic performance, have raised their admission requirements in an attempt to control the type of students they enrol. An official from Kuwait University noted that:

The experience of excess demand has contributed to Kuwait University raising their admission requirements, seeing it as a necessity to improve their academic performance, as those students with low academic achievement have a negative influence on the university's performance. (J.M., 28 November 2012)

However, the use of stricter admission requirements to improve the quality of students has been challenged by a corresponding inflation in secondary school GPAs. This inflation remains a problem, since there is no standardized test for all secondary school graduates. A graduate commented on university requirements, saying that:

The Ministry is raising the admission requirements [the GPA required for getting into higher education] every year. I don't know what they are thinking!! Are they after high achievers only? What is their policy and what is the highest percentage they are going to require for getting a chance at higher education? If it is impossible to get into university with 70 percent GPA, how much it will be in few years?...The government needs to find a solution for student numbers and the lack of sufficient places in higher education in the country. (S.2, 3 April 2013)

Therefore, the establishment of the private universities has been the only chance for many to continue their higher education. More than 60 percent of the survey sample agreed that the admission requirements of private universities are lower than those of public universities in Kuwait. Several statements given by students explain how the existence of the private higher education institutions affected their chances of getting higher education. Most responses referred to the fact that the easier access provided by private institutions increased their chances of getting higher education locally. Some of the responses were:

'It really helps, especially when the chances of getting an education in public university are low.'...'They offer better chances. If someone cannot get into a public university, they can get into a private one.'...'I got admitted to private university faster and easier than public university.'...'It is now easier to get higher education.'...'As we all know, the public university of Kuwait cannot accommodate the number of students graduating each year from high school. So I believe that the existence of private universities in Kuwait have helped in reducing the pressure on the public

university.'...'It became easier to get higher education.'...'Yes they do help in case I am accepted in the public sector.'...'The advantage of the private institutions is that they do accept lower high school GPAs than Kuwait University does.'... 'Private universities offer alternative opportunities to get higher education vs getting into Kuwait University which only accepts a small number of students.'...'It makes it easy because their requirements can be achieved.'...'My chances are higher with their existence.'

Levy (2009) in his typology of private higher education, speaks of 'demand-absorbing' institutions which exist in a setting where 'most students are not choosing their institutions over other institutions as much as choosing them over nothing' (p. 18).

The data also pointed to economic advantages private institutions offer regarding lifelong learning. The existence of the private sector, by widening the absorption capacity of higher education institutions locally, also created opportunities that had not previously existed, opportunities such as adult learning programs and classes for working students. A former minister pointed out this development, regarding it as an advantage for private institutions. She said:

They [private institutions] created chances that had never existed before for low achievers, people with outdated certificates, and employees needing to complete their further studies. (M.H., 18 March 2013)

Prior to the establishment of private higher education, there were few chances to undertake graduate studies locally. Only a few graduate programs were offered by Kuwait University, and they were highly competitive with tough admission requirements. The existence of the private higher education provides chances that never before existed for working adults to continue their graduate studies locally without having to leave the country. They make the goal of lifelong learning possible by providing the flexible schedules for employees that are lacking in public institutions. Responding to the survey question regarding how the existence of the private higher education affected their chances of getting higher education, a student commented:

The existence of private universities gave me the opportunity to continue my education and get a higher qualification/degree without the need to look for universities abroad. Kuwait University did not accept my GPA, although they lowered their standards two years after I graduated. They would now accept my high school GPA, but again I cannot apply because two years have passed, making my certificate outdated. Because of their unfair admissions, I am glad that private universities existed, especially as I have no interest in travelling and leaving my family to get a degree. (50)

Another student noted:

It [private higher education] is the only way if you need a higher certificate after ten years away from education. (30)

Thus, we can see from the discussion above that the establishment of private institutions responded to economic and labour market needs in a way that public institutions never could have, given their endemic problems of the high demands pressure and the poor efficiency.

Conclusion

In considering the major local pressures that promoted the development of the private higher education sector in Kuwait, certain conclusions have emerged. It is clear that the state of Kuwait was under considerable demand pressures similar to other states in the GCC Region. In fact, the Kuwaiti education faced challenges compounded by many different factors. Among these factors are: increased youth population; demographic realities regarding the girl-to-boy ratio; limited capacity of existing public higher education; and inconsistent policy processes that hinder public development projects. Coffman (2005) also refers to some of these factors: the excess number of females seeking education; the connection between female education abroad and Islamic values; the drop in GCC students enrolled in American universities resulting from the 9/11 incident; and the demand of Kuwait's numerous expatriates for local higher education. The public sector's utter failure to respond to these challenges was not due to financial shortages, but to the weak and random government mechanisms that allowed the factors to develop into a crisis.

However, the creation of the private sector has not completely resolved the problems that it was created to address. Student pressure continues to be a challenge facing both public and private higher education institutions. A dean at Kuwait University stated that '*if the decision were left to the university, we would opt to not accept students for the next semester*' (R.A., 13 March 2013). Thus, despite the implementation of privatization policies, most of the pressures discussed above continue to challenge higher education provision in Kuwait. However, it is highly unlikely that the Kuwaiti government will now abandon privatization policies for the further development of its systems of higher education. The question arises then – why? One possible reason for this is that the Kuwaiti policies have now become aligned to global norms. In the next chapter I will discuss why and how these norms have been embraced by the Kuwaiti state. In other words: in what ways, and to what extent, has Kuwait been influenced by global pressures to adopt privatization policies for its system of higher education?

Chapter Six: Global Influences

In Chapter Five, I discussed some of the key internal pressures that have promoted the use of private sector participation in higher education provision in Kuwait. I suggested that many of these local pressures are, at least in part, a predictable outcome of poor planning and inefficient policy processes in Kuwait. These inefficient policy processes are arguably aggravated by a culture of financial inefficiency in allocating available resources, leading many in Kuwait to favour privatization. Furthermore, as in most countries around the world, Kuwait is challenged with growing demand for higher education. I showed how this growth has been a contributing factor in the production of the PUL34/2000 policy and the promotion of private higher education. However, this increased demand would not in itself have been so significant without the government's utter failure to prepare the public sector for the largely predicted and expected increase. I noted, moreover, that other national factors motivating higher education reforms are the Kuwaiti state's desire for economic diversification, the recent labour market reforms concerning the nationalization of local work force, and a decrease in the reliance on the oil economy. Finally, there are local socio-cultural demands (women's education abroad and expatriate education) that have also fuelled the establishment of the private universities in the country.

However, as appropriate as these internal factors are in explaining the rise of privatization in Kuwaiti higher education, they are not the whole story. Globalization has challenged the traditional view that education policy is nationally bounded (Rizvi & Lingard, 2010), as reforms and practices in one locale can significantly impact other locales (Castells, 2010).

Systems learn and borrow ideas from one another in a way that can be understood through Appadurai's (1996) suggested five dimensions of global cultural flows. These five dimensions are (a) ethnoscapes, (b) mediascapes, (c) technoscapes, (d) financescapes, and (e) ideoscapes. Comparativists have referred to this practice as 'policy borrowing' (Phillips & Ochs, 2003; Steiner-Khamsi, 2004, 2012) or policy transfer (Dolowitz & Marsh, 1996, 2000). This chapter presents the findings that have emerged from a thematic analysis of the research data and are derived from both text documents and interview transcripts alongside the literature and theories of privatization. These analyses indicate that the production of higher education privatization policies in Kuwait is not a purely local or even purely rational response to local conditions. Instead, there are significant external influences that have impacted national higher education policy priorities in Kuwait. This chapter then attempts to explain in what ways, and to what extent, Kuwait has been influenced by global pressures to adopt privatization policies for its system of higher education.

International Education and Policy Formation

In an era of globalization, it is often not easy to distinguish between what is local and what is global, as the distinction is not absolute. Distance barriers have been largely reduced through the processes of globalization identified by Rizvi (2006). It can be argued that the *Westphalian* sovereignty of the nation-state has been subverted by processes of globalization. New communication technologies and high rates of people flow across borders, either physically or through technological development, are major factors that have contributed to such transformations. These flows have created new spaces to exchange ideas, thoughts, experiences, and policies. The processes of globalization have created new social spheres and complex interacting groupings all around the world. It is in these spheres and groupings that new policies are originated, steered, and diffused. International education or study abroad, found to be of large influence on imposing ideologies among local policy actors, academics in particular.

An examination of key Kuwaiti policy actors illustrates the dynamics of global flows. Most of these policy actors were educated abroad, mainly at universities in the United States, where English was their medium of communication and instruction. Accordingly, it is not surprising to find that almost all of the study participants are graduates of American universities. To mention a few:

- University of Houston (R.H., 10 March 2013)
- University of North Texas, ScM (1975) and ScD (1979) Harvard University (J.A., 25 April 2013)
- Florida State University, University of Wisconsin-Milwaukee (H.A., 11 December 2012)
- University in Nantes, France (A.F., 18 March 2013)
- University of California, Los Angeles (A.S., 27 March 2013)
- Florida State University (H.J., 13 February 2013)

A reason for this trend is that graduate programs (Master's and PhDs) did not exist locally until recently. Even now, only a few such programs can be found in Kuwait. In addition to the government's continues approach of sending students to acquire international education abroad.

The government approach of sending citizens to study abroad over the last five decades or so has produced policy actors who are mostly educated and trained abroad (i.e., Western-trained policy actors). Moreover, many have kept a sort of connection with their institutions abroad creating a local multi-national policy subculture where ideologies and practices from different countries are pooled at the local level. Understanding this fact is crucial in analysing the trends and directions of national policy production. This globalized subculture, although it is not represented systematically in official settings, nonetheless makes a substantial impact on policy decisions. Steiner-Khamsi (2004) emphasizes that 'invented communities', even though they are imagined, are still real in their impact (p. 4). They have proved to be very effective policy manipulation tools both in the past (Anderson, 1983) and in the present (Steiner-Khamsi, 2004, p. 4). A former minister of higher education points to the same phenomenon in identifying the main sources of information used concerning the production of the PUL (34/2000). She reported:

> *We have mainly used information from local experts from different educational institutions – both regional and local experts, who have mostly been educated in foreign countries and continue to have connections there.* (M.H., 18 March 2013)

Her statement illustrates the role of international (Western) education mentioned above on policy-making decisions in Kuwait. Even though policy decisions are made by Kuwait's own citizens, they often act as a conduit for ideas originating in the countries where they were educated. Considering Kuwait's history of encouraging students to go abroad for higher education, it is hardly surprising to find such international connections among academics and policy actors. These foreign-trained academics and policy actors created international networks that, in turn, are reflected in their policy actions. One participant confirmed:

> *On a personal level, academics and faculty members have memberships and connections with many organizations and agencies around the world. By these connections everyone is updated in his field of specialization and keeps up with the latest developments in his discipline.* (J.M., 28 November 2012)

An official at the PUC also stated:

> *I have experience in accreditation from my membership in ABET [American Accreditation Board for Engineering and Technology] which I held during my tenure in Kuwait University. I was responsible for the accreditation programs in my department, computer engineering, and participated three times in the evaluation team.* (F.A., 11 December 2012)

As a result of this international influence, neoliberal ideology, the international fashion of the past several decades, is highly influential among Kuwaiti policy actors. Consequently, these policy actors have actively promoted the privatization of higher education. A former minister justifying the necessity of the introduction of the PUL (34/2000) stated:

> *It is important to allow the private sector to participate in the production of higher education services and stop it from being the exclusive preserve of the government. For two reasons: First, is to enrich the higher education experience in the state with different and new philosophies of higher education. Second, most well-known and great universities in the world are private institutions, since the flexibility of the private sector in making decisions and its rapid actions contributes much to educational quality. Third, I believe that the government should not be the only [provider] sponsor of funding higher education; the society, as represented by the private sector, should participate as well.* (M.H., 18 March 2013)

An official at the PUC shares similar neoliberal views. She added:

> *In my opinion, one thing that the government overlooked or neglected while producing the Law [PUL34/2000] is the establishment of a student loan system, a financial system that allows the student to pay for his higher education. [She reported] that this is a policy that has been recently produced by the government. However, it has not yet been implemented. [According to her, a student loan law was produced the week prior to the interview 11/12/2012]* (F.A., 11 December 2012)

The study data also identifies local perceptions regarding external influences. The interview transcripts indicate a general preference for foreign, and especially Western, orientation concerning the higher education sector. Accordingly, any type of foreign connection is regarded as both an advantage and an achievement by participants. However, there is a bias towards English-speaking countries, with the greatest influence being the American system. The following statement by an official at the PUC reflects this perception of foreign relations and the degree of attention given to these relations. She said:

> *Our foreign relations are always a priority and we are always interested in knowing what is happening in the world concerning new experiences and expertise.* (F.A., 11 December 2012)

Proudly, she added:

> *We are a member of both regional and international committees and organizations such as INQAAHE and UNESCO, which considers us as a reference for its databases. However, Kuwait is a country that bears all its own financial expenses.* (F.A., 11 December 2012)

Another achievement she pointed to is:

> *Kuwait's participation in AHELO; the OECD program to evaluate higher education outcomes. Last June all final year students in both public and private HE institutions participated in the test. Our participation came even before Australia.* (F.A., 11 December 2012)

According to their website, the PUC is a member in the following associations:

- **INQAAHE**: International Network for Quality Assurance Agencies in Higher Education (full member) www.inqaahe.org

- **ANQAHE**: Arab Network for Quality Assurance in Higher Education www.anqahe.org
- Arab School for Science and Technology www.arabschool.org\
- **AROQA**: The Arab Organization for Quality Assurance in Education http://aroqa.org/en
- **ASQAE**: Arab Society for Quality Assurance in Education www.asqae.org
- **APQN**: Asia-Pacific Quality Network (observer) www.apqn.org
- **CHEA**: Council for Higher Education Accreditation www.chea.org
- **UNESCO** Portal on Higher Education http://portal.unesco.org

Even students notice this focus on Western appearance among the faculties of their private institutions. One student complained:

> *Private institutions focus too much on the foreign appearance, as opposed to the actual qualifications, of the English teachers, for instance. Their accents are totally messed up, being from Turkey and Georgia, although there are some Lebanese and Kuwaitis as well.* (S.5, 3 April 2013)

Another student points to similar foreign Western orientation. He said:

> *All of our classes are conducted in English. Our teachers come from different nationalities, mainly from Western countries.* (S.8, 3 April 2013)

Apparently Western education is generally desirable. However, there are some socio-cultural limitations. One participant expressed his disagreement with the recently proposed policies that would increase foreign involvement in decision-making in private higher education institutions. He raised an issue concerning a recent policy that strengthens the role of foreign investors in local private institutions in Kuwait, commenting:

> *With regards to partnership with international universities, the policy on franchising higher education in Kuwait is an extremely sensitive socio-cultural issue that has to be reassessed in view of the experience in other GCC countries.* (J.A., 25 April 2013)

There is a general public preference in Kuwait for Western models of education where English is the language of instruction. However, there are some religious and cultural restraints. For example, Kuwaiti families who choose an American-style University for their children may be ambivalent, despite their choice. On the one hand, they want the prestige and quality of an American education. But, on the other hand, they wish to limit the social and intellectual impact of the foreign qualities associated with critical thinking, secular attitudes, and coeducational practices (Tolmacheva, 2011, p. 6). Due to these conflicting attitudes, selectivity in policy borrowing has been exercised by participants in order to adapt to Kuwaiti socio-cultural needs, which will be discussed in the following chapter.

Although foreign education – Western education in particular – is cherished and valued locally, there is also a strong sense of independence. Most of the study participants believe that the introduction of private higher education was a national decision. A former parliament member emphasized the state's autonomy concerning the production of its national public policies, stressing that:

> *Concerning external influences, certainly there is individual participation in different international agencies from local academics seeking new knowledge and information – or even to enhance their own reputation. And the state certainly has relations with these international agencies. However, the country is very independent in implementing policies that suit its own vision and domestic interests. Since Kuwait is a rich country, these international agencies have no power to force anything on the state of Kuwait, as they do when they fund other developing countries that lack financial resources.* (H.J., 13 February 2013)

Another statement also shows a similar independence at Kuwait University. An official reaffirmed:

> *Kuwait University is an independent body; there is no such external interference on its decision-making from global organizations or agencies.* (J.M., 28 November 2012)

From the above, it is clear that education, or more precisely international education, is an effective tool of globalization on influencing policy decisions in Kuwait and that Western-trained academics act as mediators and interpreters of globalization in local settings.

The Role of International Organizations

Unlike other studies examining the introduction of privatization in developing countries, references to the role of international organizations in promoting privatization in higher education provision are minimal among policy actors in Kuwait. Generally, such references as there are consist of participants boasting about their memberships in these organizations rather than any active program being pushed by the organizations themselves.

Generally speaking, references by participants to international organizations (WTO, IMF, WB, UNESCO, OECD, etc.) are so rare as to be almost completely absent. As far as the study evidence goes, it would appear that international organizations did not have a direct or active role in steering higher education policy decisions. Accordingly, it is not clear that the data collected from the interviews is a sufficient source of information for analysing the role played by these international organizations in the introduction of privatization. In the survey data, there are only general statements concerning the influence that globalization had on privatization policy decisions. One study participant commented:

> *Although there is an absence of a clear direct foreign impact on higher education policy decisions in Kuwait, logically this decision of higher education privatization cannot have been taken in isolation from what is happening around the world. As a result of globalization, the world has become a small country. I believe that there must have been some kind of influence on the government to adopt privatization for higher education reforms.* (A.S., 27 March 2013)

An official from the ministry of higher education also affirmed that:

> *There have been numerous contacts with multidisciplinary consultancy agencies and companies to frame our privatization policies.* (J.A., 25 April 2013)

He recalled some of the most recent activities such as:

- *Korea Development Institute Ministry of Strategy and Finance, The Formulation and Implementation of National Development Plan in Kuwait, 2012/08/07*
- *Korea Development Institute Ministry of Strategy and Finance, 007 Knowledge Sharing Program: Ghana & Azerbaijan & Kuwait (In Korean) 2008/09/24*
- *Korea Development Institute Ministry of Strategy and Finance Kuwait's Strategic Response to its Developmental Challenges: Recasting its Strategic Options and Implementation Strategy from a Korean Perspective, 2008/09/24*
- *Kuwait Vision 2035. 2008. A report prepared by British Prime Minister Tony Blair*
- *The Road Not Travelled: Education Reform in the Middle East and North Africa, World Bank. 2008.* (J.A., 25 April 2013)

A former parliament member also noted:

> *At first, in the primary phase of writing the policy, we attended several conferences looking for assistance in framing our standards by benefiting from other experiences in the field of higher education privatization, in addition to recommendations offered by reports conducted by international organizations in the region.* (H.A., 11 December 2012)

Though the role of international organizations seems ambivalent, a primary analysis of their reports revealed that there are connections between their recommendations and higher education reforms in the region generally and in Kuwait in particular. Therefore, the policy documents and reports of these international organizations may be a better source for examining their influence than the explicit references by study participants.

Kuwait's memberships in the WTO, the IMF, and other similar organizations, in addition to its signing of the GATS agreement, have clearly had policy consequences. It is difficult, however, to exactly define the nature of relationship between Kuwait's participation in international organizations and the policies it has pursued. On the one hand, the hunger for international recognition might be the primary driving force leading Kuwait to implement the privatization policies recommended by international organizations. On the other hand, it is natural to be influenced merely by participating in these organizations and being exposed to the ideas circulating in them. Such participations through memberships and the type of obligations attached to them provide possible explanation of how Kuwaiti policies have been aligned to global norms.

A close examination of three reports of annual consultations that Kuwait undertook with the IMF reveals a clear promotion of privatization. These reports actively encourage the government to implement privatization policies. I have selected three consultancy reports that have coincided with the production of the higher education privatization policy (PUL 34/2000) in Kuwait. They were produced in the years 1999, 2000, and 2003.

Insights from the 1999 report clearly illustrate the call for general privatization:

> Given the uncertain medium-term outlook for the oil market, Directors welcomed the authorities' policy response, and their plans to introduce a comprehensive medium- term fiscal reform strategy centered around three components: accelerating privatization; containing the wage bill, in conjunction with labor market reform; and reducing subsidies and transfers.
> Directors looked forward to the next phase of the privatization program, which was expected to encompass the utilities sector, and lay the basis for the privatization of the telecommunications and transport sectors. These actions would not only facilitate the restructuring of the government budget, but also enhance economic efficiency and strengthen private sector participation in the economy.
> Directors welcomed the broad consensus on the need for structural reform measures aimed at enhancing the role of the private sector in the economy, encouraging foreign direct investment, reforming the Company Law, and streamlining the regulatory framework. They encouraged the authorities, and the Kuwaiti National Assembly, to approve the relevant legislation in those areas, which would help promote investment and growth, and foster competition and economic diversification. Directors stressed the essential role of private sector development in providing employment opportunities for an increasing number of Kuwaiti nationals, whose skills and salary expectations must meet the demands of the private sector. In this respect, Directors noted the authorities' efforts to narrow the remuneration gap between the private and public sectors, including by extending social allowances to Kuwaitis working in the private sector, and by improving education and training, as appropriate. Directors, however, stressed the need to preserve labor market flexibility and to keep the reform-related costs within the overall budget constraint. (IMF, 1999)

Browsing the underlined statements above, there is a clear orientation towards privatization and the empowerment of the private sector in development generally. Concerning higher education in particular, there is a stress on the role of the private sector in providing the education that prepares human capital. It is explicitly stated that expectations of this human capital must meet the demands of the private sector as stated in the following lines:

> Directors stressed the essential role of private sector development in providing employment opportunities for an increasing number of Kuwaiti nationals, whose skills and salary expectations must meet the demands of the private sector. In this respect, … and by improving education and training, as appropriate. (IMF, 1999)

The instability experienced in the oil market over the past years has been largely used as steering argument by the IMF to impose its neoliberal ideologies on policy-making in Kuwait and the promotion of privatization generally and empowering the role of the private sector.

Fig. 8 displays the trends of oil prices from 1960 to 2014. It illustrates the different phases of oil market over the period and how it has been unstable and controlled by the changing global economy and geopolitical events. Kuwait's economy largely relies on the oil market, which has been viewed as insecure economic approach to provide a strong economic foundation for the country. The IMF's approach of imposing their neoliberal ideologies stands mainly on the instability of its prices, in addition to the fact that it is exhaustible natural resource. Thus, the diversification of the country's economy and empowering the role of the private sector in economic growth and development are highly recommended by the IMF based on the ideological efficiency attached to privatization generally. Such recommendations are identified in the subsequent report.

In the 2000 report, the IMF continues to underscore the importance of privatization in suggested structural reforms and stresses fostering the role of the market as a key for successful reforms. As in the previous 1999 report, the following underlined statements from the 2000 report reveal similar influence that the IMF has had on the privatization policies implemented in Kuwait:

> Notwithstanding the improvement in the overall financial position, Directors observed, however, that Kuwait faces the medium-term challenge of raising economic growth and providing increased employment opportunities for its nationals. They underscored that the package of structural reform measures that was formulated last year aimed at better utilizing Kuwait's economic potential and laying the foundations for higher private sector-led growth and employment creation. The package was rightly focused on disengaging the government from commercial activities, privatization, promotion of foreign investment, reform of the company law, fiscal restructuring, and labor market reform.
> Directors agreed that such reforms will be key to improving business climate and promoting investment and efficiency in the economy by fostering private sector participation and attracting foreign investment. Noting that little progress had been made in approving these reforms, Directors stressed the importance of building a

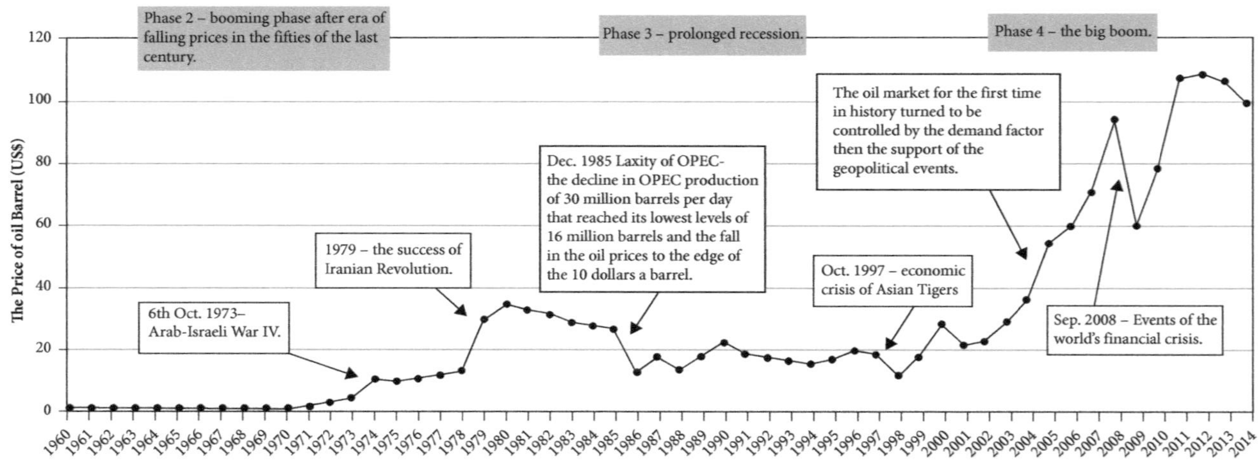

Fig. 8: The average price of a barrel of crude oil during the period (1960–2014). (Source: Al Saadoon, J. (2015, January). Oil and public finance: fast and future. In *The decline in oil prices and its reflection on the financial situation of the state*. Symposium conducted at the headquarters of Kuwait Economic Society, Shuwaikh, block 7, St.71, Villa 18) (Translated)

> broad public consensus in favor of these reforms: They encouraged the authorities and the National Assembly to work toward securing the legislative approval of these measures.
> The government has submitted to the National Assembly a package of structural reforms aimed at addressing the economy's structural imbalances, enhancing growth and fostering employment of Kuwaiti nationals. The reform package includes draft legislation on privatization (utilities, telecommunications, airline, transportation), foreign investment, opening up oil activities to foreign participation under services contract agreements, labor market reform, the company and agency laws, the corporate income tax law, and the copyright and the patent laws. A consensus between the government and the National Assembly on most of the draft bills has still to be reached, particularly with regard to implications of some of the reforms for employment, utility tariffs, and the risk of emergence of private monopolies. (IMF, 2000)

The 2003 report reveals the existence of public resistance to privatization measures, a resistance not viewed as either pleasant or progressive by the directors of the IMF. This resistance is revealed by an apparent delay in passing the proposed privatization. It reports that:

> Directors looked forward to the early passage of the Privatization Law to establish the legal and institutional framework for promoting private investment. In the meanwhile, they encouraged the authorities to move forward with early divesture of public sector activities that do not require explicit legislative action for privatization. They considered that such a step would signal the authorities' commitment to private sector-led growth and further strengthen the environment for private investment. (IMF, 2003, p.3)

Despite the reported delay, IMF encouragement for the authorities to move forward with the implementation of privatization in areas where it can be implemented without explicit legislative action that transforms or divest publicly led sector into a private sector reflects the way privatization has been implemented in Kuwait's higher education. Its introduction in Kuwait is separated from the already existed public sector, as will be further explained in the following chapter. In this way the government avoid public resistance to the introduction of the private higher education in Kuwait. Accordingly, the PUL (34/2000) authorizing the establishment of the private higher education sector had been produced. However, the above statement can be seen as evidence showing the role of the IMF in promoting privatization policies in Kuwait. They encourage the government to move forward in the implementation of privatization in areas where explicit legislation was not required in order for the government to show its commitment to private-led growth and to strengthening the environment for private investment.

These reports by international organizations are not without influence. Several survey participants note that they used the knowledge and recommendations provided in published reports on development of the Arab region, although without providing specifics. A thorough investigation into these sorts of reports led me to the Arab Human Development Reports, published in 2002, 2003, 2004, 2005, and 2009. These reports were conducted by the United Nations Development Programme (UNDP) and the Regional Bureau for Arab States (RBAS). They were mainly funded by the Arab Fund for Economic and Social Development (AFESD), as stated in all of them. The AFESD is an Arab regional institution for financial development established in 1967. It is located in Kuwait, the government of which mainly funds it. As a result, Kuwait provided data in all of its listed reports in comparison to other Arab states, data for which is almost absent or is only projected in most of these reports.

In a section focusing on higher education development, the Arab Human Development Report: Creating Opportunities for Future Generations (2002) suggests four main policies as urgently needed for a serious reform of higher education. The first policy clearly promotes the privatization of higher education, as stated:

> The responsibility of the state should continue, but higher education should be liberated from the domination of both government and the unregulated profit motive. The government's responsibility for higher education does not mean that institutions of higher education should be government-owned. Such institutions should be governed by independent boards with quadripartite representation (the state, the private sector, civil society and academia). The profit motive should be regulated to ensure the public interest, and the creation of non-governmental, non-profit organizations should be encouraged. (UNDP, 2002, p. 61)

The publication of this report was very close to the production of the PUL (34/2000). In a way, it shows the extent to which policy debate at that time was influenced by ideas generated outside the country, but promoted within it. Moreover, it also shows the extent to which policymakers and academics were affected by the circulation of the ideologies of privatization.

Kuwait is a host country for many active international organizations, and is home to branch offices of many others. The most recent that I have noticed is the establishment of the World Bank Country Office in Kuwait in 2009, an establishment which marked a new phase of collaboration with the region. Radwan Shaban, the World Bank Country Manager for the Kuwaiti office said:

> The World Bank team in Kuwait is committed to contributing its global knowledge and international experience to serve the country's vision for enhancing the economic and social welfare of all Kuwaitis. In response to the priorities identified by the government, we will focus on: human resources development, improve public sector performance, promote private sector development and economic diversification. (El Naggar, D. 2009)

As has been stated, empowering the role of the private sector is a priority.

The above discussion illustrates the embedded role of international organizations in providing consultancy and recommendations for policy reforms generally and higher education in particular as a way of restructuring the labour market and reducing public expenditure on higher education as well as promoting the role of the private sector. In the following section a specific attention is giving to a specific agreement, the GATS, and its association with the production of higher education privatization policies in Kuwait.

The GATS and Higher Education Privatization Policies

The introduction of higher education privatization in Kuwait began in earnest with the country's signing of the GATS agreement. Although there were earlier attempts to establish private higher education in Kuwait, these proposals were not taken seriously by the government. Privatization only began after the signing of the GATS. A participant reported that:

> *The first attempt to establish private universities dated back to 1993, when Abbas Maarafi and a group of 43 academics submitted a proposal to the Kuwait Investment Authority that requested a license to open a private university. It took them almost two years to get a response and was rejected, as there was no policy issued yet to allow for the establishment of a private higher education institution. In fact, there wasn't such a policy until the year 2000, when the Law of Private Universities was issued.* (W.R., 17 March 2013)

Kuwait became a signatory to the General Agreement on Tariffs and Trade (GATT) in 1963, only two years after its independence. In 1994, it became an original member of the WTO after accepting the Marrakesh agreement and signing the GATS agreement (WTO, 2012, Trade Policy Review report by Kuwait, p.23). Thereafter, proposals for establishing private higher education in Kuwait were taken seriously by the government. A former parliament member confirmed that:

> *The first official private higher education bill was proposed in the 1996 parliament. Unfortunately, it was not passed until the 1999 parliament because of the political conflict that led to the dissolving of the 1996 parliament. The HE privatization bill was put off until a subsequent parliament, and the policy was finally passed in 2000.* (H.J., 13 February 2013)

Even before final passage of the privatization law, there were proposals initiated by the government itself – specifically, the Ministry of Higher Education – concerning the same matter of establishing a private higher education sector. A former Minister of higher education stated that:

> *The idea had been existed for several years before the policy was actually produced. ...The idea began under the ministry of Dr. Mussaad Al Haroon, and then continued under Dr. Yousif Al-Ebrahim, when the Arab Open University was established – then came Al-Tabtabaee, followed by Dr. Noreyah Al Sabeeh. So there have been efforts by several Ministers. There were a number of other Ministers who advocated the idea of Higher education privatization, in addition to the support from the*

Council of Ministers. Many supported the idea, and I was one of them. (M.H., 18 March 2013)

Another former Minister of Higher Education confirmed that the idea of privatization was first proposed by the Ministry of Higher Education, although it advocated a different concept and framework from what was ultimately produced in the final version of the policy. He explained:

In the original proposal, we attempted to insure the adequacy of both financial resources and government supervision, retaining the authority to interfere if necessary... I advocated that the privatization of higher education be run by only one big private firm, which would be responsible for the establishment of the private university or universities. All private universities were to be run under this one private institution. The government, as suggested in the original proposal, would be represented by the Kuwait Investment Authority fund, as this would give the government the authority to supervise the entire processes. (A.G., 15 April 2013)

It can be argued that the production of the Private Universities Law (34/2000) is largely the outcome of the country's signing of the GATS agreement, although there are some scholars who argue against this idea. Sauvé's (2002), for example, argues that the GATS/WTO 'is not likely to be a driving force or even a major consideration behind such changes' and that the growing expansion of the private higher education has been 'occurring almost wholly independently of developments in the WTO' (p. 4). He may be right. However, it is difficult to ignore how the GATS acts as a facilitator for the expansion of private higher education in most developing countries, especially the sort of cross-border provision of higher education institutions that has proliferated in the Arab Gulf region. Rizvi and Lingard (2010) argue that 'the main assumption underlying GATS is that education is a commodified service, in which trade in not only possible but [also] desirable' (p. 171). Under this 'neoliberal imaginary', they argue that trade in higher education is assumed not to be subject to national restrictions. Ginsburg, Espinoza, Popa, and Terano (2005, p. 222) argue that the GATS agreement influenced higher education privatization policies in both Chile and Romania. They note that the impact of GATS on higher education is likely to be strong, particularly for developing countries whose restrictions are the main target of GATS policy in education area.

The GATS agreement specifies four modes of supply services, which are:

Cross Border Supply: *Provision of a service where the service crosses the border.*
Consumption abroad: *Provision of the service involving the movement of the consumer to the country of the supplier.*
Commercial presence: *The service provider establishes or has presence of commercial facilities in another country in order to render service.*

> **Presence of Natural Persons:** *Persons travelling to another country in order to provide service. (Article 1.2 of the GATS)*

All four modes are relevant to the activities of private higher education, a fact which is illustrated by the classification of higher education services according to these four modes: E- education or virtual universities fall under 'cross-border supply'; students studying in another country falls under 'consumption abroad'; Branch or satellite campuses, franchising, and twinning arrangements fall under 'commercial presence'; and teachers travelling to foreign countries to teach fall under the 'presence of natural persons'.

The connection between the GATS and the production of the PUL (34/2000) is further reinforced by examining the policy text and comparing it to the country's Schedule of Specific Commitments attached to the GATS agreement. Although the initial policy text of the PUL (34/2000) is simple and consists of only eight articles (see appendix 4), it is clear that the first article is almost a restatement of what is stated in the Kuwait's Schedule of Specific Commitments concerning foreign commercial presence, the limitations on market access, and the limitations on national treatment. According to the PUL (34/2000), it is stated that:

> It is permissible by a decree issued in response to a request by the Minister of Higher Education to license the foundation of private universities/colleges or higher institutes/branches of foreign universities where the majority of shared capital funds is wholly owned by Kuwaitis. (PUL 34/2000, article 1)

Likewise, Kuwait's Schedule of Specific Commitments, in the section on *Commercial Presence and Limitations on Market Access*, in the subsection on the *limitations on national treatments*, states that:

> Possessing, buying, selling or dealing in Kuwaiti share holding companies shares are, presently, confined to Kuwaiti natural or juridical persons. Foreigners are allowed to invest indirectly in Kuwaiti shares by means of mutual funds, expected to be listed shortly. ... Acquisition of land or real estate by foreign natural persons or foreign juridical persons are not allowed. (GATS/SC/49, 1994b, p. 1)

A subsequent version, under *Commercial Presence and Limitations on Market Access* applied in all sectors and sub-sectors, states that:

> The participation in a Kuwaiti investment company, provided the foreign participation (other than GCC citizens) must not exceed 49% of the company's capital. (GATS/SC/49/Suppl.1, 1995, p. 2)

This statement has been added to a subsequent resolution (CPU 2/ 30.3.2007) by the Council of Private Universities, which governs *the Rules of Association of Private Institutions Granting Diploma Degrees with the International Academic Institutions*. It reiterates the same limitations on foreign investment in private higher education provision in Kuwait, stating that:

> ... Encouraging parent institution to become a financial partner with the licensed corporate (body corporate) with a share not exceeding 49% of capital. ... (CPU 2/30.3.2007)

Thus, the resemblance between the GATS agreement and the higher education privatization policies in Kuwait is revealing, not only as regards the timing of the policy production, but also in regard to the similarities in the policy texts. In other words, it can be argued that signing the GATS agreement facilitated the introduction of private higher education into Kuwait by providing the critical inspiration and even the concrete texts that were missing from earlier attempts to bring private higher education to Kuwait. In fact, it can be argued that the GATS agreement may have been the deciding factor in this attempt's success, since the public desire for the establishment of private universities was already present during the earlier attempts. Since there are no identified coercive strategies experienced by international organizations on Kuwait to adopt privatization policies, then how might we explain the nature of the external influence on national policy decision to privatize?

Embracing Regional Developments

Regionalization is as important as globalization in influencing higher education policies across countries within the same region. Taking Europe as an example, and regarding 'Europeanization' as a form of regionalization, Enders (2004) makes a persuasive case that 'regionalisation in higher education is part and parcel of the globalization process, establishing cooperation among neighbours in order to counteract the pressure from other parts of the world' (p. 368). He adds that the 'basic distinction between internationalization and globalization can be supplemented, if also complicated, by the concept of "regionalisation"' (p.368).

Geographically Kuwait is located in the Arabian Peninsula with other Arab Gulf states that share similar economies, culture, traditions, religion, and history. In addition, there is formal political collaboration under the Gulf Cooperation Council (GCC), an organization that incorporates the six Arab Gulf States – namely, Kuwait, Saudi Arabia, Bahrain, Qatar, United Arab Emirates, and Oman. This homogenous cluster naturally creates a regional policy space where ideas and practices can be easily transferred. Lawn (2006) argues that these regional collaborations act as symbolic policy spaces that transcend national policy spaces producing a 'regional imaginary' (p. 273).

The survey data also reveal the influence of regional experiences and communication in affecting the national policy decision to introduce higher education privatization policies to Kuwait. A former minister of higher education recalled:

> *Kuwait was not the first country in the region to establish private universities. Dubai, if I'm not mistaken, was the leading city in the field. As a result, there were several experiences in almost similar sittings that provided us with a rich knowledge that helped us in framing our policies and creating our own private sector.* (A.G., 15 April 2013)

Regional similarities concerning higher education reforms are also noted in the literature regarding the academic boom witnessed by all of the Arab Gulf States. Over the last decade, the GCC states in particular experienced a boom in higher education. There were only eight universities operating in Saudi Arabia in 2003, for example. Now there are at least one hundred additional universities and colleges that have been created. Similar growth occurred in both Qatar and the United Arab Emirates. During this period they established 40 foreign branches of Western universities (Romani, 2009).

Another participant stressed the use of both local and regional experts and knowledge in the production of higher education privatization policy (PUL 34/2000), denying any direct foreign interference concerning the production of privatization policy. She said:

> *We have mainly used information from local experts from different educational institutions. Maybe [there was foreign influence via] regional experts or indirectly through our local experts who are mostly educated in foreign countries and continue to have connections there. However, there was no foreign pressure on us to implement the privatization.* (M.H., 18 March 2013)

The regional dimension also extends to Middle Eastern countries that have established private sectors such as Jordan. According to one survey participant:

> *We have used information from regional countries with similar experience such as Jordan, in addition to visiting some European countries regarding the same issue [HE privatization].* (W.R., 17 March 2013)

Kuwait, in addition to being in the Gulf Region, is also located in the broader region that consists of the Middle Eastern and North African countries (the MENA region). These countries share the same language and religion, and also have a history of political cooperation under the Arab League. Therefore, it is natural that the survey data indicates an exchange of ideas and practices with this broader Arabic region.

In addition to the circulation of information and practices among officials and policymakers in the region, the study data also indicates an exchange of experiences across private sectors. A former parliament member, for instance, pointed to these sorts of regional market connections. He commented:

> *From a market point of view, the recent wave of private foreign higher education that started to operate in the gulf region established that there was a great investment opportunity [in Kuwait]. This opportunity attracted Kuwaiti merchants and traders, causing them to promote the production of a privatization law.* (H.J., 13 February 2013)

A president and board member of a private institution confirmed this perception stating that:

> *Our choice for Missouri Saint Louis University to be our initial partner university has nothing to do with me having graduated from Missouri. I graduated from another branch of Missouri, not the one we are currently on partnership with. It was simply that this branch had regional experience in Oman and welcomed the cooperation. It was accordingly easy dealing with their administration.* (S.S., 5 December 2012)

The power of the regional dimension in influencing the national policy decision to adopt privatization is illustrated. Kuwaiti policy actors thus attempted to keep up and embrace regional developments in higher education. Donn and Al Manthri (2010) in their book, *Globalisation and Higher Education in the Arab Gulf States*, point to the similarities witnessed in higher education reforms across the region and attribute it to globalization. Specifically, they attribute it to the role of the 'Magistracy' (Lawn & Lingard, 2002), which they describe as a cohort of people, key players and policymakers, who travel between countries and create options, define agendas, and deliver products. These noted similar practices across the region have led the investigation to explore the reasons standing behind higher education reforms and the promotion of neoliberal ideologies in reforming their higher education systems in similar manners and timing. One possible explanation could be attributed to international organizations and their acknowledged role in the higher education promotion of privatization in different developing countries (see Chapter Two).

The Absence of Coercive Actions

In order to justify the suggested nature of the global influence on Kuwaiti policy processes, I have had to look at different distinctions of powers. There are many sources of power. Bush (2011), for example, makes a distinction between *authority* and *influence*. He argues that 'authority is legitimate power which is vested in leaders within formal organizations. ... It involves a legal right to make decisions which may be supported by sanctions' (p. 97).

Influence, on the other hand, 'represents an ability to affect outcomes and depends on personal characteristics and expertise' (Bush, 2011, p. 97).

Among the seven distinctions between *authority* and *influence* identified by Bacharach and Lawler (1980), the fifth suggests that '*authority* flows downward, and it is unidirectional; [while] *influence* is multidirectional and can flow upward, downward, and horizontally' (as cited in Bush, 2011, p. 97). Based on this distinction and the data presented above, I argue that external impact on national policy processes in Kuwait is better described as an influence than as an authority or pressure, since there are no coercive practices noted in the data. Most factors identified result from a circulation of ideologies through the processes of globalization suggested by Rizvi (2006); and the country's desire for international acceptance, a factor that I will discuss further below.

The autonomy achieved by a small country like Kuwait is a baffling matter for many scholars. Apparently, Kuwait's success in mediating global influences stems mainly from its financial wealth, as was shown in the earlier literature review concerning the historical emergence of the state of Kuwait and the crucial role of oil in its rise as a civil nation-state (see Chapter Three). Drawing on Bourdieu (2003), Rizvi and Lingard (2010) argue that 'the amount of 'national capital' possessed by a given nation is a determining factor in the degree of autonomy for policy development within the nation' (pp. 67–68). Therefore, they stress that national capital, which may consist of economic, political, and cultural capital, can be seen to mediate the extent to which nations are able to be context-generative in respect of the global field (Rizvi & Lingard, 2010, p. 68). Drawing on Bourdieu's (1984) opposition between 'the tastes of Luxury [or freedom] and the tastes of necessity', Marginson (2008), similarly, argues that 'the potential for self-determination is confined to freedom from material necessity' (p. 312). However, he adds that self-determination, as derived from resources is also conditioned by historical relations of power, by the imagination, and by the capacity of agents to work within their limits (Marginson, 2008, p. 312). He stresses that understanding the conditions of agency is essential, as they reveal the possibilities that a nation has to work with. Considering all of these factors, it can be argued that Kuwait's global position – what Marginson (2008) refers to as its 'global agency' – is restrained by its lack of martial power, its small population, and its small landmass. However, its agency is not confined by financial needs.

The conditions that Kuwait attached to the GATS agreement provide an illustration of the autonomy the government has in shaping and limiting the intervention of international organizations such as the WTO. Signing the GATS did not extract the autonomy Kuwait has over its national higher education policy decisions. The country's Schedule of Specific Commitments, attached to the GATS agreement, clearly imposes limitations on both foreign access to the local market and on the foreign commercial presence in the country. It states:

> ... foreign commercial presence should be either through a Kuwaiti Agent working in the same field of services or related to it (official agency contract must be registered with the Ministry of Commerce and Industry). Or: through a partnership with the capital of Kuwaiti Company, in which Kuwaiti portion should be 51% at least, and the aggregate portion of foreign capital should not exceed 49%. (WTO, 1994b GATS/SC/49: p. 2)
>
> Foreign commercial presence, must add some economic interests to the country, like high technology transfer, research and development programs, technical or marketing assistance and educational or training of local manpower, including a condition to employ 30% of his workforce with Nationals. (WTO, 1994b GATS/SC/49: p. 3)

Foreigners are only allowed to invest indirectly in Kuwaiti shareholding companies. The same laws are subsequently applied to the establishment of the private higher education sector, as is clearly stated in the policy:

> It is permissible by a decree issued in response to a request by the Minister of Higher Education to license the foundation of private universities/colleges or higher institutes/branches of foreign universities where the majority of shared capital funds is wholly owned by Kuwaitis. (Article 1, PUL34/2000)

The investigation of the external factors that influence the production of higher education privatization policies in Kuwait illustrates the degree of autonomy that characterizes national policy decisions in Kuwait. As mentioned earlier, there is no evidence of coercive action forcing the government to adopt privatization in reforming its higher education sector.

According to Rizvi and Lingard (2010) 'coercion involves an imposition of policies upon a weaker system under threat of sanctions' (p. 42). Bush (2011) similarly argues that 'coercion is backed by the threat of sanctions ... [and also] rests on the ability to constrain, to block, to interfere, or to punish' (p. 99). This is apparently not the case in Kuwait. A former parliament member confirms the independence of the country concerning the production of the PUL (34/2000), or at least I should say in his perception. He explained:

> *Certainly there is individual participation in different international agencies by local academics seeking new knowledge and information – or even to enhance their own reputation. And the state certainly has relations with these international agencies. However, the country is very independent in implementing policies that suit its own vision and domestic interests. Since Kuwait is a rich country, these international agencies have no power to force anything on the state of Kuwait, as they do when they fund other developing countries that lack financial resources.* (H.J., 13 February 2013)

The following statement by another participant reflects the same autonomy. He stated:

> *There have been numerous contacts with multidisciplinary consultancy agencies and companies. ... However, the influence of the recommendations presented by these and other agencies was negligible due to numerous socio-political reasons.* (J.A., 25 April 2013)

The above statement suggests the authority that policy actors have over national policy decisions, an authority that indicates that the adoption of policies is voluntarily. However, the absence of coercive practices does not suggest that globalization played no role in the promotion of higher education privatization or the more general adoption of neoliberal ideologies in Kuwait. Dale (1999) notes that globalization also employs non-coercive and discursive mechanisms to achieve national compliance. Below I will provide several concepts that can help us to understand and explain the influence of globalization on Kuwaiti policy decisions.

Soft Governance

'Soft governance' is a concept found in policy literature that is useful in describing one way in which global processes influence the production of national policies in Kuwait.

Governance (as opposed to 'government') is defined by Lawn (2006) as a:

> [N]ew paradigm, representing a shift from hierarchy and state hierarchies, and referring to a set of institutions and actors that are drawn from, but also beyond, government. [He explains that] The legitimacy of governing authority cannot be demanded but has to be negotiated and its relation with its partners in civil society is one of steering, guiding and contracting, within recognition that supported networks are unstable and fluctuating. In turn, civil society (in Habermas's terms, associations, organizations and movements) assumes a role in discussing and influencing the purposes of the relation and its purposes. (p. 280)

Soft governance, on the other hand, refers to the power of the language. Nye (2004) uses this concept of 'soft power' to describe the shortcomings of the current American foreign policy which uses 'hard power' – armed force and economic coercion – as its primary resource and tends to ignore alternatives. Soft governance, on the other hand, relies on the soft tools of networking, conferences, seminars, consultations, advisory groups, publications, etc. (Lawn, 2006). These practices frequently appear in the survey data, a fact that indicates that Kuwaiti policy actors are highly involved in these sorts of activities. These processes of cultural exchange and institutions for seeking economic and policy assistance are crucial in forging international alliances. Lawn (2006) argues that the cultivation of relations with allies, along with the search for economic assistance and cultural exchange, are necessary to win support abroad (p. 273). This reality explains the Kuwait's desire for international recognition as a way to strengthen its relations with allies and offset its strategic vulnerability explained earlier in Chapter Three.

Ahonen (2001) extends the metaphor of soft in governance with 'an exploration of policy- making upon practices, procedures, and conventions that have no binding character as to their implementation' (as cited in

Lawn, 2006, p. 279). Such practices have created a broad policy space whose effects are neither binding nor consist of hard laws. The policy spaces created by these practices represent a new 'soft governance' mode. These policy spaces are created through expert exchange, unilateral secondment of experts, observatories, advisory committees and working groups, information networks with contact points, information gateways, consultation of stakeholders, work of advisory committees and working groups, work of consortia in framework programmes, peer reviews, information exchange, monitoring, conferences, seminars, colloquia, round tables, symposia, certain types of applied research, and programmed research and development in education and training. According to the survey data, the production of the Private Universities Law (34/2000) was accompanied by considerable consultation and significant efforts to seek assistance abroad. However, this consultation and assistance brought no compulsion. None of the advice was binding and none of the assistance had strings attached. According to one participant:

> *There have been numerous contacts with multidisciplinary consultancy agencies and companies. ... However, the influence of the recommendations presented by these and other agencies was negligible due to numerous socio-political reasons.* (J.A., 25 April 2013)

In their book, *Globalisation and Higher Education in the Arab Gulf States*, Donn and Al Manthri (2010) argue that 'there are powerful influences, structural, procedural and personnel, exerting pressure on nationally defined agendas and concerns for curriculum, institutional development and administration' in the six Arab Gulf States (p. 156). Their examination of the G8/BMENA (Broader Middle East and North Africa) ministerial meetings reveals the existence of a 'magistracy' (Lawn & Lingard, 2002), a cohort of people, key players and policymakers, who travel between countries and create options, define agendas, and deliver products in a given region. They indicate a considerable influence for this 'magistracy' in shaping educational policy agendas in the region. This magistracy is responsible for introducing new concepts to the region, concepts such as: centre of excellence, use competencies, TVET linkages with the labour market, ... quality and autonomous accreditation bodies, ... continuous learning and lifelong learning, ... (and more importantly) include private sector and civil society in education policy development (p.152). This type of 'magistracy' plays a great role in educational policy decisions, in the Arab Gulf States generally and in Kuwait in particular.

Language seems to be a central feature of the techniques of 'soft' governance. The language of policy documents and reports is therefore an important indicator of the manner in which 'soft' governance operates on national policy processes. The IMF consultancy reports (IMF, 1999, 2000 & 2003) that were discussed previously provide indicators of this sort of influence. Although these reports are entirely non-compulsory, taking the form of suggestions and recommendations, it is the power of the language used that has this magistracy effect.

Features of 'soft governance' and 'magistracy influence' can be seen in these reports that use language such as:

> Directors welcomed the broad consensus on the need for structural reform measures aimed at enhancing the role of the private sector ...
> [Directors] encouraged authorities ... to approve relevant legislations ... to promote investment and growth, and foster competition and economic diversification.
> Directors looked forward to the next phase of privatization ... Directors stressed the essential role of the private sector ...
> Directors hoped that the National Assembly would act speedily on these [privatization] proposals ...
> Directors stressed the importance of building a broad public consensus in favor of [privatization] reforms ...
> Given the uncertain medium-term outlook for the oil market, directors welcomed the authorities' policy response to introduce a comprehensive medium-term fiscal reform strategy centered around three components: accelerating privatization; containing the wage bill, in conjunction with labor market reform; and reducing subsidies and transfers.
> Directors encouraged the authorities to take advantage of the current favorable macroeconomic conditions and buoyant private sector, and step up the pace of implementation of their strategy. In particular, they encouraged accelerating reforms to reduce state involvement in the economy, promote private investment, and improve the functioning of the labor market.
> Directors looked forward to the early passage of the Privatization Law to establish the legal and institutional framework for promoting private investment. In the meanwhile, they encouraged the authorities to move forward with early divesture of public sector activities that do not require explicit legislative action for privatization.
> Directors encouraged the authorities to improve the budget structure by reducing current expenditure, particularly on wages and subsidies, in conjunction with civil service reform and adjustment of prices of goods and services provided by the public sector toward cost recovery. On the revenue side, they stressed the need to boost non- oil revenue, and encouraged the authorities to work with regional partners toward the introduction of the value added tax.(IMF, 1999, 2000 & 2003)

The question that arises then is what made policy actor to comply with such recommendations and giving them priority in policy decision.

Needs for Global Recognition

The country's desire for international recognition, as noted in the previous section, to sustain its survival from the surrounded threats acted as an indirect steering power of policy decisions. International recognition for Kuwaiti educational diplomas and certificates, in the same vein, is utterly necessary in order to maintain a credible education system in Kuwait. As a result, the necessity for this international recognition exerts a strong influence on higher education policy decisions. This complete dependence on international recognition is due to the lack of graduate programs and courses in the country and, in addition, to the absence of traditional higher education culture. At Kuwait University for example, international recognition is crucial for its graduates to be able to continue their further studies. An official from KU stated:

> *In the case of Kuwait University, it has to meet international standards for quality and accreditation for its graduates to be accepted seeking their further studies abroad.* (H.J., 13 February 2013)

Another participant from the same university bluntly stated that:

> *In the region we are [the business school of KU] the only college recognised by the United States through the ASS.* (J.M., 28 November 2012)

Moreover, the PUC also aims for Kuwaiti private higher education to be internationally recognized. A PUC's official stated:

> *Our aim for our private higher education is to achieve international recognition and to be accredited by international accreditation bodies.* (F.A., 11 December 2012)

Even private institutions seek international recognition, even if it might be only to fulfil their licensing requirements. However, most private institutions also market their foreign affiliations to the public. A President of a private university stated:

> *We have four different agencies to evaluate our programs to ensure the quality of our education provided. These are: New England, DUSP, ABET, and also the PUC. We are providing education that is recognised internationally, not just by the PUC.* (S.S., 5 December 2012)

Thus, adherence to international standards is a common goal for both the public and private sectors.

Students also valued the continued approach of Kuwaiti higher education institutions to conform to international standards, as it improves their chances if they consider continuing their studies abroad. A student from a private institution endorsed the university's approach of having examinations graded externally at universities abroad, saying:

> *I believe that the ACK is the private university with the strongest active connection with the mother universities abroad, especially compared to other private institutions in Kuwait. This is because we are graded mostly from the mother universities in Australia – Victoria University is one of them. A large percentage of our work was sent to be graded in Australia. Most of our assignments and exams are*

> *marked externally in the mother university abroad, which is a big university as you may know. Accordingly, we can easily transfer to study in our affiliated institutions abroad.* (S.8, 3 April 2013)

Therefore, the hunger for international recognition is driven by a nationally perceived necessity. This need to adhere to international standards has acted as a type of external influence and frequently steers national higher education policy decisions.

Policy Borrowing and Transfer

Policy transfer (also known as policy borrowing) is defined as 'a process by which knowledge of policies, administrative arrangements, institutions and ideas in one political system (past or present) is used in the development of policies, administrative arrangements, institutions and ideas in another political system' (Dolowitz & Marsh, 2000, p. 5). The impact of policy transferral on policy-making provides a useful explanation for the adoption of privatization in Kuwait. In an era of globalization, educational systems are increasingly looking to what others are doing and hoping to use the experiences of other systems to improve their local systems. Countries reforming their education systems frequently look abroad for best practice and seek to import policies, practices, and programs that appear to incorporate best practice. Thus, ideas, policies, and what are considered best practices in one locale are sought after by policymakers, with the intention of improving and developing provision in other systems (Dolowitz & Marsh, 2000). In so doing, they appear to contribute to the increasing globalization of education. Accordingly, and given the high level of interaction with global society among policymakers in Kuwait, the production of the PUL (34/2000) could be a good example of the phenomenon of transferring policies, ideas, and programs from what are perceived to be the best practices in the world today. Study participants frequently note practices abroad with regard to the implementation of privatization policies in the higher education sector. According to a former parliament member:

> *At the initial stage, we looked at different experiences in the field of higher education privatization in order to search for better practices to learn from in the application of our own privatization polices.* (H.A., 11 December 2012)

Other participants also refer to practices in other countries as examples of better ways of doing things. For example, an official at the PUC noted:

> *Student loan systems have been implemented in many systems around the world, which in my opinion is the only thing that the government left out from the initial privatization policy [PUL34/2000], as it allows students to pay for their own education with easy loans. This policy will reduce government expenditure on higher education as well as increasing student accountability for their higher education.* (F.A., 11 December 2012)

A former minister also stated:

> *It is important to allow the private sector to participate in the production of higher education services and stop it from being the exclusive preserve of the government... [noting that] most well-known and great universities in the world are private institutions, since the flexibility of the private sector in making decisions and its rapid actions contribute much to educational quality. Third, I believe that the government should not be the only [provider] sponsor of funding higher education; the society, as represented by the private sector, should participate as well.* (M.H., 18 March 2013)

Not only is policy borrowing a favoured practice, it has become a de facto obligation for private institutions to implement programs from the world's best practices, as implied by the policy regarding eligibility to be parent institutions below:

> The (Parent) Educational Institution is qualified in accordance with the adopted Standards and Criteria of the Private Universities Council no. (PUC 16/d 25-02/2006) which stipulates that the institution must be among the best 200 universities listed in the latest appendix of the Times Educational Magazine. (PUC 2/ 30-4/ 2007)

Therefore, the role of policy transfer illustrates the how higher education privatization is implemented in Kuwait. Policymakers look at other best practices with the hope of adopting what best fits their national needs.

In order to understand the nature of the influence of policy borrowing (or policy transferring) as an external force influencing policy decisions in Kuwait, I applied Dolowitz and Marsh's (2000) suggested continuum of policy transfer. They hold that policy transfer can be, in varying degrees, both voluntary and coercive. To establish a sharp and unbridgeable distinction between voluntary and coercive transfer is to oversimplify the process. Accordingly, they suggest that policy borrowing and transfer is a 'continuum that runs from lesson-drawing to the direct imposition of a programme, policy or institutional arrangement on one political system by another' (Dolowitz & Marsh, 2000, p. 13), as shown in Fig. 8.

In the continuum above Dolowitz and Marsh (2000) note that lesson-drawing highlights the fact that actors engage in policy transfer as a 'rational response to a perceived process' (p. 14). As an example, the authors note that 'dissatisfaction with the status quo' may warrant actors to engage in a voluntary policy transfer in which programmes elsewhere are examined. The aim is to see the transferral of these programmes to the local system (perfect rationality). Somewhat less voluntary is the situation where the actors are not perfectly rational, as when they act with limited information. In this case the choice to transfer policy may be based on an inaccurate assessment of the real situation or mistaken information about the nature of the policy and how it operates. In an even more coercive transfer, national governments are compelled to transfer and adopt certain programmes and policies by virtue

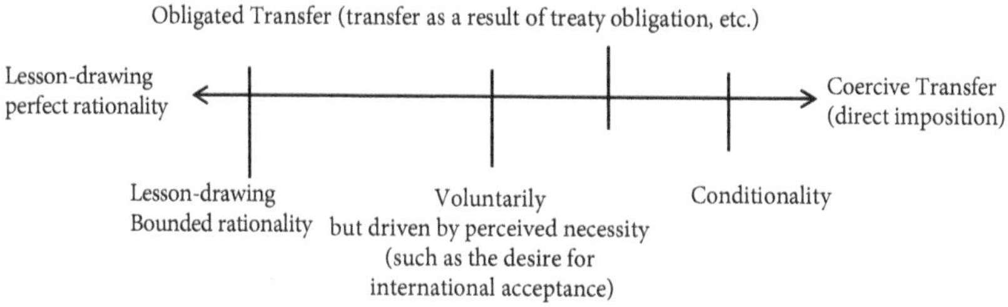

Fig. 9: Policy borrowing and transfer continuum. (Source: Dolowitz & Marsh, 2000)

of being a member of an international organization and as part of their obligation to that organization. However, it should be remembered that policy borrowing and transfer might not always strictly be viewed as voluntary or coercive; policy borrowing and transfer can be a mixture of both 'voluntary decisions and coercive pressures' (Dolowitz & Marsh, 2000). For example, as members of an international organization, nations are forced to comply with the organization's policies and directives, which can be termed coercive transfer. On the other hand, Dolowitz and Marsh (2000) argue that, because nations voluntarily join an international organization and collectively shape its edicts, the choice to transfer policy is, in this situation, both 'obligated' and 'negotiated' (Dolowitz & Marsh, 2000).

In Kuwait policymakers were looking for better practices to solve the problems of their higher education system because of the dissatisfaction with the local conditions, as presented in the previous chapter. This fact indicates that the adoption of privatization was voluntary. However, being a full member of the WTO and a signatory to the GATS agreement would obligate the government to comply with the WTO's policies and directives, a situation that could be viewed as coercive. The IMF's reports, for example, encourage the government to adopt privatization and foster the role of the private sector in its development processes. One such report states:

> Directors agreed that such reforms will be key to improving business climate and promoting investment and efficiency in the economy by fostering private sector participation and attracting foreign investment. Noting that little progress had been made in approving these reforms, Directors stressed the importance of building a broad public consensus in favor of these reforms: They encouraged the authorities and the National Assembly to work toward securing the legislative approval of these measures. (IMF, 2000)

Also:

> Directors looked forward to the early passage of the Privatization Law to establish the legal and institutional framework for promoting private investment. In the

> meanwhile, they encouraged the authorities to move forward with early divesture of public sector activities that do not require explicit legislative action for privatization. They considered that such a step would signal the authorities' commitment to private sector-led growth and further strengthen the environment for private investment. (IMF, 2004, p.3)

The above two excerpts show that the adoption of privatization can be both voluntary and coercive in varying degrees and ways. The language used (in the above statements and elsewhere) suggests that directors are using the country's desire for international recognition, which in itself is voluntary, in order to impose their ideologies and policies on national policy decisions. These decisions can, therefore, be said to be 'obligated'. However, they can also be said to be 'negotiated' when one takes into account the conditions that Kuwait added to the GATS agreement. Also increasing Kuwait's voluntariness level is the scope of action it gains by exercising selective adoption of different programs from different educational systems.

Based on the data presented in this chapter and the suggested theoretical justifications for the adoption of privatization for higher education reform in Kuwait, I will suggest a heuristic conceptual framework that could be useful in analysing the sources of external factors influencing the processes of national higher education policy production in Kuwait. To some extent, it provides a general understanding of the role that the processes of globalization have in affecting policy-making in the country, as illustrated in Fig. 10 below. A thematic analysis of the text documents and interview transcripts highlights four major external forces that influence higher education policy decisions in Kuwait. Although the suggested framework does not eliminate other possible influences, it is confined to the purpose of this study. The dashed line surrounding national policy decision-making in Fig. 10 is used to suggest the openness of the process and the possibility of other influences that have not been revealed in the data. Study data indicates that there are four major external factors steering national policy decisions in Kuwait.

First – and most evident in the data – is the internationalization of policy actors and their openness to global experience and practices, which largely related to their international education. The government's long-standing practice of sending Kuwaiti students to complete their higher education studies abroad has created policy actors with a thoroughly Westernized policy outlook. This outlook has been shaped by what are considered to be the best systems in the world today. Most of these policy actors have created networks and communities that allow for the circulation of ideologies and policies. Thus, the internationalization of policy actors through international education is the first major influence. Secondly, there are regional influences, which arise either by means of similar established communities or by means

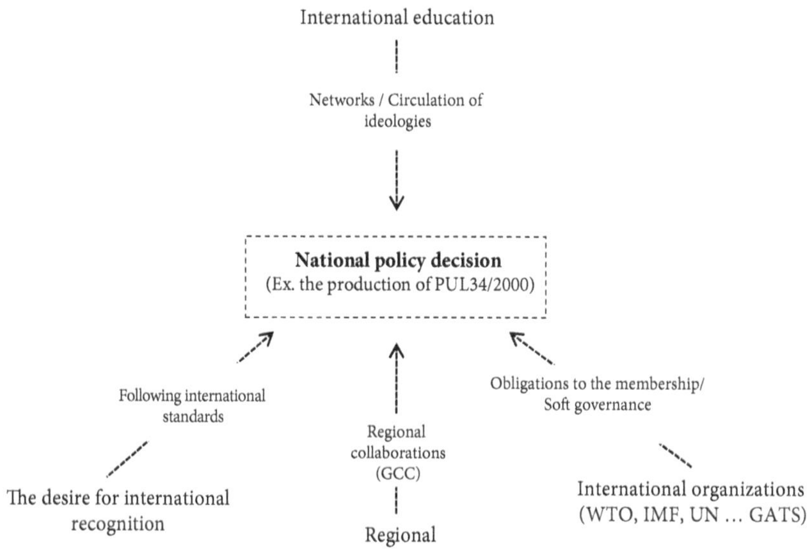

Fig. 10: Heuristic conceptual framework of global influence on higher education in Kuwait.

of agreements between the countries in the region. Such collaborations stimulate governments to embrace regional as well global development.

A third influence emerges from membership in international organizations and from the signing of international agreements. International organizations, although they may be joined voluntarily, nonetheless require that the member countries follow their rules. Likewise, with international agreements that, although they may have been signed voluntarily, nonetheless create obligations that the country must follow. International organizations also subtly impose ideologies and policies by using soft governance techniques that rely on the use of language. Finally, the fourth major influence is the country's desire for international recognition, a desire that forces the state to follow specific policies in order to comply with international standards. Taken together, these four modes of regional and international influences exert a powerful force on decision-making. However, it should be noted here that most of these external influences are indirect and non-coercive and their degree of influence is varied and unsystematic.

Conclusion

From the above, it can be concluded that external influences on Kuwaiti national policy decisions are more voluntary and negotiated than coercive.

The country's autonomy in deciding its national public policies may, to a great extent, be attributed to its financial capacity and its oil wealth. Nevertheless, there are international factors that play a crucial role in steering Kuwait's policy decisions – sometimes directly, but more often indirectly.

International forces such as the Westernization of national policy actors, the obligations to international organizations, and the need for international recognition all play an important role in Kuwaiti policy-making. However, the study finds no direct coercive action from external powers affecting national policy decisions in Kuwait.

The absence of coercive forces directly imposing higher education privatization on Kuwait raises the question of how external influences interact with national pressures in order to produce privatization policy. Globalization is not uniform in its effects. Nor is it an irresistible force that imposes a predetermined outcome, forcing different nation-states to adopt identical policies. Instead, it is mediated and steered by local forces that shape the influences of globalization according to local contexts. The internal and external factors by which higher education privatization policies are promoted in Kuwait do not operate separately or in isolation from each other. The nation-state continues to play a significant role as mediator in processing external influences brought about by globalization. Rizvi and Lingard (2010) similarly argue that 'the state is not powerless in the face of globalization' (p. 67). Accordingly, the following chapter will present the interplay between the local and global factors in the production of higher education privatization policies in Kuwait. It will illustrate how external influences have been mediated to respond to local pressures in the production of privatization policies.

Chapter Seven: Globalization, the State and Privatization Policies

In contrast to Chapter Five, Chapter Six indicated that there are significant external influences that have influenced national higher education policy decisions in Kuwait, concerning, in particular, the production of privatization policy and the establishment of the private higher education sector. Almost all of those external pressures were found to be outcomes of the processes of globalization identified earlier in Chapter Two. However, there was no coercion identified. On the contrary, most influences have followed a 'soft' way of governance, or developed as a result of national desire for global recognition. Education policy formulation is a broad field and the influences on it are hard to confine to local, national, or regional borders. Both the local pressures and global influences that promote privatization in the Kuwaiti higher education system do not occur in isolation from each other. They are interrelated and interconnected. The separation applied in the previous two chapters was only for the purposes of analysis.

Mann (2000) argued that influences on education policy could often be traced across multiple socio-spatial layers: local, national, international (relations between nations), transnational (passage through national boundaries) and global (as cited in Rizvi & Lingard, 2010). In addition, there is also a regional layer to consider (Rizvi & Lingard, 2010). Consequently, under the influence of globalization, policy decisions are formulated across all the different dimensions of the world's spaces today (local, regional and global). The processes of policy formulation are interrelated and it is often difficult to separate the different threads of influence from each other. Accordingly, in policy analysis it is important to discern the interactions between the different dimensions of the multilayered educational policy field: local, regional and global, as these dimensions are interrelated and affected by the processes of globalization (Rizvi & Lingard, 2010). Likewise, Marginson and Rhoads' (2002) 'glonacal agency heuristic' also captures this global and local embeddedness, as explained in Chapter Four (p. 281).

Globalization is not a uniform, universal or monolithic force that works in only one direction and forces purely passive nation-states to adopt identical policies. Rather, it is mediated and steered by local forces that shape its influences according to local context. This is an argument that has been supported by the global diversity witnessed in the implementation of privatization in higher education systems across the regions presented earlier in Chapter Two. Rizvi and Lingard (2010) also emphasize that 'Global processes do not affect all educational systems in the same way. They are filtered through particular national political and cultural traditions, as well as the specific ways in which policymakers engage with global pressures' (p. 42). Both the local and global pressures promoting higher education privatization policies in Kuwait have not been in effect separately, or in isolation from each other. They influence each other, and each contributed to the final policy formulation. Green (1997) argues that globalization and internationalization do not necessarily result in the 'demise' of local, national, and regional education systems. If this is so, privatization is not entirely due to globalization. At the same time, it cannot be attributed to local factors alone. Rather, both local and global factors have contributed to the policy production.

Wangenge-Ouma (2008), for example, in his study on funding policy shifts in Kenya, argues that, although Kenya's higher education funding policy shift from free higher education to greater cost sharing was mostly caused by its encounter with globalization, nonetheless, local social, political and economic dynamics exerted a significant influence. With or without globalization, the policy of free higher education had to stop at some point. Thus, the policy shift was not exclusively due to the often blamed globalization and its processes, as identified by Rizvi (2006), or the World Bank in this context (see Chapter Two). Rather, prevailing local conditions also required this policy shift, as Kenya simply did not have sufficient resources to support free higher education (Wangenge-Ouma, 2008). Thus, globalization only expedited these changes, although perhaps 'precipitately' (Wangenge-Ouma, 2008, p. 226).

The nation-state then continues to play a significant role as mediator in processing influences of globalization. The role of the state has changed, but it has not been eliminated (Sassen, 1996). It is simply not the case that the nation-state is losing significance. Rather, 'the state itself has been a key agent in the implementation of global processes, and it has emerged quite altered by this participation' (Enders, 2004, p. 369). Rizvi and Lingard (2010) also argue that 'the state is not powerless in the face of globalization', as 'it is possible ... to resist the global dominance of neoliberalism' (p. 67). However, the capacities of nation-states to manage their national interests vary, not only between nation-states, but even within nation-states. This variation is mainly because the educational policy field is 'multilayered', a field that is 'stretched from the local to the global' (Rizvi & Lingard, 2010, p. 67).

In this chapter I argue how global processes are influential in the production of privatization policies in Kuwait; however, the state is not entirely powerless. Given the fact that Kuwait would be financially capable of sustaining and expanding its public higher education system, this chapter will capture the unique interplay between both local and global pressures that led to the introduction of privatization. Kuwait's engagement with global processes is complex. It has to respond to local demands/needs in ways that rearticulate its understanding of privatization. This chapter will illustrate how global pressures have been mediated, altered, and justified in response to local interests. It argues that global processes have been mediated by the state to address long-standing local higher education problems, thereby producing an adjusted (or adapted) form of privatization. Thereby, Kuwait rearticulates the ways in which it understands privatization.

Globalization from Above

As presented in the previous chapter, clearly policy actors are highly influenced by the processes of globalization by way of their education abroad or by way of other tools of exchanging information and ideas. Conferences, consultancy, partnerships with global groups – all of these international institutions play a role in introducing globalization into Kuwait, as was noted in Chapter Six. Thus, national policy decisions on privatization are also influenced by globalization from above. Dolowitz and Marsh (2000, p. 10) similarly noted that it is becoming increasingly clear that policymakers, at both the national and international levels, are relying on the advice of consultants, whether individuals or firms, who act as policy experts in the development of new programs, policies and institutional structures.

Accordingly, international organizations play an important role in the promotion of privatization in Kuwait, despite the absence of coercive actions. Also noted is that the country has voluntarily become involved in partnerships with global organizations such as the WTO, the UN, the IMF, and the World Bank. These partnerships require annual meetings with the consultants from those organizations. It should be noted that these consultations and the resulting recommendations on policy-making in Kuwait have no binding character as to their implementation, as is shown in the following statement:

> *There have been numerous contacts with multidisciplinary consultancy agencies and companies. ... However, the influence of the recommendations presented by these and other agencies was negligible due to numerous socio-political reasons.* (J.A., 25 April 2013)

However, despite the lack of influence of specific recommendations, the overall ideological influence exerted by international institutions on policy decisions in Kuwait is hard to overlook. Dolowitz and Marsh (2000) also noted that international governing organizations (IGOs), such as the OECD, the G-7, the IMF and the UN and its various agencies, are increasingly playing a role in the spread of ideas, programs, and institutions around the globe (p.11). These organizations also influence national policymakers directly, through their policies and loan conditions, and indirectly, through the information and policies spread at their conferences and reports (Dolowitz & Marsh, 2000). It is this indirect influence that appears most frequently in statements given by study participants. In fact, most of them refer to the use of information and ideas from external experts and organizations. One participant, for example, stated that:

> *At first, in the primary phase of writing the policy, we attended several conferences looking for assistance in framing our standards by benefiting from other experiences in the field of higher education privatization, in addition to recommendations offered by reports conducted in the region.* (H.A., 11 December 2012)

This sort of deliberate seeking of international input, along with the consultancy reports of the IMF discussed in Chapter Six, clearly indicates the influence of globalization from above on the introduction of privatization into Kuwait and the empowerment of the market with regard to its higher education.

In addition to the types of influence shown above, international nongovernmental organizations (NGOs) are also increasing their influence over global public policy through their ability to spread ideas and information on an international level. As Gordenker and Weiss (1996) put it:

> Nongovernmental organisations (NGOs) have in increasing numbers injected unexpected voices into international discourse about numerous problems of global scope. Especially during the last 20 years ... interests have become active in political work once reserved for representatives of states. In their own ways, NGOs ... grope ... towards a modicum of global governance ... NGOs have now become an integral part of the process of setting agendas. ... and in carrying the results not only to governments but to other NGOs and individuals. (as cited in Dolowitz & Marsh, 2000, p.11)

With regard to the nine main categories of policy actors identified by Dolowitz and Marsh (2000) – elected officials, political parties, bureaucrats/civil servants, pressure groups, policy entrepreneurs and experts, transnational corporations, think tanks, supra-national governmental and nongovernmental institutions and consultants – they notice that the role of the last two in policy processes is becoming increasingly evident (p.10). Dolowitz and Marsh (2000) also argue that, although only consultants, IGOs, and NGOs are acting as agents of coercive policy transfer; they are also agents of voluntary policy transfer, a fact that complicates any potential model of policy transfer. Unlike most categories of actors involved in the policy transfer process, they act as agents of both voluntary and coercive policy transfer. More importantly, both can be used by other actors to help in their efforts to transfer, or force others to transfer, policies (Dolowitz & Marsh,

2000). When international organizations, such as the IMF and the World Bank, get involved in policy transfer, they often recommend that particular consultants be hired (Dolowitz & Marsh, 2000, p.10). They argue that the role of these international consultants has complicated the distinction between voluntary and coercive policy transfer and made it less clear, which they suggest could be also further complicated by time.

Thus, although most indicators point to privatization in Kuwait being voluntarily, there might be some influences of a coercive character emerging from an initial voluntary decision by the state to join such organizations. Dolowitz and Marsh (2000)'s conceptualization of the role played by consultants and international organizations explained in Chapter Six provides an explanation of the nature of the external influences on Kuwaiti policy processes. Their framework explains how voluntary decisions could become coercive over time. Given the local realities presented in Chapter Five, a privatization policy had to be produced at some point, especially considering the existence of growing public demand. Sauvé (2002) observes that 'the [market] for trade in [higher] education services is big, diverse, innovative and growing fast. … [Such] changes … have been occurring almost independently of developments in the WTO', which introduced the GATS (p. 4). However, I disagree with Sauvé's (2002) conclusion that the GATS/WTO 'is not likely to be a driving force or even a major consideration behind such changes' (p. 4). The case of Kuwait provides strong support for my disagreement, as the data presented in the previous two chapters clearly shows that, despite local discontent, higher education privatization was placed on Kuwait's policy agenda only after the country's signing of the GATS agreement.

Significantly, there was no private higher education institution in Kuwait before the signing of the GATS agreement. However, just after signing, the policy was created, and within a decade or so private higher education expanded so rapidly that it now accommodates as many students as the public sector. At the present, there are a total of seventeen licensed private institutions, either fully operating (eight in 2009) (Al-Atiqi & Alharbi, 2009; PUC, 2011) or '*expected to open in the next few years*' (F.A., 11 December 2012). They are all operating under the supervision of the Private Universities Council (PUC):

- Gulf University for Science and Technology (GUST)
- Australian College of Kuwait (ACK)
- American University of Kuwait (AUK)
- Kuwait Maastricht Business School
- American College of the Middle East (ACM)
- Arab Open University (AOU)
- Box Hill College Kuwait

- Kuwait Technical College
- American University of the Middle East (AUM)
- College of Aviation Technology
- Kuwait Institute for Science and Technology
- Kuwait International Law College (KILC)
- Algonquin College – Kuwait
- British College of Kuwait (BCK)
- American University of Medical Sciences
- Community College in Kuwait

Most of these institutions offer two-year diplomas and four-year Bachelor's degrees. Some even offer Master's programmes, mostly in business management, such as the MBA program offered by the Kuwait Maastricht Business School and GUST.

It should be noted that the GATS offers some degree of choice. However, while it is possible for a country to 'opt out of [or be excluded from] the multilateral trading system altogether (Sauvé, 2002, p. 11), it is unlikely that many nations would want to pursue this course, particularly if they view trade in higher education as representing an opportunity. Moreover, while (as noted above) nations currently have the opportunity to restrict what service sectors will be subject to GATS rules, it should be remembered that '[t]he GATS ... contains an overarching commitment to successive future negotiations to increase coverage and expand the agreement ... aimed at achieving a progressively higher level of liberalisation' (Sinclair, 2002, p. 4). As EI and PSI (1999) note, in accordance with the 'so-called rollback rule', it is expected that, as time goes by, member countries will open up their markets further, gradually lifting more and more restrictions on trade (p. 18). These expectations are noted by a study participant with regard to the current policy debate about partnerships with international universities. He expressed his opposition to the new policy, arguing that:

> *The policy on franchising higher education in Kuwait is an extremely sensitive socio- cultural issue that has to be reassessed in view of the experience of other GCC countries.* (J.A., 25 April 2013)

This statement reflects the fact that the GATS's expectation of further liberalization has been successful in influencing current policy debate in Kuwait, a fact that further supports the argument that the GATS and higher education privatization policy in Kuwait are in many ways associated with each other.

Policy Processes and the Role of the State

Despite global pressures on the state in promoting privatization, it is not powerless in the adoption of privatization policies for its higher education.

In this section the focus will be on the state, its policy processes, and their consequent deficiencies that placed privatization on the policy agenda.

The Kuwaiti Constitution guarantees a democratic system of government. It states:

> The System of Government in Kuwait shall be democratic, under which sovereignty resides in the people, the source of all powers. Sovereignty shall be exercised in the manner specified in this Constitution. (Article 6, Democracy)

Despite the Amir's appearance of superior authority discussed earlier in Chapter Three, policy processes and legislations are often the outcomes of a shared participation between both the public and the government. There are three central authorities in the State of Kuwait: first is the legislative power that is represented by the Amir and the Parliament with its 50 elected members. Second is the executive power represented by the Amir, the Cabinet, and the Ministers. Third, and above all, is the judicial authority represented by both civil and constitutional courts. Selected passages from the Constitution will illustrate the different levels of power concerning national policy processes. The Constitution section IV, Powers, chapter I: General Provisions, states that:

> The system of Government is based on the principle of separation of powers functioning in co-operation with each other in accordance with the provisions of the Constitution. None of these powers may relinquish all or part of its competence specified in this Constitution. (Article 50, Separation and Constitutionality of Powers)
> The legislative power is vested in the Amir and the National Assembly [the parliament] in accordance with the Constitution. (Article 51, Legislative Power)
> The executive power is vested in the Amir, the Cabinet, and the Ministers, in the manner specified by the Constitution. (Article 52, Executive Power)
> The judicial power is vested in the Courts, which exercise it in the name of the Amir within the limits of the Constitution. (Article 53, Judicial Power)

All policies produced must be approved by these three central authorities.

Although it seems simple and systematic at a glance, in practice policy processes are much more complex. Unfortunately, policy processes have not functioned well for some time. To explain, the following statement by a study participant briefly reflects the problematic condition of policy processes and political practices in Kuwait over the last two or three decades. He stated:

> *Haphazardness characterised policy processes in the State of Kuwait, plus corruption through socio-economic connections, a problem damaging the entire public sector. Policies in the state of Kuwait are random, and they are not referred back to the Constitution before their production as should be done.* (S.G., 5 December 2012)

His statement suggests a crucial factor affecting the dynamics of policy processes and policy decision-making in Kuwait – that is, 'connections', or what it known locally as *wasta*. He refers to the pervasive phenomenon of the decisive role of socio-economic relations in decision-making, a factor that permeates the entire public sector. It is the residual effect of the early governance of the state, discussed in Chapter Three, which has been reinforced through the formation of the modern state of Kuwait. Another participant also reinforces this view. He commented:

> *The processes of policy production in the State are idiosyncratic, based on the individuals who are in charge and their personal interests. They are not random processes because to some extent planning and plans do exist in the country. However, the implementation is selective and based on the personal opinions and interests of whoever is in power.* (A.S., 27 March 2013)

The above statement suggests that public policies are sometimes created without regard to actual public needs. Instead, public policies tend to reflect only the personal decisions of influential individuals (policy actors) and may be based on a narrow view of reality, a view that is far from being the result of any kind of systematic study. This explains why interviewees, when discussing individuals in power, frequently point to their socio-economic backgrounds. They are especially likely to do this when asked about policy production processes. An example of this tendency is the first response a study participant gave when asked about the production of the Private Universities Law (34/2000). He responded:

> *The only thing I would say is that the policy was issued when Professor Yosif Al-Ebrahim was the Minister of Higher Education, who is well-known because of his affiliation with the Merchants' community.* (H.A., 11 December 2012)

He carefully noted Al-Ebrahim's connection with the merchants (the private sector) before proceeding to any discussion regarding his role in the policy production process.

This overdependence on the personal opinions of influential policy actors is exacerbated by an apparent lack of available research and studies that could inform policy decisions and direct policy discussion toward actual public needs. According to one participant, most public policies are produced under pressure and are mainly the result of trade-offs between the government and the different socio-political groups that constitute the parliament. Important policy decisions are rarely informed by any research, study, or planning that might lead policymakers to respond to actual public needs. He complained bitterly stating that:

> *Unfortunately, due to political pressures and trade-offs, public policies are produced without sufficient studies, resulting in the production of distorted unplanned laws.* (A.F., 18 March 2013)

Policy decisions, then, are not grounded on adequate studies. Instead, they are determined by policymakers' perceptions of their own current situation and their socio-political associations, which are traditionally inherited. Apparently, there is a gap between the need for research and the policy production processes. As noted by a participant:

> *Policy processes are not random processes because to some extent planning and plans do exist in the country. However, the implementation is selective and based on the personal opinions and interests of whoever is in power.* (A.S., 27 March 2013)

But perhaps the problem is not a lack of available policy research. One official at KU notes the existence of studies, which were submitted to the government and neglected for years. He said:

> *In 2005, KU submitted a study proposal to the government showing the need to establish three new public universities, and until now it is still frozen and no real actions have been seriously taken!* (R.A., 13 March 2013)

Thus, the apparent lack of studies and research may not be due to the lack of professionals and local experts. Rather, it may be that the nature of Kuwait's policy production process discourages the commissioning and utilization of research. The gap between research and policy production would thereby be caused by defective policy production processes rather than being a cause of them. This political reality has produced long-standing problems.

Norton (1993) noted that in the Arab Gulf States generally, rhetoric has long focused on solidarity and unity; however, the reality in these states is the persistence of socially familiar and divisive forms of associations such as the family, the clan, the tribe, and the sect. Norton (1993), accordingly, argues that these authoritarian states have been successful in breeding social particularities and exploiting cleavages to the detriment of the development of democratic institutions and meaningful political participation. The State of Kuwait, however, is one of the few Arab States that enjoys a great degree of democracy and active public political participation in policy decisions (Norton, 1993). Despite this fact, the anti- democratic practices used by the other Arab Gulf States have found their way into Kuwait's political practices. Given what has been revealed by the data, I tend to agree with Norton's apparently cynical argument about the region. Not only that, but it apparently applies to Kuwait as well as the other Arab Gulf States.

The persistence of various social, political, and economic associations among policymakers is exacerbated by the government's ban on the formation of the political parties, discussed earlier in Chapter Three, that might otherwise mediate between these associations and give stability to alliances between them. The resulting fragmented nature of Kuwaiti politics has negatively affected policy processes and resulted in polarized and inconsistent policy decisions. According to Dar (2012), increased polarization of political preferences leads to an increase in disagreement over various political issues, often resulting in legislative 'gridlock' and erratic policy-making (p. 781). This explains the political instability pointed to by most participants as a major factor in the long-standing higher education problems in Kuwait. A former member of the parliament noted that:

> *Public policies are dependent on the political stability of a country, which means if a country is politically stable and its constitutional authorities represent societal views, public policies will be produced following that vision. However,[in our case] the state suffers from ongoing crises and frequent political turns of fortune that result in the hindering of many development plans and vital projects. This is because of the disruption of political cycles and shifting them to a new parliament with a different balance of political powers and a different list of priorities. This political turbulence leaves the production of public policies at stake.* (H.J., 13 February 2013)

In this passage, he is referring to the recurrent dissolutions of the parliament over the last two decades. This repeated dissolution of parliament creates inconsistency in public policies and results in many stalled higher education development projects.

Drawing on Isaiah Berlin, Hannah Arendt, and others' perception of the characteristics of ancient democracies, Tétreault (1995) explains the inefficiency of Kuwait's policy processes by using the concepts of positive and negative liberty. 'In broad terms, negative liberty means freedom from – from interference, coercion, or restraint – while positive liberty means freedom to, or self-determination-freedom to act or to be as one wills' (Heyman, 1992, p. 81). Positive liberty here refers to 'the power to act as one thinks fit, within the bounds of civil law' (Heyman, 1992, p. 84). Negative liberty, on the other hand, 'requires that individuals remain free of state control except where necessary for the good of the community' (Heyman, 1992, p. 85). 'This is negative liberty in the sense we most commonly use the term today – freedom from unjustified interference by government ... liberty can be expressed in terms of specific rights – the constitutional rights against governmental interference with life, liberty and property, with free speech, and so on' (Heyman, 1992, p. 85). Both are commonly deemed necessary to a healthy and fully functional liberty. Accordingly, Tétreault (1995) argues that the recurrent suspensions of the parliament are the result of the absence of the negative liberty that would create effective constitutional limits on state power. Such negative liberty as exists is constantly jeopardized by the actual and threatened suspensions of the Constitution. This situation sets up a vicious cycle in which the frequent suspensions of the Constitution are both a result of and a cause of the absence of negative liberty in Kuwait.

Tétreault (1995) examines the patterns of public liberty in Kuwait and how these patterns affect the public's ability to identify needs and transform them into policies. She explains that:

Fig. 11: Caricature 1, illustrating the absence of negative liberty explained by Tétreault (the white building is the Parliament building and the man's outfit is representation of the government). (Source: unknown, n.d.)

> [Positive liberty] is the primary social and institutional manifestation of democratic practice in Kuwait. Exercised in protected spaces, positive liberty exerts a strong and effective check on state power. However, positive liberty is limited by physical and ideological constraints as well by its fundamental nature. Positive liberty is the freedom of the strong. It does not guarantee the rights of the weak to political status, material sustenance, or personal safety – rights that require state intervention to create and protect. As a result, the benefits of positive liberty are enjoyed disproportionately more by economically and socially better off Kuwaitis than by the economically dependent and/or declass, though even for the relatively powerful, the benefits of positive liberty are attenuated by the absence of negative liberty. (p. 3)

Therefore, despite the many characteristics of positive liberty manifested in policy processes in Kuwait, the absence of negative liberty hinders the practice of consistent and stable policy processes. Sarcastic caricatures from national newspapers remarkably capture the conditions of the poor policy processes in Kuwait (see Figures 11 & 12). Not surprisingly, this instability has resulted in inefficient policy decisions that have marginalized higher education problems for years. This inefficiency is a problem noted by study participants, and has frozen some long-standing higher education development projects for years. As an example, one participant pointed out:

> *Jaber University ... is a new public university that we have done the report for, and it has been submitted to the Minister who should establish the management board and commence its activity in September this year, but it has not been commenced up to this date.* (W.R., 17 March 2013)

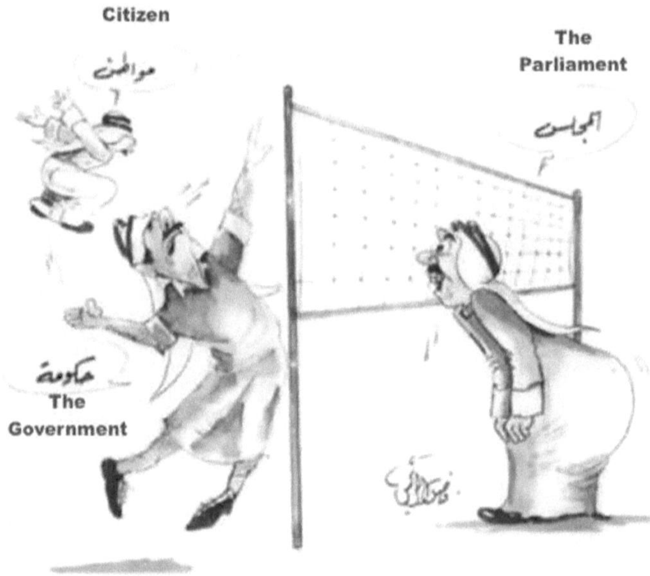

Fig. 12: Caricature 2, implies the de facto role of the Parliament in the face of the government. (Source: Al-Rayyes, F. Wednesday 9-4-2014, *Al Qabas* newspaper)

Another such project is called *Al Madinah Al Jamee'iah* (or University City). This projected city is intended to accommodate three new public universities. According to participant:

> *There is the law of the establishment of* Al Madinah Al Jamee'iah, *an academic city that will house many universities in a single place, and which is now in development. This is in addition to the state development plan that is working on establishing three new public universities, such as Jaber University of Applied Sciences.* (H.J., 13 February 2013)

When participants are asked the reason that they were unable to finish these projects during their tenure in the Ministry, they often refer to the accumulation of unresolved tasks from previous governments. One study participant declared that:

> *When we are given high positions in the government we are unable to innovate or develop the sector that we are in charge of by producing constructive new policies. This is because we will often be bombarded with piles of paper work and [the burden of] fixing problems the ministry has had for years. As a result, there will be no time for us to concentrate, think, or innovate.* (S.S., 5 December 2012)

The recurrent suspensions of parliaments result in a situation where tasks accumulate in most of the country's institutions, where many problems, plans, and projects are shifted from one government to another without being resolved. This accumulation of the past problems results in the creation of conditions that would be unmanageable in the best of circumstances. However, they must be faced in a climate of severe time constraints due to often incomplete political cycles. It has been explained earlier by a former parliament member that:

> *The State suffers from ongoing crises and frequent political turns of fortune that result in the hindering of many development plans and vital projects. This is because of the disruption of political cycles and shifting them to a new parliament with a different balance of political powers and a different list of priorities. This political turbulence leaves the production of public policies at stake.* (H.J., 13 February 2013)

The inconsistency in policy production processes, I argue, is largely due to the fact that the Kuwaiti Constitution does not allow the formation of formal political parties. Permanent political parties could give a consistency to political agendas that would not be disrupted by the frequently terminated parliaments. Permanent political parties would also increase public accountability. However, the reality is that formal political parties are forbidden and, as a result, policy production processes are largely affected by the frequent suspensions of the parliament. The continued reliance on pre-existing informal political groupings, presented in Chapter Three, to steer policy processes in Kuwait is far from achieving any efficiency or stability in the processes of policy production. Accordingly, public policies are produced based on momentary, often individual, decisions that lack any research, evidence, or planning. Study participants frequently observe the results of this method of policy production – namely, '*short-sighted government policies that focus only on addressing the urgent immediate issues and often result in unintended consequences*' (S.G., 5 December 2012) and (A.F., 18 March 2013).

The higher education sector, accordingly, suffers from many deficiencies. However, the main policy debate was dominated by the urgent increased demand for higher education and the limited capacity of public institutions. In fact, policy debate has been dominated by the growing demand pressure for higher education places since the mid-1990s. A former parliament member emphasized that:

> *The main debate back then was about the increased number of students and the lack of higher education places offered by public institutions. More specifically, there were thousands of high school graduates without higher education spaces.* (H.J., 13 February 2013)

Others also pointed out the limited capacity of the existing higher education institutions relative to the increasing number of general education graduates. One study participant stated that:

The existence of Kuwait University as the only university in the state for such a long time, in addition to the increased number of high school graduates that exceeded the actual capacity of the existing public higher education institutions, led to the government searching urgently for possible solutions to accommodate the excess number of students. (F.A., 11 December 2012)

Most study participants stressed that the major challenge was to find an immediate solution to the problem of existing high school graduates who lacked any higher education opportunity. One participant stated that:

The main demand was to find the best and fastest solution to secure higher education places for all eligible seekers. (H.J., 13 February 2013)

Clearly, the government faced a critical situation and had to respond to an immediate social demand. Its situation was further complicated by the existence of long-standing problems that several governments had failed to resolve. These presented inefficient and unproductive public policies that have been faced with the widespread ideology (the myth) of market efficiency. Therefore, privatization has been viewed as the tool to escape the proven public inefficiency in addressing higher education problems for years:

It is important to allow the private sector to participate in the production of higher education services and stop it from being the exclusive preserve of the government… [noting that] most well-known and great universities in the world are private institutions, since the flexibility of the private sector in making decisions and its rapid actions contribute much to educational quality. Third, I believe that the government should not be the only [provider] sponsor of funding higher education; the society, as represented by the private sector, should participate as well. (M.H., 18 March 2013)

Privatization and Public Bureaucracies

By the year 2000, Kuwaiti higher education faced growing failure and needed urgent action. Given the disastrous state of Kuwaiti policy processes and the resulting inefficiency and inconsistency, the government was clearly unable to address long-standing higher education problems within a relatively short time. Yet, the urgency of the situation of the excess student demand required the government to act promptly. According to a former parliament member:

The main debate back then was about the increased number of students and the lack of higher education places offered by public institutions. More specifically, there were thousands of high school graduates lacking any local higher education opportunity. (H.J., 13 February 2013)

Thus, the production of the Kuwaiti privatization policy can be seen as a way to avoid the consequences of government failure in addressing higher education problems that had been unresolved for years. The following statement by a participant clearly indicates the lost faith in the government to improve higher education publicly. He said:

> *All circumstances were calling for a private university.* (S.S., 5 December 2012)

This argument is further supported by examining the structure and the method of establishment of the private sector in Kuwait. The private sector is placed under what amounts to an autonomous branch of government, and its management is kept as isolated from the ordinary public sector as possible. According to an official from the Council of Private Universities (PUC):

> *Decision-making in the PUC is independent from the government and the instability that the state is facing these days. The Minister of Higher Education does not have much influence at our board meetings, as our board meetings only occur every three months and we only require the attendance of the Minister of Higher Education in order to finalise our previously arranged decisions.* (F.A., 11 December 2012)

Both the structure and governance of the Private Universities Council (PUC) provide an illustration of how it has been organized in order to avoid the bureaucratic nature of the government and its unstable inconsistent policy processes (see Fig. 12). The PUC is a semi- nongovernmental organization that comprises nine specialists appointed by the Council of Ministers and is chaired by the Minister of Higher Education (Al-Atiqi & Alharbi, 2009). It constitutes four specialized committees. The PUC adopts a business model of a flat structure, which emphasizes the role of line managers and gives them greater responsibility within the organization (Al-Atiqi & Alharbi, 2009). They argue that this business model is a critical factor in the success of the PUC and the development of the private higher education sector in its initial stages, as the title and organizational structure of the PUC has been modified recently to be more bureaucratic with more specialized units similar to other public institutions as shown in Fig. 14.

Despite the autonomy that has been attached to the PUC, it continues to represent the government's authority over the private sector. Ironically, it exerts a more effective influence over the private sector than the ministry has over the more directly governed public higher education institutions. The reality is that the state has more authority in controlling the private sector, since its sustainability is highly connected with the recognition and licensing by the PUC, which also constitutes a major source of income to most private institutions. Such authority over the public sector does not exist. Public institutions, Kuwait University in particular, have more autonomy in their decisions, since their existence is not conditioned by following similar standards and regulations. It is worth restating here that public and private higher education sectors in Kuwait are not both governed by the same rules and regulations. Rather, the standards and rules set by the PUC as conditions of licensing do not affect the public sector. The private sector views these rules as unfair and sees them as eliminating fair competition between them as private institutions and the public sector. Demanding that the ministry should treat both sectors equally, a participant from the private sector complained:

> *The public sector suffers from many problems but the ministry has done nothing to control such poor provision. However when it comes to us [private institutions], we have to go through the licensing procedures and control every time we want to expand and open a new program, for example. At least, the council should differentiate between a newly established university and a well-established one like us.* (S.S., 5 December 2012)

Another example is the implementation of the gender segregation law, which was passed in 1996 (see Chapter Five). It was not implemented at Kuwait University until 2002, and even then not at all of the colleges due to resistance from the faculties and student unions. At private institutions, however, delay or resistance was impossible as their licence was at stake. Even some private providers opted to operate only for girls, such as Box Hill College Kuwait. Some found ways to implement the law without affecting their overall academic objectives and resources. In most others, the implementation of the gender segregation law was partial. In these, gender segregation was implemented in about 50 percent of the classes, but not in all of them. The decisions on how to allot classes between the genders were made either in accordance with student preferences or with student numbers, taking into

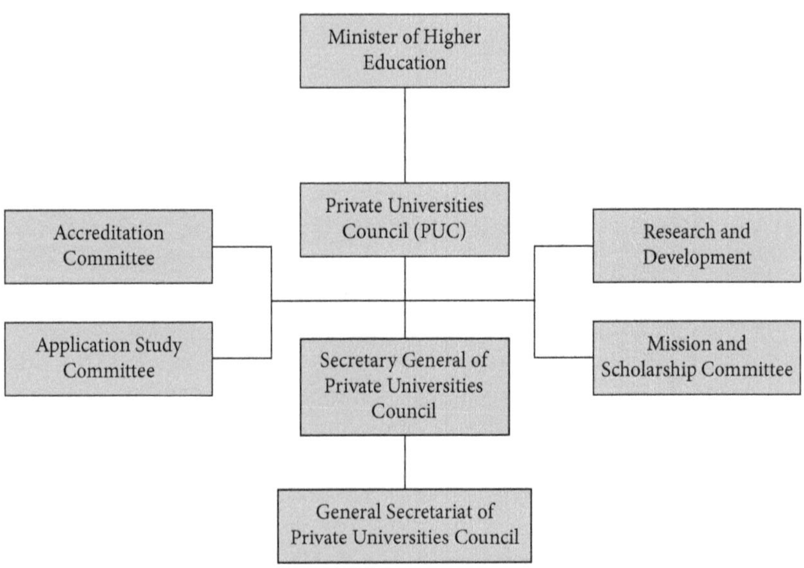

Fig. 13: Initial organizational structure of the Private Universities Council (PUC). (Source: Al-Muhareb et al., 2009)

account the ratio between the number of girls and boys enrolled in a given subject. Cost efficiency and the availability of adequate lecturers were also factors.

A closer look at both the organizational structure and the governance of the PUC illustrate the attempt to decentralize decisions regarding the operation of the private institutions. The PUC consists of eight members chaired by the Minister of Higher Education. A Secretary General is appointed by the council of ministers to manage the operations of the PUC. He is consequently given both administrative and financial authority according to the Cabinet Resolution no. 1179/2006, *Adding a New Article to the Executive Bylaws of the Law for the Establishment of Private Universities* (34/2000). An administrative member from the PUC stated that:

> *The General Secretariat was commissioned in order to implement PUC decrees, but had no formal executive power until Nov. 2006 when the Council of Ministers formally recognized it as the sole executive arm of the PUC and provided it with administrative and financial authority.* (F.A., 11 December 2012)

At present the council is an autonomous governmental body. Its eight board members, according to the law (34/2000), shall not be involved, directly or indirectly, in the business of running private education throughout the period of their membership:

> A Council shall be formed entitled 'Private Universities Council' under the chairmanship of the Minister of Higher Education with eight highly qualified higher education experts as members. Council members shall have no direct or indirect contribution to any private educational institution throughout the period of their membership. They shall be appointed by a Cabinet decision based upon a request by the Minister for a three-year renewable period. The Private Universities Council may form temporal / permanent sub-committees from amongst its members, and may add field experts to their membership and assign some of its functions to them. (PUL 34/2000: section 1, article 2)

There are four standing committees of PUC: Accreditation Committee, Application Study Committee, Research & Development Committee, and Mission & Scholarship Committee (illustrated in Fig. 10). According to PUL 34/2000, the PUC, through these committees, must fulfil the following missions:

- Examine applications for founding private educational institutions (see Fig. 12).
- Determine academic requirements for private educational institutions; approve their educational programs and review their performance to ensure commitment to the provisions of their founding decree.

- Approve standards and conditions that need to be complied with by academic programs at any private educational institution; and reconsider those standards and conditions whenever the need to do that should arise.
- Accredit certificates granted by private educational institutions and equate them based on the relevant rules and criteria.
- Consider whether to suspend or cancel the activities of private educational institutions or even merge them.
- Look into any other matter referred by the Minister. (PUL 34/2000)

The establishment of the Council was followed by sets of policies, procedures, and resolutions, issued between 2000 and 2007, which were designed to organize and supervise private universities and colleges in Kuwait. The main policies and regulations issued so far by the PUC are: the Executive Bylaws of Law no. 34/2000 for Establishment of Private Universities (2000); Board of Trustees Membership of private Universities and Colleges (2004); Regulations for Agreements with the Associate Universities (Quality control) (2005); Criteria for Adding New Academic Programs in Licensed Universities and Colleges (2005); Conditions for Accreditation of Study Certificates Issued by Private Institutions (2006); Cabinet Resolution Adding

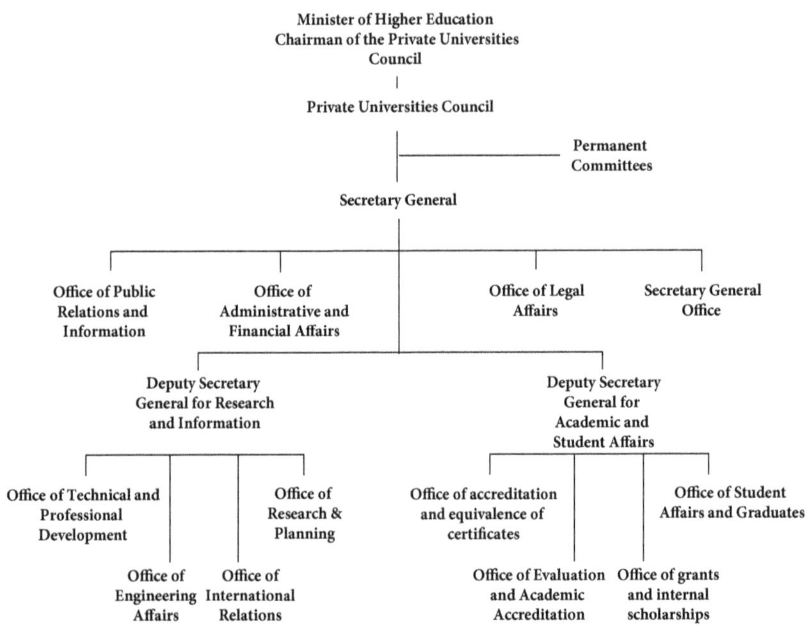

Fig. 14: Current organizational structure of the General Secretariat of Private Universities Council (PUC). (Source: http://www.puc.edu.kw, 2018)

a New Article to the Executive Bylaws of the Law for the Establishment of Private Universities (2006); Rules and Procedures for Private Educational Institutions License Applications (2007); and Rules of Association of Private Institutions Granting Academic Degrees with the International Academic Institutions (2007).

A chronological review of the above rules and laws shows that the purpose of the initial law in 2000 was, to a great extent, to allow the establishment of the private institutions in order to expand the local provision of higher education without increasing government expenses. Subsequently, several laws have been issued to control and manage privatization by shifting authority to the PUC and away from the unstable Kuwaiti policy processes. The result is that policy-making for the private sector is separated from policy-making for the public sector. Even the Ministry of Higher Education is kept at a distance. This system creates a division between the public and private higher education sectors in Kuwait by placing them under different governance, rules, and measures. Thus, the difference in governance structures causes differences in their performance and ultimately their outcomes.

A review of the history of the production of the PUL34/2000 law will illustrate the involvement of the private sector in the process from the beginning. Microplanners, working both inside and outside the existing system of higher education played an essential role, illustrating the role of international education on policy formation discussed in Chapter Six. Apparently, given the generous subsidies offered by the government (see appendix 3), there was considerable enthusiasm from the market for starting for-profit universities, as is evident from the number of requests provided to the PUC to open private higher education institutions directly after the production of the policy – 50 requests in the period from 2001 to 2003 (Al-Atiqi, Alharbi & Ali, n.d.). A participant who was involved in the preparation of the executive bylaws of the PUL34/2000 law said that:

> *While we were in the process of preparing the executive bylaws for the law, there was a fear of shortages in the number of applications to be received from the private sector. However, the number of Applications exceeded 37 and only 17 were agreed on and licensed.* (F.A., 11 December 2012)

The government, through the establishment of the Private Universities Council (PUC), attempted to organize the process of private provision in the higher education sector, trying to avoid most of the pitfalls associated with its implementation in other countries. Experts were allocated to identify useful standards and regulations, and to organize and control the implementation of the policy. An involved policy actor stated that:

> *The preparation began with the establishment of a Committee of academics to study the whole idea of privatization – based on their experience in the sector and*

from the experiences of privatization in other countries of the world – in order to ensure a secure implementation of the law without affecting the nature of higher education ... The committee worked, from the beginning, and great efforts were made while working on the regulations of the Law, in an attempt to avoid all of the drawbacks of privatization in higher education and to ensure that the process would not undergo market orientation as happened in other experiences around the world. (F.A., 11 December 2012)

A dean at KU who was involved in the early stages of establishing the private higher education sector stated:

We offered our experience to the private sector by providing them with the standards that would assure the quality of higher education services they provide, such as suitable educational facilities and the appropriate ratio between the numbers of faculty members and students, and the minimum qualifications required for their faculty members, to mention few. (H.A., 11 December 2012)

The government made a great effort to limit the negative aspects of market influence on higher education provision both before and after the production of the policy. For instance, the original proposal, according to a previous Minister of Education, is considerably different from what has been implemented:

In the original proposal, we attempted to insure both an abundance of financial resources and an adequate degree of governmental supervision, giving it [the government] the authority to interfere if necessary ... I advocated that the privatization of higher education be subsumed under a single big private firm. This firm would be responsible for the establishment of a private university or universities. Thus, I emphasized that all private universities should be run under one institution.
The government side, we suggested should be represented by Kuwait Investment Authority [an autonomous government body] as the funding provider, which would give the government the authority for supervising the entire processes. (A.G., 15 April 2013)

Despite variations in the implemented policy, the government still provides considerable financial support for private institutions. For example, the government offers the POT (Counter-Trade Offset Program), a system that provides them with the land. It also delivers a program of internal scholarships that provides private universities with guaranteed clients (government sponsored students). A participant from the private sector noted that:

Being granted a license by the Council yields couple of privileges: land on 20-year lease to build a campus and an annual quota of scholarship students. (J.A., 25 April 2013)

Private institutions generate their funds through five different sources, these are: paid-in capital, Loan facilities, Enrolment fees, the Offset program, interstate funding programs, and Government facilities. Each is described in appendix 2.

The council follows licencing processes that, to a great extent, guarantee the sustainability of any private institution prior to its establishment. Proposals for new private institutions are sent to the Licensing Committee, which then examines them. Based on a careful examination of the proposed institution, the committee recommends approval, dismissal, or sometimes resubmission. The licensing procedure consists of two reviews. Initially, a preliminary application is submitted for a preliminary review. If approved, then, it will then be supplemented with a detailed application. The diagram in Fig. 15 briefly explains the licensing processes the PUC is following for each application.

The considerable support provided by the public sector, and even academics, for the creation of private institutions suggests that the establishment of private institutions offers them a chance to realize their own visions of providing a better education – an education that will not be distorted by the dysfunctional policy processes that have hindered public higher education for decades. However, the question that must be asked is: Has the existing private sector fulfilled this ambition? Unfortunately, it seems that a lack of legislative experience resulted in the production of a poor policy text that is unable to control the intended implementation. A participant claimed that:

> *The policy text is too simple and does not take into account all of the measures needed to insure the quality of provision in private institutions, even with the existence of the PUC and its committees. This is because the rules and standards issued by these committees cannot be legally enforced on the institutions, as standards were not included in the original policy text. As a result, any action taken by the PUC against private institutions can be challenged in court by private institutions. Thus, the degree of authority given to the PUC over private universities is disputed.* (A.F., 18 March 2013)

The above claim should be given extra weight, since this study participant has a law background. In addition, the simplicity of the policy text of the law, which only consists of eight articles, also supports his claim. A financial analysis conducted by the PUC to monitor the financial performance of the private sector supports the above statement. It concludes that the governance actions by the Private Universities Council (PUC) are still evolving (Al-Atiqi & El-Azma, 2007), mainly because of the following outcomes:

- While the return on investment has improved with time, most institutions still show a shortage of liquidity.
- There is a considerable discrepancy between the ownership capital put into the institutions when compared to the income earned from students, a difference that reflects the lack of financial experience on the part of the regulatory agency that conducts the early licensing stage. (p. 22)

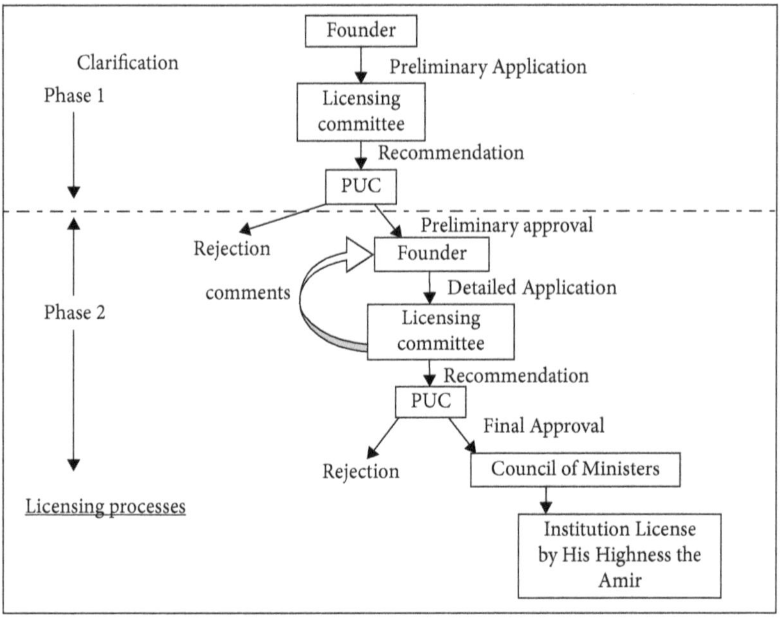

Fig. 15: Licensing processes for the private institutions. (Source: presentation by Al-Atiqi)

The study suggests that these outcomes are the result of deliberate financial decisions by the private companies. It is probably a deliberate strategy to not supply more funds than necessary in order to create revenue-generating campuses. This strategy makes perfect sense from an investor perspective, but is hardly desirable for providing quality education to students. These findings above support economic arguments against privatization raised by its opponents discussed early in Chapter Two, such as Tilak (1991), who argues that the market can be criticized in its inability to ensure an optimum social investment in higher education that is a quasi-public good.

Therefore, it can be argued that the PUC lacks the necessary financial competence to supervise the private sector. The PUC does not have its own accounting resources for examining financial issues. It tends to rely on external authorized accounting offices to audit the financial performance of the private institutions. According to a PUC official:

> *We require that annual financial reports, conducted by an authorized external accounting office, be provided by each private institution.* (F.A., 11 December 2012)

During the course of my fieldwork, I found a serious loophole in this process. Some private institutions own their own independent authorized accounting offices. These institutions can use their 'independent' authorized accounting offices to conduct the financial report required by the PUC. Needless to say, one can seriously question the reliability of the resulting reports. I discovered this fact when I arranged an interview with the president of a private university. Since he was not aware of the main focus of my research, because he did not spend time reading the plain language statement, the university president arranged for the meeting to be at his accounting office. After I explained the focus of my research to him, he openly wished that he had arranged to meet at the university instead, saying that:

> *If I had known, I would have met you at the university, not here. So I could show you the university.* (S.S., 5 December 2012)

Thus, more attention from the PUC needs to be placed on controlling the private sector's activities in running their higher education institutions.

Privatization from Below

Combined with globalization from above, Kuwait's problematic policy processes and their impact on the higher education sector constituted a major force driving higher education privatization in Kuwait, acting as a form of globalization from below. The local realities presented earlier in Chapter Five supported such an argument. These realities have raised both academics and policymakers' 'dissatisfaction with the status quo' (Eta, 2014, p. 4). This dissatisfaction, in turn, caused academics and policymakers to engage actively and voluntarily in the promotion of higher education privatization. This section will present data showing that the establishment of the private sector was largely a local decision, taken in response to local public needs. Despite the influence that globalization has from above, as has been represented by the GATS agreement and IMF recommendations and other external factors presented in Chapter Six (See Chapter Six), the production of privatization policy in Kuwait was also an outcome of 'globalization from below' (Falk, 1993, p. 40), a process depending on local actors who are influenced by the processes of globalization, illustrating the role of the state in the production of privatization.

The nature of policy processes discussed early in this chapter illustrates the role of individuals, microplanners, and small groups on policy decision-making in Kuwait. Policy discourse in Kuwait is, to a great extent, steered by microplanners, individuals in power. This characteristic of policy-making in Kuwait has been rooted in the early formation of the state as explained in Chapter Three. The significance of these individuals can be illustrated in the initial responses by participants when they were asked about the production of higher education privatization policy. One participant initially responded:

> *The only thing I remember is that the policy was issued when Prof. Yosif Al-Ebrahim was the Minster of Higher Education.* (H.A., 11 December 2012)

Another participant noted:

> *The idea was initiated under the ministerial cycle of Dr. Mussaad Al Haroon, then transferred to Dr. Yousif Al-Ebrahim when the Arab Open University was established. Then came Al-Tabtabaee, followed by Dr. Noreyah Al Sabeeh. So there were efforts from several Ministers.* (M.H., 18 March 2013)

And some others referred to their socio-political association, saying that:

> *This policy has been produced when Dr. Mussaad Al Haroon was the minister of education, who is known of his association with the merchants.* (A.F., 18 March 2013)

It is important to note that dissatisfaction with public policies regarding higher education generated public demand for higher education reform. According to a study participant:

> *The position was that the State needed to expand the provision of higher education in order to keep up with the youth educational boom because Kuwait University was no longer capable of accommodating all those [high school] graduates.* (S.G., 5 December 2012)

The role of microplanners has been maintained through the data that revealed an early attempt to establish a private university in 1993 by a group of academics, although it ultimately failed due to the absence of the required legislation. A participant recalled:

> *The first attempt to establish a private university dates back to 1993, when Abbas Maarafi led a group of 43 academics and submitted a proposal to the Kuwait Investment Authority requesting a license to open a private university. It took them almost two years. Ultimately, it was rejected, as there was no policy issued to allow the private higher education yet. In fact, there was none until 2000 when the Law of Private Universities has been issued.* (W.R., 17 March 2013)

Of course, during that period public higher education was still recovering from the impact of the Iraqi invasion, which had left the education sector, as well as the entire country, with massive physical and financial losses (Abd-El-Bary, 1993), not to mention the loss in the numbers of non-Kuwaiti staff and faculty members. Having said that, such a proposal could have expedited the reconstruction of the education sector; it could have been an investment opportunity for people wishing to rebuild their country.

Another participant also noted that:

> *Officials and academics at Kuwait University were disturbed by the escalating political pressure that, for years, forced the university to enroll increasing numbers of high school graduates, more than the university could accommodate.* (H.A., 11 December 2012)

This explains the active involvement of academics in the promotion of higher education privatization despite their theoretical rejection of the core concept of privatization, which treats education as a private good, concurrent with the theoretical arguments of Samuelson (1954), Friedman (1962), ... and Savas (2000) presented in Chapter Two. Their main goal was to reduce the pressure on public institutions. Accordingly, actors from Kuwait University played major role in promoting the production of privatization policy. A participant recalled:

> *On January 1997, an assembly of Kuwait University (KU) faculty members chaired by Prof. Shaib A. Shaib, former president of KU and current president of Gulf University for Science and Technology, was formed with the intention to discuss the feasibility of establishing a private university. The discussion produced a conceptual framework for a private university contributing to higher education in Kuwait in the face of rapidly growing social demand and the shrinking capacity of KU, the only institution of higher education at that time.* (J.A., 25 April 2013)

He added:

> *The proposal by KU faculty prompted the government to consider the private sector as a viable partner in contributing to the national goals in higher education.*
> *Accordingly, in 2000, the Private Universities Decree, No. 34 was issued establishing the Private Universities Council (PUC) chaired by the Minister of Higher Education and giving it the mandate to ensure conformity in licensing private higher education institutions. The establishment of the Council was followed by a set of policies, procedures and resolutions, issued between 2000 and 2007, designed to organize and supervise private universities and colleges in Kuwait.* (J.A., 25 April 2013)

There were also proposals from the Government, here represented by the Ministry of Higher Education. A former Minister claimed that the idea of establishing the private sector was a government's. However, it was proposing a different approach that had nothing similar to what was ultimately implemented in the PUL (34/2000). He stated:

> *In the original proposal, we attempted to insure both an abundance of financial resources and an adequate degree of governmental supervision, giving it [the government] the authority to interfere if necessary ... I advocated that the privatization of higher education be subsumed under a single big private firm. This firm would be responsible for the establishment of a private university or universities. Thus, I emphasized that all private universities should be run under one institution.*
> *The government side, we suggested should be represented by Kuwait Investment Authority [an autonomous government body] as the funding provider, which would give the government the authority for supervising the entire processes.* (A.G., 15 April 2013)

Therefore, there were joint efforts on micro levels that promoted the establishment of a private higher education sector. These joint efforts included representatives from academia, the government, and the private sector.

However, given that academics usually support the idea of the public good of higher education, it is surprising that Kuwaiti academics have played such a key role in the production of the privatization policy. A former parliament member argued that:

> *A crucial factor contributing to the production of the law at that time [1999] was the assemblage of academics in both the parliament and the government, simultaneously led by the minister of higher education, which placed the law on the priority list of that parliament. Having said that is not to deny that there are both commercial and political dimensions to the idea of privatization. Politically, there were alarms and warnings that KU, the only public university, was no longer able to absorb the increasing numbers of students. As a result, the debate was about the need for more higher education institutions. Commercially, on the other hand, the beginning of the third millennium saw a wave of private higher education spread throughout the Gulf region, a trend that created an important investment opportunity that attracted Kuwaiti merchants.* (H.J., 13 February 2013)

The participant's commercial argument represents the regional influence discussed in the previous chapter on local policy decision in Kuwait.

However, despite the local appeals for the establishment of private higher education that are noted by the data above, the role of globalization is not thereby eliminated. The role academics have had in promoting the production of privatization policy provides an illustration of the influence of the 'globalization from below' noted by Falk (1993). Kuwait's academics and policy actors have been trained abroad, mostly in first world universities and mostly during the past several decades. Thus, they have been exposed to policy spaces that are broader than the local policy space. According to the data presented in the previous chapter, they are also highly active in their connections with the global world through memberships with international and regional organizations, conferences, networks and partnerships with higher education institutions abroad. Rizvi and Lingard (2010) argue that, 'policies are not only located within discourses, but also in [social] imaginaries that shape thinking about how things might be 'otherwise' – 'different from the way they are now' (p. 8). Given the problems suffered by public higher education, Kuwaiti academics are influenced by the global imaginaries that promote neoliberal views of privatization; views that see privatization as promoting the greater efficiency associated with the marketplace.

Despite the neoliberal influence noted among policymakers in the previous chapter, the initial introduction of privatization to a great extent eliminated the role of the market. It deliberately avoided the kind of commercialization adopted by higher education reforms in other countries. A former Minister of Higher Education declared that:

> *The original idea of private universities, initiated during my ministerial years, is entirely different from what has been implemented recently. In our proposal,*

we stressed the 'not-for-profit' nature of private higher education. We suggested handing the responsibility to a single big private firm run by either one university or a network of private universities in order to ensure accountability. The government authority over the supervision would then be guaranteed by having the Kuwait Investment Authority provide the main source of funds. (A.G., 15 April 2013)

A former parliament member reaffirmed that:

Initially, the first idea suggested was to establish not-for-profit higher education institutions. (H.J., 13 February 2013)

In contrast, the established private sector consists entirely of for-profit institutions. A participant confirmed that:

All the existing private higher education institutions are nothing but for-profit institutions. Their financial resources are derived mainly from tuition fees and government subsidies--both direct and indirect. Even worse, most of those private higher education institutions are owned by branch companies that are in turn owned by mother corporations, in the big market, which already suffers financial problems. (A.F., 18 March 2013)

Thus, the final outcome of the privatization policy production process was not the outcome that was initially intended. Levy (2006) talks about the unanticipated outcomes of policy processes. These sorts of policy outcomes are associated with the type of process called 'microplanning [that] is consistent with pluralist rather than state-centered models' (Levy, 2006, p. 223). The term 'microplanning' refers to a process in which multiple policy actors, operating at different levels and acting mostly unintentionally, nonetheless work towards open-ended policy objectives (Levy, 2006). Education policy processes in Kuwait can be described as a sort of microplanning. This process is illustrated by the efforts at different micro levels of actors that all share similar objectives regarding the need to expand the provision of higher education in order to improve its efficiency and/or to generate profits. The end-product is a privatization policy that allows the participation of the private sector in higher education provision while the government continues to offer higher education for free (via an internal scholarships program which will be discussed further in this chapter). The coexistence of these radically different approaches to higher education shows how different micro level efforts came together in the final education policy.

There is still opposition to the for-profit approach allowed for private institutions in Kuwait, despite the general acceptance of their existence. This opposition is shown in a previously quoted statement by a participant who noted:

They [private institutions] greatly rely on government resources that provide them with the land and easy customers [students]. Some of these institutions, such as the International Law School, have enrolments are purely governmental. There is no competition whatsoever. I am not sure if they really care about their academic quality! (A.F., 18 March 2013)

Another study participant expressed similar doubts about the commercial activities followed by most private institutions in Kuwait. A former president of private institution stated:

Although I see private universities as a necessity, their quality needs more policy attention. There is a general commercial mentality that affects the performance of most private institutions in Kuwait, which places their academic quality at stake. The first announcement in the newspaper for one private institution called investors to great investment opportunity, while nothing was mentioned about providing better education! Education provided by the market needs more supervision. Institutions are too focused on profits. Even with the PUC supervision, they know how to get around those rules. I urgently call on private institutions to reinvest some of their profits into improving their institutions academically by hiring better staff members and providing better research resources for their students. (S.G., 5 December 2012)

He suggested:

Taking into account all the support (financial and otherwise) offered by the government, private universities' profits should be controlled by law. I suggest a separation between the board of owners and the administration, as this separation is very important for the academic improvement. Any interference by owners in the administrations is destructive, even if they are academics themselves, since they will naturally be driven by profit making. The law needs to be modified to make these institutions not-for-profit. (S.G., 5 December 2012)

He referred to the Turkish model of private higher education as an example, noting that:

The law states that they must be not-for-profit institutions owned by foundations, such as the case of COCH University. (S.G., 5 December 2012)

Thus, even though higher privatization policy is the outcome of an 'assemblage' of efforts, even though it is implemented at a micro level of planning, and even though it is the result of a 'globalization from below', nonetheless, it is the market that dictates the final outcome – a private higher education system that is driven by the need to generate profits. However, even this hunger for profits demonstrates the local nature of the driving force. Recall the Schedule of Specific Commitments that Kuwait attached to the GATS agreement, discussed in the previous chapter. This treaty addendum guarantees a majority share of the ownership of private institutions to Kuwaiti citizens (the merchants). This incentivizes local Kuwaiti merchants to become a driving force behind privatization. Thus, even where there is a clear international influence in the form of a treaty, it works to incentivize local actors to work from below in creating a privatized higher education sector. Although I noted connections in the previous chapter between the production of privatization policy and the consultant reports by the IMF and the GATS agreement, the study participants themselves paid no great attention to this sort of influence. This fact indicates that higher education privatization was more in response to local needs than it was to global forces. The desire of the private sector for profits, the desire of educators to avoid an overpopulated KU, and the desire of the government to avoid the discontent created by demographic changes – these are the primary concerns that appear in study participant comments. In the background though, there is always the desire for international acceptance and the fear of being left behind in a rapidly changing world. According to Dolowitz and Marsh (2000), transferring what is considered fashionable and modern may be done to gain international acceptance, and privatization is without any doubts a global trend. As Savas (2000) noted, 'the trend is unmistakably away from the government and toward … privatization' (p. 3).

Despite the above and illustrations of state power that are further to come concerning Kuwait's policy-making, there are still global factors limiting its power. At the higher education level, for instance, there is always the need for international recognition and acceptance, which has been represented by the data above. On an economic level, however, although the state is privileged with its natural rich resources, this wealth is highly controlled by the global market that controls its prices. The oil market has been through different phases that affected its prices through the years, as is illustrated in Fig. 8 in Chapter Six. Kuwait's economy is highly dependent on its oil wealth. Given the previously illustrated inefficiency in policy processes that claimed to be impulsive, spontaneous, and inefficient generally, one can expect that the state is likewise inefficient in utilizing its oil income. Jassim Al Saadoon (2015, January), in a presentation entitled 'Oil and public finance: past and future', in a symposium concerned with the current decline in oil prices and its reflection on the financial situation of the state, argued that the state has failed to deal with the four different phases of the oil market since the 1960s. After almost two decades of a flourishing market that supposedly left the state with sufficient financial surpluses to make it financially stable in the face of any sudden changes in the oil market, unfortunately, the current decline in oil prices has revealed weaknesses in the economy, resulting in sudden major changes in different public sectors in an attempt to limit public expenditure. In this sense, I could argue that state power is limited by the global economy and the rules and agreements that control its income from the oil revenues, represented by OPEC and the Organization of Arab Petroleum Exporting Countries (OAPEC), the main purpose of which is to ensure the stabilization of oil markets in order to secure an efficient, economic and regular supply of petroleum to consumers, a steady income to producers, and a fair return on capital for those investing in the petroleum industry.

Recontextualization of Privatization

Policy borrowing does not consist of slavishly copying a given policy. Instead, there are processes of local adaptation, modification, and resistance to global forces in education (Steiner-Khamsi, G., 2004). Phillips and Ochs (2003) also propose 'internalization/ Indigenization' as a significant final stage in processes of policy borrowing. In their theoretical typology, they consider 'internalization/Indigenization' as a series of four steps in the overall process of borrowing. These steps are: impact on the existing system/ modus operandi, the absorption of external features, synthesis, and evaluation (Phillips & Ochs 2003, pp. 456–457). Carnoy and Rhoten (2002) also discuss the process of 'recontextualization' in acknowledging that context affects the interpretation and implementation of such 'borrowed' policies (cited in Phillips & Ochs, 2003, p. 457), which provides an illustration of the state power in rearticulating its understanding of globalization. Accordingly, this section will examine how privatization has been recontextualized and mediated to respond to Kuwaiti public demands.

The particular form of higher education privatization implemented in Kuwait represents a mixture of several different forms of privatization that are blended together to produce a context-specific private sector, one that arguably responds to local needs. Alerted by others' experiences in the field of higher education privatization worldwide, the government made a great effort to control the negative impact that privatization could have on higher education. Because of Kuwait's wealth, the government was able to organize, control, and supervise the establishment, provision and growth of the private sector. This control can be illustrated by the authority that was given to the Private Universities Council over the private providers.

Thus, privatization was recontextualized to match national needs. In fact, higher education privatization in Kuwait is extremely distinctive, not only because of the authority given to the government, by means of the PUC, over the private provider. It is also different because of its other responses to local legislative requirements and both social and cultural needs.

Legislative Adjustments and the Introduction of an Internal Scholarship Program

Savas (2000) noted that legislative barriers are the greatest obstacles to privatization. Some countries, Savas explained, are 'saddled' with constitutional requirements that protect GOEs (government-owned enterprises) and seem to prevent their privatization unless the constitution is amended. According to the Constitution of the State of Kuwait, education has to be provided by the state to all citizens free of charge. Following up on the statement that 'Education is a fundamental requisite for the progress of society, as assured and promoted by the State' (Article 13), Article 40 states:

> Education is a right for Kuwaitis, guaranteed by the state in accordance with law and within the limits of public policy and morals. Education in its preliminary stages shall be compulsory and free in accordance with law. (The Constitution, 1961)

In the Constitution, the explanatory note (article 40) elaborates:

> ... [there is] nothing in this constitutional text that prevents the free provision to extend to all other levels of education, as is now the case in Kuwait and as it is hoped always to remain.

Despite the implementation of the privatization policy, higher education in Kuwait continues to be provided by the government as a public good. The use of 'hoped' in the above quoted passage from the Constitution is in consideration of the financial ability of the state to continue the provision of higher education as usual, a matter that has never been an issue for the country yet. Accordingly, the recently introduced privatization policy has not affected the public sector. It has been implemented independently of the public sector's operations. The only thing that both sectors share is that they are both under the governance of the Minister of Higher Education. Thus, the above-mentioned constitutional requirements explain an important aspect of the way in which privatization was implemented in Kuwait, specifically how the pre-existing legislative requirement of free education mediated the way that privatization was paid for. According to a participant:

> *There were many obstacles and problems that faced the initial phase of the policy production. The idea of private universities was relatively new to the region, and there was great resistance to private sector involvement in education [the idea of privatizing higher education], mainly concerning the issue of who would be paying the students' expenses.* (W.R., 17 March 2013)

Another participant from the public sector even refuses to use the term 'higher education' privatization, claiming that:

> *First of all, there is no privatization of the higher education sector happening in Kuwait. It is only the government allowing private universities to operate in the country.* (J.M., 28 November 2012)

The continuous government provision for higher education is clear with the increasing numbers of students' enrolments in the private higher education sector via the internal-scholarship program of the PUC, illustrated in Fig. 15.

Privatization in the public sector usually begins by the contracting out of public services. This private sector interference in the public sector, as recent privatization literature calls it (see Savas, 2000), does not seem to have occurred in the Kuwaiti context. Most privatization practices in the public sector, such as contracting out services, have mostly been restricted to non-educational activities, such as cleaning, printing, security services, etc. There has been no general transfer of public higher education services to private contractors. Higher education, then, continues to be freely and directly provided to Kuwaitis in accordance with the Constitution, despite the introduction of privatization policy PUL (34/2000). Higher education privatization has been implemented independently from the existing public sector.

Working out privatization within the legislative system in this way was recommended by the IMF consultants. The production of the PUL (34/2000) is apparently an implementation of their recommendations, which stated that:

> [Directors] encouraged the authorities to move forward with early divesture of public sector activities that do not require explicit legislative action for privatization. They considered that such a step would signal the authorities' commitment to private sector-led growth and further strengthen the environment for private investment. (IMF, 2004, p.3)

The divestiture of the higher education public sector is not allowed by the Constitution. As a result, this suggests that the privatization policy in Kuwait is designed so that it will not touch the public sector. This method of introducing higher education privatization is a clear response to IMF's recommendation represented in the above statement.

However, a major objective of the establishment of the private sector is to address the demand pressure on public institutions. It is there to serve the same constitutional goals that public sector higher education was created to achieve. Accordingly, privatization policy must be mediated so that it will respond to the demands of the constitution. In its second article, the PUL (34/2000) stipulates that:

> The aims of private universities are to contribute to the fulfilment of Higher Education and the applied education goals, in order to realize the coordination between these objectives and the evolving needs of society.

The law's explanatory note states that the law was passed in order to address the issue of the limited number of places at the University of Kuwait and the resulting inability to accommodate increasing numbers of high school graduates. Both articles 3 and 6 of the law's executive regulations (see appendix 4) concern the Private Universities Council's competence regarding the establishment of rules and procedures for student admission to private educational institutions, tuition fees, and the scholarships system. The law's provisions and executive regulations also needed to fill a legislative gap in the Ministry of Higher Education's decree that limited its authority to scholarships outside Kuwait only.

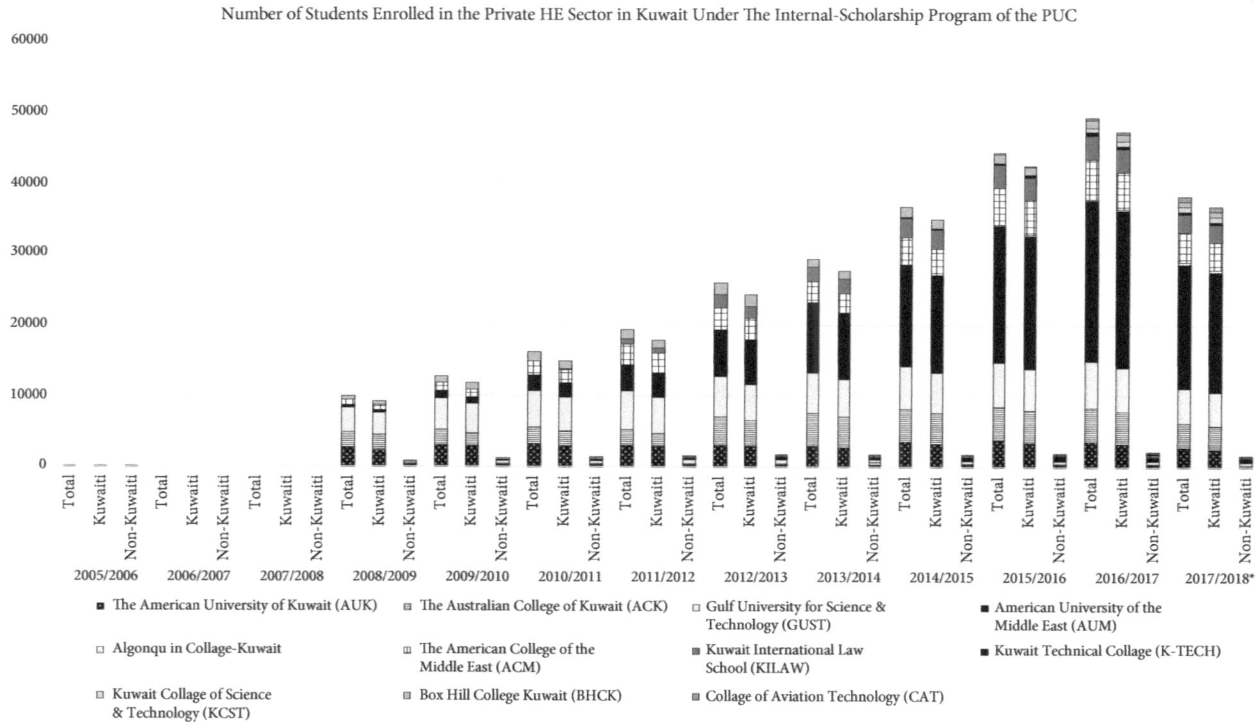

Fig. 16: Number of students enrolled in the private HE sector in Kuwait under the Internal-Scholarship Program of the PUC. (source: PUC 2018)

Accordingly, the Private Universities Council issued a policy decision on local scholarships in its March 2006 meeting in order to meet the goals of the law. The new policy required that private educational institutions were to pay 20 percent of the tuition fees, while the government would pay the rest (Al-Atiqi, Al-Rashed, & Al-Ali, 2010).

Eventually, the government found a way to continue providing higher education as a public service through the newly established private higher education sector by the introduction of the internal scholarships program. According to a PUC official:

> *[The government] covers the financial cost of more than 80 percent of the total enrolments in the private sector.* (F.A., 11 December 2012)

The implementation of the local scholarships program responds to the government's demand for an efficient way to address rising higher education expenditures (Al-Atiqi & Alharbi, 2009). A study by officials at the PUC stated that:

> Each year, the scholarships program allows the state to save 50% more than the alternative costs of funding additional governmental educational institutions or foreign scholarships. In light of the delay in the taking over the University of Kuwait's new headquarters in Al -Chadadiyah, planned for 2014, the scholarships program seems to be the only available cost-effective solution to absorb high school graduates. (Al-Atiqi, Al-Rashed, & Al-Ali, 2010, p. 119)

The same study noted:

> the state's budget has more than doubled during the last five years while, during the same period, the number of seats available for the students admitted yearly in the University of Kuwait and in the Public Authority for Applied Education and Training combined has increased by no more than 25%. (p. 119)

The above quote confirms that financial deficiency was never the issue in the policy debate in Kuwait. Better efficiency in using public resources, on the other hand, has always been a priority.

The introduction of the internal scholarships program was also intended to overcome the inequality that might arise as a result of the difference in students' financial ability to pay tuition fees. Equity in private higher education is closely linked to the ability to pay. The introduction of tuition fees plays a significant role in escalating social exclusion among citizens. Regarding the privatization of funding sources, Camilleri (2008) argues that it is almost impossible to create an equitable system with private funding. He found that tuition fees create an obstacle in this form of privatization, as the increase in tuition fees is generally disproportionate to the increase in family incomes. The Higher Education systems in many countries of the world have been criticized for their lack of equal opportunities in Higher Education provision, favouring affluent students at the expense of lower-income students.

For example, Ali Al-Hawat (2007) says that higher education institutions are facing a funding crisis manifested, inter alia, in the lower-income students' incapacity to participate in the available learning opportunities. Al-Hawat suggests ways to support education, such as the Public Private Partnership, in financing students' tuitions fees, which can be seen in the introduction of the internal scholarships program mostly funded by the government (as cited in Al-Atiqi, Al-Rashed, & Al-Ali, 2010, p. 120).

Private universities and colleges have been accepted by Kuwaiti society as a result of the introduction of such scholarships. This acceptance is reflected in a growing demand for private universities that, over the first three years, has exceeded the designed plan by a rate of not less than 15 percent. In fact, on average, 20 percent of the students who applied to private universities were not admitted (Al-Atiqi, Al-Rashed, & Al-Ali, 2010, p. 123). This program has given unique educational opportunities to students who do not wish to study abroad, but still want an educational environment and educational programs similar to high quality universities and colleges in developed countries. Why many students would prefer to get their education locally is a matter that will be discussed in the following section. Thus, equity as a claimed disadvantage of privatizing higher education, discussed in Chapter Two, has been addressed in the Kuwait's implementation of privatization through the internal scholarship program.

Responding to Social and Cultural Needs

The implementation of the privatization policy in Kuwait can also be justified as a response to both social and cultural needs. Drawing on Silova's (2004) example of the Latvian case, where national governments have become innovative in using global rhetoric for national purposes, Donn and Al Manthri (2010, p. 24) argue that 'the Gulf [higher education] transformation is not an evitable result of Globalization'. They emphasize the role of the nation-state in processing the inputs of globalization into local policy decisions. With respect to the local cultural and religious factors discussed above, the power of the state is clearly shown in the privatization law (article 6: law 34/2000), which states:

> Private universities/colleges and branches of foreign universities shall abide by the following:
> 1. Operate its buildings to <u>ensure gender segregation</u> in all departments, disciplines and student activities.
> 2. Observe <u>Islamic values</u> and <u>time-honoured traditions</u> in relation to student dress and activities.

Among the factors promoting the establishment of private international institutions were cultural and religious concerns about education abroad, particularly for women as was discussed in Chapter Five. According to a study participant:

> *one of the advantages brought by the establishment of the private higher education sector in Kuwait is its way of solving some cultural and religious issues concerning traveling abroad to study, more for girls than boys.* (S.G., 5 December 2012)

Article 6 from the law (34/2000) also embodies a considerable local challenge for the privatization policy to overcome – namely gender segregation. This legislative obstacle was initially created by the gender segregation law (24/1996), which applies to all higher education institutions in Kuwait. A former parliament member stated:

> *A major problem that faced the production of the private universities law was the recent production, at that time, of the 'gender segregation law' on higher education institutions, which was passed by vote of the national assembly.* (H.J., 13 February 2013)

The segregation law applies to both public and private institutions. The difficulties for the private sector in following it emerge from two sources. The first concerns the financial resources required from private institutions in order to separate the different genders physically. Gender segregation requires a substantial increase in faculties and other facilities. This is the issue that led to the recent creation of private colleges for girls only, such as Box Hill College Kuwait. The second difficulty emerges from the incompatibility between the objectives of the law and the objectives of most imported international higher education systems. Despite these issues, the law has been implemented, although the opposition is expressed. While visiting most of the private institutions in Kuwait during the fieldwork, it became clear that the segregation law has been implemented in one way or another. In most private institutions, the implementation of the law required that 50 percent of the classes be gender-segregated, leaving the other classes to be populated based on the availability and student preferences. A previous president of a private university declared that:

> *The private universities law has been hampered by the issue of segregation and mixing sexes … Prof. Imad Alatiqi when he was the General Secretary of the PUC helped me during my working years as president of the AUK [American University of Kuwait] in how to deal flexibly with the segregation law; While I initially rejected the implementation of the segregation law, later I decided to apply it partially, as in 50 percent of the classes.* (S.G., 5 December 2012)

Most private institutions also made modifications to their imported curricula in order to match national interests. This recontextualization is illustrated in the alterations made for imported curricula due to national, cultural and societal considerations. A current president of a private university noted:

> *The curriculum implemented from the foreign institutions has been altered to match both cultural and societal needs.* (A.S., 27 March 2013)

For example:

> *We substituted the subject of American history with the history of Kuwait, and the American economic studies with Kuwaiti economics and so on …* (A.S., 27 March 2013)

Such decisions, along with many others, made some participants criticize the nature of private institutions' international partnerships with their mother institutions abroad. They claim that these partnerships are 'shallow' and 'superficial'. According to a participant:

> *Most private universities' partnerships are superficial and inactive, as there is no active academic connection between the local providers and their mother institutions abroad.* (A.F., 18 March 2013)

The ineffectiveness of the partnerships discussed above is possibly the result of the government strategy that requires that the majority of a private institutions' ownership be reserved for Kuwaiti investors. Here we see the consequences of the limits on foreign investment in the local private higher education sector that was included in the 'Schedule of Specific Commitments' attached to the GATS agreement (see Chapter Six). This is in addition to the impact of labour market reforms and the policy of Kuwaitization represented as local pressure in Chapter Five, which is also applicable to staff employment in private higher education institutions. These strategies provide other illustrations of the state power in mediating global influences to match national interests, as it gives a predominance of decision-making power in the private sector to local actors.

Although the establishment of the private higher education in Kuwait contradict Levy's (2006) argument of the unanticipated explosion of the private higher education globally, as it was an outcome of anticipated policy, the policy has, at the same time, resulted in unanticipated outcomes. Unintendedly, the production of the PUL 34/2000 has also responded to a politically neglected social need that concerns non-Kuwaitis' higher education. This is simply because they have not been mentioned in any of the higher education privatization policies produced, nor have they been the focus of policy debate through the production processes of the policy, which is to be expected as they have no political representation in the parliament. However, they have been referred to by the study participants only as an unplanned added pressure on the established private institutions that have been allowed to expand in response to growing demand by Kuwaitis' (see Chapter Five), which further resulted in shifting the demand pressure to the private sector. The establishment of the private sector offered non- Kuwaities

Tab. 6 Students enrolled at Kuwait University.

Academic year	Kuwaiti students	percent of Kuwaiti students	Non-Kuwaiti students	percent of Non- Kuwaitis	Total
2001/2002	15809	90.7%	1626	9.3%	17435
2012/2013	30925	88.5%	4014	11.5%	34939

(Source: Kuwait University Statistics)

Tab. 7 Kuwaiti and non-Kuwaiti students enrolled in the private higher education sector (Fall semester 2005/2006).

Private Institutions	Kuwaiti students	percent of Kuwaiti students	Non-Kuwaiti students	percent of Non-Kuwaitis	Total
Arab Open University-Kuwait	2721	43%	3573	57%	6294
Gulf University for Science and Technology (GUST)	1119	84%	218	16%	1337
Kuwait Maastricht Business School (KMBS)	254	75%	83	25%	337
American University of Kuwait (AUK)	530	69%	237	31%	767
Australian Collage of Kuwait (ACK)	370	73%	139	27%	509
Total	4994	54%	4250	46%	9244

(Source: www.puc.edu.kw)

opportunities that have rarely existed before in the public sector, as represented in their enrolment rates in the private institutions as revealed by the PUC first published statistics of the academic year 2005/2006 (see Tab. 7), in contrast to their enrolments rates in Kuwait University as illustrated in Tab. 6. Since public education in Kuwait is free through all its levels up to postgraduate studies, it has mostly been exclusively for Kuwaitis, except for a few cases of non-Kuwaitis – mostly students whose mothers are Kuwaitis, citizens of the other GCC countries, the children of diplomats, children of non-Kuwaitis faculty working in public higher education, or top non-Kuwaiti high achievers from high school.

The demographics of the State of Kuwait, discussed earlier in Chapter Three and as it can be illustrated in Figure (16 & 17), show how Kuwaitis constitute only one-third of the total population. On the other hand, there is a significant majority of non-Kuwaitis in the country whose educational needs need to be addressed by the policy. The percentage of non-Kuwaitis

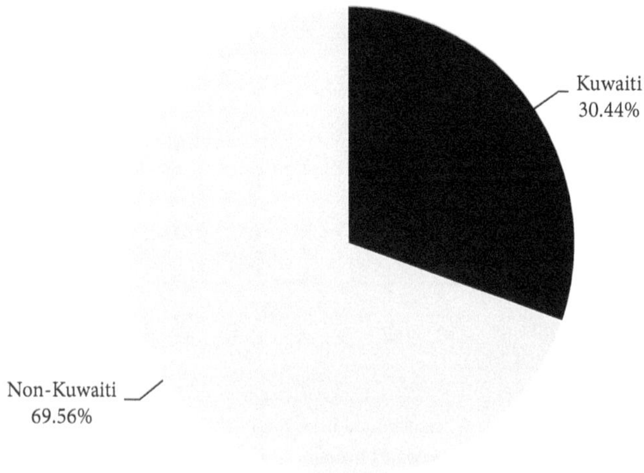

Fig. 17: Total population of Kuwait June 2018. (Source: www.paci.gov.kw)

has been following similar rates since the early formation of the modern state of Kuwait, as revealed by the following censuses across the decades: 1965, (63.9 percent); 1975, (69.1 percent); 1985 (72.3 percent); 1995, (58.5 percent) (CSB, 2015). Their high percentages resulted mainly from the state's efforts to fill the shortages in the nationals' work force, as in other GCC countries.

Interestingly, however, their distribution across the different age groups in comparison with Kuwaitis reinforces the fact that their presence in the country is highly related to employment and the workforce (see Figures 18 & 19). While only 15 percent of the Kuwaiti population is in the workforce, above 84 percent of the non-Kuwaiti population is in the workforce (PACI, 2018). These percentages have been reflected in the school age population of the two categories of the population.

Non-Kuwaitis' demands for higher education have been represented in their enrolments in the first years following the establishment of the private sector, when their enrolments were almost equal to Kuwaitis in the academic years 2005/2006 and 2006/2007, as shown in Tab. 9. However, after the establishment of the internal scholarships program in 2006, which publicly funded Kuwaiti students to continue their higher education in the private sector, the gap has widened between the two social groups in the private sector. For example, while non- Kuwaiti students constituted 46 percent in the academic year 2005/2006, they only constituted 29.5 percent in the academic year 2011/2012 (see Tab. 8). Another significant illustration is the percentages of students from each social group across different private institutions, which has been almost stable across the years (see Tab.

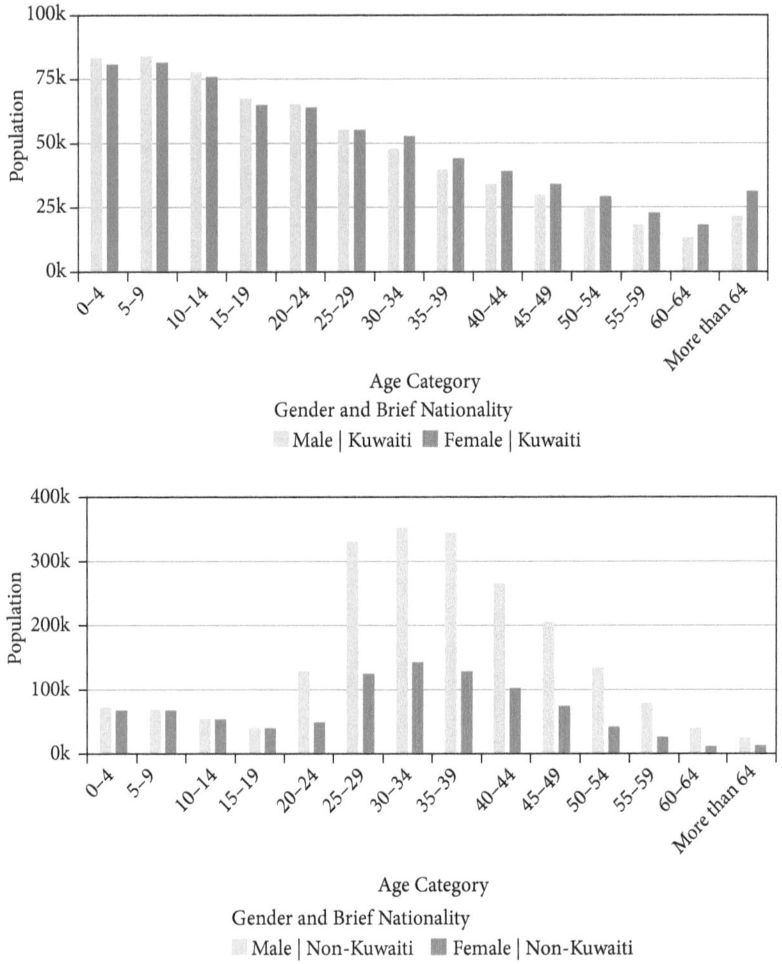

Fig. 18: Population by gender and brief nationality June 2018. (Source: www.Paci.gove.kw)

8 & 9), showing that non-Kuwaiti students have been concentrated in the Arab Open University. This concentration can be attributed to two major factors: first is the relatively low tuition fees of the AOU in comparison to the fees charged by the other institutions, and the second could be the language of instruction, which is mostly Arabic in this university in particular. Therefore, despite the fact that the introduction of the privatization policy (PUL34/2000) has been designed to respond to the needs of Kuwaitis, it has been at the same time unintentionally responding to non-Kuwaitis who wished to continue their higher education in the country.

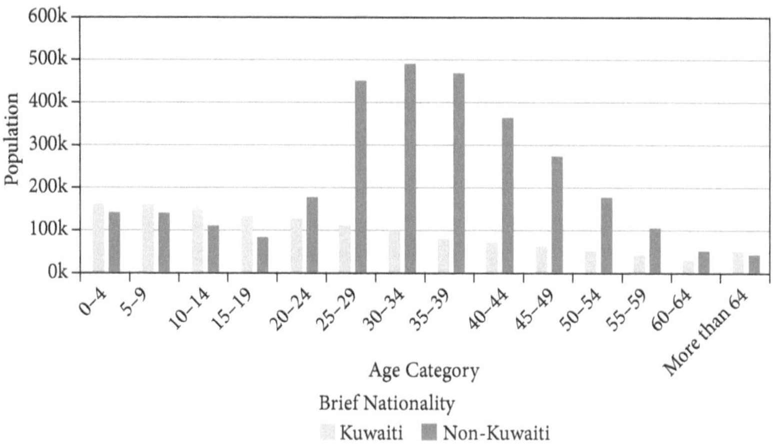

Fig. 19: Population based on nationality and age groups 2018. (Source: www.PACI.gov.kw)

Tab. 9 Kuwaiti and non-Kuwaiti students enrolled in the private higher education sector (Fall semester 2011/2012).

Private Institutions	Kuwaiti students	percent of Kuwaiti students	Non-Kuwaiti students	percent of Non-Kuwaitis	Total
Arab Open University-Kuwait	1850	38%	3023	62%	4873
Gulf University for Science and Technology (GUST)	3009	85%	516	15%	3525
Kuwait Maastricht Business School (KMBS)	191	53%	169	47%	360
American University of Kuwait (AUK)	1692	74%	596	26%	2288
Australian Collage of Kuwait (ACK)	1769	78%	508	22%	2277
Box Hill Collage Kuwait (BHCK)	639	89%	76	11%	715
American University of the Middle East (AUM)	1388	92%	117	8%	1505
American Collage of the Middle East (ACM)	982	90%	106	10%	1088
Kuwait International Law School (KILAW)	719	98%	14	2%	733
Total	12239	70.5%	5125	29.5%	17364

(Source: www.puc.edu.kw)

Tab. 8 Numbers of Kuwaiti and non-Kuwaiti students in the private higher education sector in Kuwait.

Academic year	Kuwaiti students	percent of Kuwaiti students	Non-Kuwaiti students	percent of Non- Kuwaitis	Total
2005/2006	4994	54%	4250	46%	9244
2006/2007	6160	58%	4374	42%	10534
2007/2008	7429	61%	4733	39%	12162
2008/2009	8319	65%	4441	35%	12762
2009/2010	9402	65%	4940	34%	14342
2011/2012	12239	71%	5125	29%	17364
2012/2013	24188*	94%	1650*	6%	25838*
2013/2014	27547*	94%	1725*	6%	29272*
2014/2015	34844*	95%	1780*	5%	36624*
2015/2016	42478*	96%	1818*	4%	44296*
2016/2017	47279*	96%	1976*	4%	49255*
2017/2018*	36633**	96%	1510**	4%	38143**

(Source: http://www.puc.edu.kw/)
*Internal-scholarship students only.
**Summer course numbers not included.

Conclusion

Although privatization is promoted by the processes of globalization, the nation-state is still active in mediating those influences and shaping them to match local interests. In Kuwait privatization was introduced to serve the interests of the state. Privatization solved local political problems concerning the development of Kuwaiti higher education, especially when capacity of the public sector was overwhelmed. Thus, privatization in the Kuwaiti context is more of an outcome of globalization from below than it is an outcome of external pressures forcing the government to privatize. There were no coercive practices on the government to adopt privatization policies. Rather, insofar as there was direct global influence at all, it entered by way of the consultancy services of international organizations such as the IMF.

With the above discussion in mind, we can now construct a broad overview of the interplay between the local and global factors that promoted the introduction of the privatization policy. It can now be argued that the higher education privatization policy pursued by the Kuwaiti government in 2000 reflects a neoliberal agenda promoted endogenously by local academics (globalization from below) that came to dominate positions in both the parliament and the government in the 1990s. This globalization from below was reinforced exogenously (globalization from above) by the policy recommendations of the IMF, the UN, and the World Bank. Perhaps not coincidentally, the government initiated the establishment of the private sector directly after the signing of the GATS agreement. Thus, the changes that took place in the Kuwaiti higher education system resulted from a confluence of ideas and actions of both 'endogenous' (or local) factors and 'exogenous' (or global) factors.

The Kuwaiti higher education privatization policies are products of a convergence of both the dynamics of globalization and local contextual imperatives. By the late 1990s the Kuwaiti state seemed incapable of addressing the crises of higher education. It had shown itself to be incapable of accommodating the growing demand within a short period of time due its inconsistent policy processes and its long-standing inability to complete public sector projects. This governmental incapacity seemed to argue against relying on a public-sector solution to its higher education crisis. However, given Kuwait's tremendous financial capability, perhaps its political difficulties might not have completely precluded a public-sector solution. An additional influence was required in order to push Kuwait toward higher education privatization. That additional influence was the neoliberal ideology that promised a superior efficiency for privatization and market-based solutions. Thus, the confluence of local issues and international globalization ideology, working together, created the privatization policy in Kuwait.

Chapter Eight: The Conclusion

In this study I have noted that the growing student demand for higher education and the resulting financial challenges have encouraged most governments around the world to adopt privatization policies. However, because of its rich oil wealth, Kuwait does not have the financial pressures that drive other governments to adopt privatization policies. Despite its wealth and financial capability, Kuwait has nevertheless followed the global norm in pursuing the privatization of its system of higher education. Since the financial arguments for the adoption of privatization policies are not applicable to the State of Kuwait, one naturally wonders what forces and influences have compelled Kuwait to embrace privatization.

Accordingly, the main purpose of this study has been to explain the reasons for Kuwait's adoption of higher education privatization policies. In addition, it has provided a contextual illustration of the intersection between global pressures and local realties in influencing the processes of national policy decision-making. It should be noted that this book does not claim to provide an account of how privatization policies have been implemented in Kuwait, nor does it assess the merits or outcomes of these policies. Rather, it is concerned with the processes associated with the production of privatization policies in Kuwaiti higher education.

There has been a remarkable concurrence in privatization policies witnessed in all of the GCC countries over the last two decades, including Kuwait. These privatization policies, which resulted in the authorization and expansion of private higher education institutions, have garnered strong public support and been praised by their governments (Coffman, 2005). Despite these generally known phenomena, there is little in the policy literature that would explain or reveal the factors that led such rich governments to adopt privatization policies for their higher education systems. For this reason, this study has also aimed to investigate the pressures that triggered the privatization policy in Kuwait. These pressures, once discerned, could potentially apply to other countries in the region, given their political, economic, and historical similarities. However, despite the overall similarities of the GCC countries, Kuwait has its own unique characteristics in its political system and policy processes. These unique characteristics were presented throughout this book, but especially in Chapter Three. In our discussion, we found that Kuwait's semi-democratic system and the influence of its people in making policy made the findings of this study applicable only to the Kuwaiti context.

To address these objectives, the study was mainly guided by the question of how might we explain Kuwait's adoption of a privatization policy in its higher education in year 2000? To answer this key question the following sets of sub-questions were raised. Firstly, 'Why was this policy developed in Kuwait; who were the main policy players; and what interests does the policy serve?' Secondly, 'What were some of the local and global pressures that led to the production of a privatization of higher education policy in Kuwait?' And finally, 'How does this case study of Kuwait illustrate the ways in which global processes influence the production of national policies in higher education?' In order to answer these questions, the study followed a continuum qualitative methodological approach, collecting data mainly from interviews and policy documents. This data was supported by insights from a guided student survey.

In Chapter Two I provided a conceptual framework for understanding privatization, its introduction to higher education, and the ensuing expansion of private higher education worldwide. Chapter Two also tracked the intellectual foundations of the concept of privatization and attempted to provide an overarching conceptualization of privatization as an existing phenomenon, discussing its theories, forms, and global practices. This chapter also outlined the global debate surrounding the introduction of privatization into higher education systems and evaluated its advantages and disadvantages. In the course of that discussion it became clear that most arguments explaining the introduction of privatization policies into higher education systems ultimately appeal to financial pressures. It was this realization that revealed the difficulty of explaining privatization's introduction to the Kuwaiti higher education system.

In order to generate a broader understanding of the Kuwaiti context of the study and the nature of Kuwait's policy processes, Chapter Three provided a historical, socio-economic, and political understanding of Kuwait. This local context provided a foundation for the policy analysis in the chapters that followed. It illustrated how the problematic nature of Kuwait's policy processes initiated most of the country's higher education dilemmas. It also showed how these policy processes had a similarly destructive impact on the other sectors of the country (Kinninmont, 2012). The purpose of Chapter Three was not to devalue the unique Kuwaiti democratic experience, but only to point out that there is a need to improve the functioning of both the government and the Parliament alike.

While in both Chapters Two and Three I laid the foundations for my research, in Chapters Five through Seven, I presented the findings that investigate the key questions I set out to address in this study. In order to answer the question raised above and to realize the aims and objectives of the study, I mainly used a qualitative approach that relied heavily on data collected from interviews and policy documents. To broaden the scope of the data, I followed a 'continuum qualitative approach', or mixed methods approach, proposed by Laura L. Ellingson (2011), which encourages the utilization of multiple tools and methods to add depth, richness, and complexity in understanding the phenomenon under investigation.

Accordingly, I added a student survey that mainly provided me with insights that reflect generally on the students' impressions of privatization policy implications. My findings are derived from the data collected mainly from interviewing policy actors and academics from both public and private sectors, in addition to policy documents and reports from regional and international organizations. Using a thematic analysis of data from the various sources, as explained in Chapter Four, I examined the following factors: local pressures; global influences; and the intersection between these different dimensions, globalization, the state, and privatization policies.

Key Findings

Chapter Five argued that there are major local pressures that promoted the introduction of higher education privatization policies. The decisive local pressure consisted of the rapidly growing demand pressure, a pressure that challenged the limited capacity of the public education sector. This demand pressure is shown to be the result of the demographic growth in the youth population in the country. This demographic growth has been so rapid that the school age population now constitutes a majority of all Kuwaitis. This overwhelming demographic confronts an extremely limited supply of available pubic higher education. The data suggested that this limitation in the capacity of public education has not been a result of financial shortages. Rather, it has been the consequence of inefficient policy processes that produce inconsistent public policies. These erratic and, indeed, random policy processes have hindered the performance of existing public higher education institutions and crippled the development of new ones. This lack of coherent policy formation also applies to the broader state sectors, as has been reported by Kinninmont (2012) in a briefing report on Kuwait's semi-democratic experience. As a result of the increasing demand pressure, the quality of public higher education was negatively affected. Like other state sectors, higher education was vulnerable to electoral cycles that were disrupted by the frequent dissolutions of parliaments. These disruptions, in turn, rendered parliament unable to plan long-term policies. This is not to underestimate the role of private sector in promoting the policy of privatization, noting in particular to the often overlapping roles that complicate the differentiations between each academics, policy actors and businessmen. The negative effect of the increasing demographic pressure on public higher education, along with the lack of constructive political response, made policy actors in general, and academics in particular, into avid promoters of privatization for Kuwaiti higher education.

Local pressures can also take the form of social and cultural needs. In particular, cultural restrictions on having women educated abroad increased the need to provide international higher education locally. Another significant social need was the provision of higher education to non-Kuwaiti residents. Despite the fact that non-Kuwaiti residents were a majority of the population, their opportunities for completing their higher education locally were extremely limited. In fact, they were almost non-existent before the year 2000. The establishment of private institutions has provided them with new opportunities, although this was not a primary intention of the privatization policy. Additional pressure to expand higher education in Kuwait emerged from labour market reforms. The policy of Kuwaitization imposes on private companies the obligation to employ specific quotas of Kuwaiti nationals. This requirement to hire Kuwaiti nationals has caused the private sector call for better-qualified Kuwaiti graduates to match their needs. Given the above key findings, Chapter Five concluded that there were crucial local realities that, even in the absence of global trends, would have promoted privatization as a policy choice for Kuwait.

Chapter Six focused on the global dimensions of policy influence. It argued that, alongside the local realities presented in Chapter Five, there were also global influences. These global influences entered into Kuwait in many ways. Some appeared to be a sort of 'globalization from below'. That is to say, academics and policy actors were influenced by their international education and the high rates of global flow of people and ideologies. There was also the role of international and regional organizations. These organizations have hidden commitments to neoliberal policies, as argued by Rizvi (2006) (see Chapter Two). These international and regional organizations acted as an external global influence on national policy decision-making in Kuwait. However, their role in the Kuwaiti context was rather different from the sometimes coercive role they have played in many countries. In Kuwait and the other GCC countries international and regional organizations have mostly exerted influence by acting as consultancy agents, introducing neoliberal ideology by the non- coercive tools of soft governance. These tools consist of persuasive means such as networking, conferences, seminars, consultations, advisory groups, publications, etc. (Lawn, 2006). External global influence was also seen in the GATS agreement that Kuwait signed in 1995. This treaty clearly expedited the production of higher education privatization policies in Kuwait. Note the close proximity between Kuwait's signing of the GATS treaty and the production of the PUL (34/2000). In addition, the resemblance of Kuwait's ultimate policy text was too close to the Schedule of Specific Commitments attached to Kuwait's GATS agreement to be a mere coincidence. Thus, while it was true that Kuwait was financially independent, it nonetheless lacked the technology, skills, and expertise required to unilaterally achieve the economic development to which it aspired. This deficiency, among others, created limits on state power and opened the door for external global pressures to influence local policy decisions.

Given Kuwait's close proximity to Arab Gulf States that share similar economies, culture, traditions, religion, and history, in addition to their formal collaboration under the GCC regional organization, it was not surprising that there was a regional policy space that allowed for the natural flow of ideas and practices among the policy decision-makers in the region.

Given that the region, over the last two decades, has witnessed an unprecedented emergence of private higher education, Kuwait's embrace of such trends was a natural response to the challenges it faced. Despite references to global influence on Kuwait's decision to privatize higher education presented in Chapter Six, it should be emphasized that there were no coercive actions practised by external agencies on Kuwaiti policy decisions. Rather, global pressures have taken the shape of soft governance, using such tools as the pursuit of international recognition and the national habit of policy borrowing. These factors, along with the international education of Kuwait's policymakers, constituted a global influence that was both external and voluntary. Therefore, Chapter Six provided an explanation for the introduction of privatization policies in Kuwait that showed that privatization was adopted mostly for ideological reasons, rather than because there was concrete evidence of its appropriateness in addressing Kuwait's higher education problems.

Chapter Seven examined the intersections and the interplay between local pressures and global influences. It argued that, despite the indisputable role of globalization in influencing the production of higher education privatization policies in Kuwait, the role of the state was not thereby nullified. The nation-state continued to play an important role in mediating global processes at the national level. Privatization in Kuwait was simultaneously promoted endogenously by local actors, illustrating the globalization from below, and reinforced exogenously by the international and regional organizations (such as the WTO, the IMF, and the UNESCO). As a result, privatization policies were promoted in Kuwait on the ideological assumption that they would provide a more efficient and better quality higher education in Kuwait without any concrete evidence of their appropriateness for addressing Kuwaiti higher education problems.

The role of the state in mediating privatization policies in Kuwait is illustrative largely through exploring the type of privatization it has implemented. The significant role played by the Kuwaiti state made Kuwait's engagement with global processes a complex one. The State of Kuwait had to respond to local needs in a way that rearticulated the way it understood privatization. This complexity is shown in the form of privatization implemented in Kuwait. Privatization had to be mediated and recontextualized in response to local requirements. This mediation was most clearly seen in three major areas. First, privatization had to address the legislative requirement of free education for all eligible Kuwaitis as mandated by the Kuwaiti Constitution. After all, ordinarily private education is available only to those who can pay.

How could the Kuwaiti state compel or induce private institutions to accept financially disadvantaged students? This matter was resolved by the formation of the Internal Scholarship Program that changed the previous policy that only allowed the government to offer scholarships for studying abroad. Second, Kuwaiti privatization had to address local demands for better education. Privatization policies, therefore, moved away from local measures of quality towards global measures through the implementation (borrowing) of internationally recognized educational practices. Kuwaiti policy stipulated that a private institution in Kuwait must implement programs and be affiliated with universities from among the best 200 universities listed in the latest appendix of the *Times Higher Education* magazine. Finally, an examination of the governance structure established for regulating the private sector revealed that, by placing the private sector under a semi-independent governmental organization such as the PUC, the regulatory structure was intentionally organized so as to prevent the previously established public bureaucracy from affecting the development of the private higher education. The private sector was placed under different governance, rules, and regulations than the public sector. As a result, private institutions are more independent from the direct impact of general policy processes than public institutions. On the other hand, private institutions also have policy obligations, imposed by the PUC, that potentially threaten their very existence. Technically if private institutions do not follow PUC rules, their licence might be at stake. Private institutions are intentionally placed under a close governmental supervision by the PUC that, to some extent, negates their autonomy in order to control quality, a factor that might otherwise be neglected in favour of generating profits.

In practice, privatization is complicated, a fact which makes answering the question of 'what interests does the policy serve?' a complex one. An official public policy can control the establishment of private higher education providers, and maybe their operation, but there are definite limits to this control. The culture and mentality of the people involved cannot be eliminated from the equation. These factors will influence the private higher education sector, despite the fact that it has been placed under different governance from the public sector. I argue that the privatization policy has established a new dimension of policy tension. Earlier, in Chapter Five, we saw that the government bureaucracy and the problematic political environment continue to affect and hinder the processes of private institutions. Not only must private institutions deal with ministries of the government other than the PUC, but they must also maintain personal connections within the PUC itself. Several interview participants noted the assistance they had received because of their personal connections with PUC officials. The most striking illustration of this phenomenon is the fact that one person, who played an active role in the formation of the privatization policy and subsequently chaired the PUC, is now running one of the well-established private institutions.

It is widely believed in Kuwaiti political circles that the establishment of private higher education created a win-win situation, where both the government and the market benefit at the same time. As mentioned earlier, Savas (2000) argued that rich countries might be able to afford inefficient and ineffective government services. But they too are wasting resources that could be put to better use by society (p. 289). Accordingly, even taking into consideration all of the public operational costs that have accompanied the establishment of the private higher education – the PUC with its various committees and employees, the physical and financial subsidies offered by the government to help the establishment of the private institutions – private providers are nonetheless offering the government an opportunity for a more efficient use of public expenditure on higher education. Specifically, private higher education institutions provide local alternatives that are cheaper than external scholarships would be.

Formerly the government had to fund expensive external scholarships due to the lack of available local public education capacity. The availability of local private higher education institutions saves the government from sending thousands of students abroad to complete their higher education studies every year.

On the other hand, private institutions are quite privileged. They are guaranteed clients in the form of the publicly funded students that are injected by the government into those institutions. As a result, they have almost guaranteed profits. Therefore, both the government and the private higher education providers benefit financially from the policy of privatization. Ostensibly, the law places strict restrictions on the members of the council (the PUC) – specifically, that they shall have no direct or indirect connection to any private institution throughout the period of their membership. In practice, however, it is more complicated.

Although private sector decisions have been shielded from the stagnating effect of Kuwait's usual public policy processes, it is very difficult to completely isolate the PUC and private institutions from the government and its ministries. Given the overwhelming dependence of private institutions on government subsidies in the form of student grants and scholarships, it can be said that 'most private institutions are not totally private, at least from a financial standpoint' (Tilak, 1991). For this reason, there has been and always will be a tension of interests that will be difficult to control by policy.

The Kuwaiti experience presents a unique case with regard to the potential financial challenges of higher education privatization policies. Unlike most countries, as noted earlier by Levy (2011), the private higher education sector in Kuwait simply did not exist prior to its privatization reform. It was this new public policy (PUL 34/2000) that allowed the private sectors' establishment, albeit with high government involvement. Despite the heavily subsidized nature of Kuwaiti privatization, private higher education continues to be viewed by policymakers as an unambiguous public good. This is largely because financial capacity has not thus far been an issue. However, given the state's total dependence on oil revenue, will its troubled and inefficient policy processes be capable of ensuring its continued financial sufficiency in an unstable oil market? The lack of coherent and long-term policy vision could place Kuwait in a critical position that would ultimately have grave implications for the public resources available for its higher education sector. Privatization and market mechanisms cannot therefore be counted on to supply a magic 'invisible hand' that will permanently fix all of the problems of higher education sector.

The global focus on higher education for competitiveness in the knowledge-based economy has led to the danger that local policymakers will uncritically accept whatever reforms are fashionable throughout the global community. In particular, there are concerns that an external program of reform may be unsuited to local needs. Given the contextual blindness of international agencies (Verger, Edwards Jr, & Altinyelken, 2014), it should be local policy actors who make the final decisions regarding the type of international education imported. It is imperative that these decisions be made based on whether the proposed reforms actually fulfil the local needs, rather than simply because of their global success. After all, what will work in some contexts might not work in others. Samuelson (1954) argues that 'the solution "exists"; the problem is how to " 'find' it"' (p. 389). While the solution is always there, the most critical task is how to implement it within the existing contextual realities.

Emerging Issues

Almost after two decades from the establishment of Kuwait's first private higher education institutions, access demand continues to be a major pressure in Kuwait on both the public and private higher education sectors. The future of private higher education in Kuwait is difficult to predict. Its ultimate sustainability is not the issue here. However, it should be pointed out that, if the planned expansion of the currently underdeveloped public institutions is ever completed, private institutions might face serious challenges in attracting students, especially among the publicly funded cohort that constitutes the majority of their current enrolment.

The current debate on the value of private higher education institutions is dominated by two major considerations: academic performance and financial performance. Assessing the academic standards of private institutions is a daunting issue. Participants from the private sector like to stress their association with international academic and professional accreditation agencies. These accreditations are in addition to the standards required by the mandatory national institutional accreditation. The issue of academic quality, however, must be addressed and enforced by national policies in order to avoid biased assessment practices that could occur both inside and outside the PUC domain. Also affecting quality is the fact that private institutions typically end up with lower academic achievers, at least as determined by the local exam system. This problem has forced most private institutions to modify their academic standards in order to accept lower academic achievers. The resulting presence of lower achievers in turn forces private institutions to modify their learning processes to accommodate them. In order to address this problem, both public and private higher education institutions should be placed under the same big umbrella of rules and regulation not only by recognizing their given qualifications.

Nearly a decade after the implementation of the privatization law, the PUC has finally begun imposing a requirement that private higher education institutions engage in research and development, a major feature of universities in benefitting society. However, private institutions regard R&D, like all of their programs, as investment opportunities that should bring about good financial returns. Accordingly, they have asked that the PUC offer them financial resources similar to what the government provides to public institutions. Private institutions have further insisted that they cannot adopt research programs and activities in areas of limited student interest, since they must always focus on areas that bring in a good return on investment for both students and institutes. They have further demanded the development of national policies to financially support research and development in their private institutions on equal bases with those of the public one.

Private institutions' financial performance is another issue in the current debate over privatization. For example, some participants note a need to establish not-for-profit universities, or at least require private institutions to reinvest part of their profits into their institutions. The study participants feel that, in view of the large financial subsidies private institutions receive from the government, they have an obligation to reinvest some of their profits into improving academic quality. Some participants even suggested there was a need to evaluate and rewrite the initial policy of privatization in order to achieve this goal.

It has been fifteen years since the passage of the privatization law (PUL 34/2000) and nearly ten years since its implementation. We have arrived at a point where its fruits have become clearer. Now is the time for evaluating this law, to ask the questions: Do private universities play the role that privatization proponents claimed for them? Did they solve the dilemma facing Kuwaiti higher education? Did they reach the desired quality of provision? Did they manage the cost of higher education in a way that matched government expectations? These are all questions that are open for further study. Indeed, they are questions that must be investigated in order to fill a serious gap in the literature with regard to evaluating higher education privatization, both in Kuwait and in the larger Gulf region.

Appendix 1: The Shift from the Traditional Rule and the Merchant Resistance

The issue of sharing power was essential to the stability of the kingdom. The system of governance discussed above characterized the early years of Al Sabah and lasted until Mubarak Al Sabah succeeded to the rulership in 1896 by force. This sheik assassinated his two brothers with the support of several Bedouin tribes, which then provided the new sheik with personal protection in that critical time (Al hajeri, 2004). This shocking incident of shedding family blood by a member of the royal family has never been repeated in Kuwaiti history. The interesting thing is that the Kuwaiti prominent merchant families ultimately accepted Mubarak's rulership, in return for his promise that he would uphold justice and never take a decision without consulting them (Al-Rashid, 1995, p. 149). On the one hand, that indicates how essential the issues of power sharing and the stability of the rulership were. On the other, it illustrates the type of relationship that existed between the rulers and the Bedouin tribes who provided protection for Mubarak. The Bedouin have always been known for their loyalty to the rulers. Their extreme loyalty has been criticized by the other social groups as distorting the process of policy-making and preventing it from representing the real public interests of the modern State of Kuwait (Ghabra, 2011).

Under Mubarak's strong rule, Kuwait flourished. The population of the City doubled and the wealth of its merchants increased substantially. However, Mubarak proved to be autocratic in his ways of governance. He departed from the Al Sabah traditions of consulting with the merchant families and keeping taxes low. He raised taxes substantially by raising customs duties on all imports and exports, as well as imposing a new tax on property (Shuhaiber, 1981, p. 25). Mubarak's autocratic rule and oppressive taxes made the merchants aware of their lack of political power. So, in 1921 and 1938 they demanded a formal way of political participation in decision-making. These attempts at establishing the consultative councils of 1921 and 1938 were mainly dominated by the merchants and illustrated their early political consciousness as a group. Even then, they were attempting to curtail the power of the Al Sabah by establishing a formal political process where power would be shared between them. Not surprisingly, these attempts faced stiff resistance from Al Sabah (Crystal, 1990).

The attempt by the merchant community to form a Consultative Council in 1921 was embodied five suggestions to the Emir. As one historian relates,

> The sudden death in 1921, of Sheikh Salam, the successor of Mubarak, caused a succession problem. A group of prominent merchants seized the opportunity and

submitted a handwritten petition to the ruling family that addressed the succession issue and pressed for political reforms. The petition included five main suggestions which were:

1. The reform of the house of al Sabah so that no differences may occur in appointing the Ruler.
2. The naming of three nominees for the office of Ruler: Sheikh Ahmad al Sabah, Sheikh Hamad al Mubarak and Sheikh ʻAbdullah al Salim.
3. Once the ruling family agrees on one of these three nominees, the decision then should be presented to the government (the British) for its endorsement.
4. The appointed Ruler becomes the president of a Consultative Council, majlis shura.
5. Members of the Council shall be elected from among al Sabah family and the people to administer the affairs of the country, with justice and fairness. (Shuhaiber, 1981, p. 52)

Not surprisingly, these suggestions were rejected by Al Sabah, as they were fully aware of their implications, especially the last two. The merchants were clearly aiming at creating a formalized formula of sharing power. Although Al Sabah officially rejected the suggestions, nonetheless a council was formed that consisted of twelve members. However, it was headed by the leading merchant instead of the ruler. In this way, the traditional approach of allowing the merchants to advise the ruler was to continue, but only as an indirect involvement by way of non-binding advice from the council. The following ruler promised the people that he would not decide on any important issue without the council's approval. However, AI-Qana ʻi (1987) described these consultations as being 'fruitless'. This was because every member was convinced he was right, and no majority rule was enforced. As a consequence, the Council rarely met and the Ruler reverted to the traditional practice of informal consultation.

Despite the failure of the 1921 council, Kuwaiti political activists continued to exert pressure on the ruler. Over the years the merchants became more and more dissatisfied with the informal consultations with the Amir, as these consultations occurred only has his discretion and were in any case non-binding. The merchants once again directed their criticism against his autocratic rule and demanded some type of formal participation (Baz, 1981, p. 116). Anti-government agitation was fuelled by the prevalence of corruption and poverty. It was further inflamed by the monopoly of Al Sabah family on capital accumulation in a declining economy. These discontents resulted in growing demands for social reforms (Ismael, 1982, p. 73). Many of these problems – the poverty and declining economy – were caused in part by the imposition of a blockade by the Saudis in 1922 and the failure to reach an agreement with them on transit and import duties. These factors were exacerbated by the decline of the pearl industry due to the competition from Japanese cultured pearls (Shuhaiber, 1981).

Consequently, the 1930s witnessed more political activities and challenges to the regime than before, as can be illustrated by the incidents associated with the formation of the consultative council of 1938.

This 1938 council was preceded by the formation of a secret organization known as the 'National Bloc' or *Al Qutlah al Wataniyah*. This organization was formed by leading Kuwaiti merchants and other influential figures who had been influenced by regional reforms in Iraq, Dubai, and Bahrain and who wanted similar reforms in Kuwait (Shuhaiber, 1981). The Bloc's programme of reform was eventually printed in the Iraqi newspaper *al Zaman*. It demanded a general improvement in the provision of social services, the halt of non-Arab immigration, the encouragement of Arab immigration, and a greater cooperation with Iraq (Shuhaiber, 1981). As a result of this publication, the National Bloc was approached by the British, who were concerned about this possible threat to Al Sabah rule, since they had a common interest with Al Sabah being in power. The Bloc assured the British that their intention was not to challenge the rule of the Al Sabah, but that they were seeking a representative government.

Accordingly, the National Bloc decided to act publicly and approached the ruler, requesting the formation of a legislative council (Shuhaiber, 1981). The British played a role in convincing the Sheikh to be flexible and accept the formation of the council, since they were in favour of political reforms and the creation of a representative government, as long it did not undermine their own power (Abu-Hakima, 1983). One of the primary pressures that played a role in convincing the ruling family to allow political participation was the Iraqi claim on Kuwait. This threat was a major factor in forcing Al Sabah to grant partial democracy, since greater political participation would help ensure the continued existence of Kuwait under their rule. Among other things, this incident illustrates the British interference with the state's public affairs in order to secure their own interests. This type of external pressure on the Kuwaiti policy decisions is discussed more extensively in Chapter Seven.

The Consultative Council of 1938 that resulted from these machinations was tasked with drafting a constitution. It based the new constitution closely on the 1923 Egyptian Constitution. Like its model, the proposed Kuwaiti constitution included five articles that gave the Council considerable rights in the administration of both domestic and foreign policies. A controversy arose, mostly concerning the public interference with international affairs. These articles state that:

Article One: the people are the source of power represented by the Council of their elected representatives.

Article Two: This enumerates the areas that the Council has to establish their laws: Law of the Budget, Law of Justice, Law of Public Security, Law of Education,

> Law of Public health, Law Improvements which basically deals with the infrastructure of the country, Law of Emergency which ensures public security in the event of an emergency.
> **Article Three:** The Council is the place of reference for all treaties, concessions, monopolies, and agreements, both internal and foreign. If any of these (I.e. existing ones) have to be renewed, it shall not be considered to have become legal unless seen and approved by the Council.
> **Article Four:** As the state has no court of appeal, the powers of such a court will rest temporarily with the Council until such time as a special court is established for that purpose.
> **Article Five:** The president of the Council represents the executive authority in the State. (Shuhaiber, 1981, p. 60)

It was clear that this draft undermined the power of Al Sabah by shifting the source of political power to the people through their elected council. For this reason, the reigning Amir initially refused to sign it. He only did so under the pressure from the British and from Sheikh Abdullah Al Salim, a member of the Sabah family who supported the idea of the council from the beginning out of his ambition to become the next Amir. After a few months, the British also showed dissatisfaction with Council involvement in foreign affairs, as this was an area that had been a primarily British concern. The British now realized that the extension of the council's authority jeopardized their own interests in Kuwait. Specifically, they were annoyed by the council's interference in the Kuwait Oil Company (Al-Rumaihi, 1987; as cited in Al Hajri, 2004). The British realized that they preferred the previous exclusivity of dealing directly and only with the ruler, with the council acting only in an advisory role (Baz, 1981). As a result, only after five months, the council was dissolved by the Sheikh.

In an attempt to mend the relations between the Ruler and the people, a new election was held and new council was formed, with twelve re-elected members from the old council. Sheikh Ahmad al Jaber, then reigning Amir, submitted a new Constitution to the council, which gave the ruler the power to veto the council's decisions. This action transformed the council into an advisory body, giving the ultimate power to the ruler. The council rejected the drafted constitution and the Amir once again dissolved the council. The Council in turn refused accept the order of dissolution. There was a call for public resistance to the ruling family by a Kuwaiti merchant Muhammad Al Munayas, who was immediately executed (Crystal, 1990, p. 50). This incident explains the reluctance, in later years, of opposition groups to come into open conflict with Al Sabah. Only recently, with the coming of Arab spring, has it become evident that even Kuwait is not immune to political instability (Kuwait Security Overview, 2012).

After the execution of Muhammad Al Munayas, political activities and reform movements took a different form. They were pursued through voluntary organizations and associations that were broadly based and included more of the public sector than just the merchant families (Smith, 1999). Most important of these associations was the institution of *Diwaniyya* or reception hall. Most associations were not independent from the government control.

However, the *Diwaniyya* was an autonomous social space, where the government traditionally had no right to interfere. As Norton (1993) argued, it was (and is) the essential element of the Kuwait civil society:

> Arguably, the essential element in Kuwaiti civil society is the diwaniyya, the 'meeting places which have historically been behind many political events. The *diwaniya* is traditionally a male gathering, but [in recent years some women have started their own *diwaniyat*]. It is well understood that no candidate could win election if he did not visit most, if not all, of the *diwaniyat* of his district. When the law of gatherings prevented the holding of any meeting without prior permission from the authorities, the *diwaniya* was excluded.' As Ghanim al-Naijar notes, Kuwait's pro-democracy movement started in a *diwaniyya*. (p. 210)

These organizations and social spaces have, over the years, called for Arab Unity, national independence, and a constitutional government (Al Mughni, 1993, p. 34). In early 1950s Kuwaiti nationalists asked the people of Kuwait to demand the following:

> ... Ask for the formation of a Constituent Assembly which will prepare a Constitution and which will guarantee your natural freedom, put an end to despotic rule and bring forth a national independent government which will be formed by the people themselves. (Al Mughni, 1993, p. 34)

The most serious challenge to Al Sabah came in 1959 when a rally was held at the Shuwaikh Secondary School to commemorate the first anniversary of the creation of the United Arab Republic (Al Mughni, 1993, pp. 35–36). Reformists expressed their views on Arab Unity and attacked the autocratic rule of Al Sabah with forceful demands for immediate reforms, especially on the issue of popular participation in the government. Jasim Al Qatami, a leading Kuwaiti Arab nationalist, announced that:

> The Al Sabah became the Rulers of Kuwait 300 years ago. They ruled autocratically and arbitrarily then. They cannot expect to do the same in the latter part of the twentieth century. Either they grant the people the necessary reforms at once, or the people will take power for themselves. (Smith, 1999, p. 98)

Realizing the significance of this event, Al Sabah imposed strict and repressive controls on all political activities and voluntary organizations, not to be lifted until 1961 (Al Mughni, 1993, p. 70). Only the *Diwaniyya* was excluded. However, Al Sabah knew that they needed to deflect public criticism. To do so, they formed the Supreme Council, consisting of ten Al Sabah members who enacted some internal reforms against incompetence, extravagance, and corruption, especially in departments controlled by members of the family (Smith, 1999, p. 98).

The conflict between the influential social groups did not terminate, at least formally, until the production of the Constitution of 1961 that determined the rights and the duties of each group towards others. Under this constitution, supreme authority was reserved to the ruler, the *Amir* who had to be from Al Sabah family. However, the new constitution permitted relatively more open space for public participation in policy decisions through the elected parliament.

Appendix 2: Sources of Funds to Private Institutions

Source of fund	Description
1. *Paid-in capital*	Most educational providers in Kuwait are owned by registered corporations. The law PUL 34/2000 stipulates that founder's equity for private institutions must have a local (citizens) majority. This equity is determined at the time of license application within the feasibility and financial study. The ample availability of funds within the local private sector enables most institutions to be founded without the need for foreign capital. *Table 1* lists the founder's equity for the operating institutions.
2. *Loan facilities*	Kuwait has an advanced banking system that can be tapped to supplement owner's capital. Current licensing procedures allow for loan facilities to a limited extent, typically not exceeding owner's equity. Inspection of common-size financial statements for operating institutions reveal that total liabilities amount to 42 percent of total assets, of which 30 percent are current liabilities.
3. *Enrolment fees*	Most institutions charge students on a credit-hour basis. This would range between KWD 130 and 170 per credit, and students register in a semester-based system with 12 to 18 credits per semester. The tuition fees are a major source of revenue for institutions that allow tuition fees to cover operating expenses as well as future expansion. Tuition fees are agreed upon during license application. The Private Universities Council (PUC) allows for a reasonable fee structure that is compatible with the standard of living. The enrolment data proves that society accepts the current fee levels, alongside enrolments that match up with, to a reasonable degree, feasibility study expectations. Further elaboration will be made later on in the paper. The fee structure is not allowed to increase before five years have elapsed.

Source of fund	Description
4. *The Offset Programme*	This programme was established in 1992 by the Kuwaiti Government. It is defined as the derivation of particular financial commitments from foreign companies and agencies that provide imported goods and services to the Government of Kuwait. Under the Offset Programme, foreign companies that wish to sign supply contracts of a value equal to or greater than KWD 1 million with the Government of Kuwait are required to invest, inside or outside of the state, in projects adding value to the national economy. Under this programme, the offset obligation is equal to 30 percent of the contract value to be executed within eight years of the contract award. As an incentive to invest in counter-trade offset obligations, the Government sets a multiplier for certain developmental projects in order to lower the offset burden. A three multiplier means that a contractor can invest KWD 1 million and obtain credit for KWD 3 million; the multiplier for educational projects being typically 3.5. Certain academic institutions have benefited greatly from the Offset Programme. One institution has obtained major engineering, aviation and marine science equipment from offset obligations, valued at more than KWD 12 million. The audited results of this provider show that the offset grant constituted 24 percent of its total assets in 2006. With this programme, they were able to develop a major expansion from a diploma programme to a Bachelor of Technology Programme. The Offset Programme is also a major provider of student scholarships for students to pursue their tertiary education. This activity is the result of an agreement with the Ministry of Higher Education (MOHE).
5. *Interstate funding programmes*:	There are numerous funding programmes of this type, whether related to trust foundations or to UN organizations. The programme that made the largest impact in Kuwait and many Arab States is the Gulf Programme for Support of United Nations Developmental Agencies (AGFUND). Chaired by Prince Talal bin Abdul Aziz Al- Suood. This programme established the Arab Open University (AOU) in 2001. The AOU was housed in Kuwait by an agreement with the Government and now has branches in more than seven Arab countries. This agreement was ratified as Law 31/2002 in the State of Kuwait. In Kuwait itself, more than 6,000 students are currently enrolled in the AOU Kuwait branch with a tuition fee that is roughly 500 KWD per year. UNESCO signed an agreement with the AOU Chairperson in October 2001 to provide information and communication technologies (ICTs) equipment and personnel training to the University. This will include video conferencing equipment and satellite linkages for distant education and electronic library. The project value was USD$1.55 million.

Source of fund	Description
6. *Government facilities*	Several Government programmes are in place for the direct and indirect support of private universities. A crucial one is the land grant facility. An agreement was reached with the Ministry of Finance (MOF) and the municipality to allow private institutions to sign long-term leases on state lands for their campuses. In a compact country like Kuwait, this facility proved very beneficial. Other programmes of interest are the scholarships granted by several Government agencies for their employees to study in private institutions. These programmes provided institutions with additional sources of revenue to supplement revenue from the self- paying students. The biggest programme of this kind is the scholarships for new high school graduates, which started this year. The PUC secretariat negotiated with the Ministry of Finance a budget of USD$11.5 million for support of 1,068 students in 2006/2007, which constituted 80 percent of the tuition cost. The purpose of this programme is to provide fair access to the otherwise limited tertiary education seats within the country. Not directed to institutional funding, this programme is partially supported by the institutions themselves by means of subsidized tuition. It is to be noted in this context that all institutions had achieved profitable status before this programme commenced.

Appendix 3: Establishment of Private Universities Law (PUL 34/2000)

In accordance with the constitution; and in consideration of law no. 29 for 1966 regulating higher education and its amendments and law no. 63 at 1982 establishing the Public Authority for Applied Education and Training, we have ratified and promulgated this law passed by the National Assembly; the articles whereof are hereinafter detailed.

(Article 1)

It is permissible by a decree issued in response to a request by the Minister of Higher Education to license the foundation of private universities/colleges or higher institutes/branches of foreign universities where the majority of shared capital funds is wholly owned by Kuwaitis.

(Article 2)

A private university aims at contributing to the promotion of the goals of higher education and applied education; in a manner optimally meeting all envisaged society's developing needs and performing research services.

(Article 3)

The decree founding a private university shall prescribe its legal status, regulating provisions and constituent colleges and higher institutes. It defines the mode for forming their boards of trustees, related functions and financial resources. It also defines academic degrees offered and stipulated prerequisites.

(Article 4)

A private university shall have an independent honorary character as of the date of promulgating its founding decree in the Official Gazette; and shall be represented by the university president before other parties and in courts of law. The university shall have the right to the ownership of its movable and immovable assets and to the signing of contracts; including contracts of sale, mortgage, loaning, accepting donations, grants and wills, and initiate legal actions that are not in conflict with its set goals.

(Article 5)

The university shall operate under the supervision of the Ministry of Higher Education in all that is relevant to the provisions of this law and related executive bylaws, the provisions of the founding decree and related executive bylaws, which guarantee that the university will adhere to the provisions. Whenever the need arises, a temporal managing board for the university may be appointed by a cabinet decision to last for maximum two years.

(Article 6)

Private universities/colleges and branches of foreign universities shall abide by the following:

1. Operate its buildings to ensure gender segregation in all departments, disciplines and students activities.
2. Observe Islamic values and time-honoured traditions in relation to students' costumes and activities.

(Article 7)

The rules and provisions prescribed under this law shall apply to all colleges, higher institutes and branches of foreign universities founded under licence of Article I.

(Article 8)

Based on a request by the Minister of Higher Education, the Cabinet shall issue the executive bylaws for this law within six months from the date it goes into effect.

(Article 9)

All ministers shall execute this law, each in his field of competence.

The Emir of the State of Kuwait Jaber Al-Ahmed Al-Sabah

Issued at Bayan Palace on 11th July 2000.

Appendix 4: PUL 34/2000's Explanatory Note

Kuwait University was established in 1966 and it is being regulated from that time and until now under the law No.29/1966 about the higher education, while the Kuwaiti society, from this date, has leaped and changed to a large extent and the higher secondary schools' graduates' number has increased and the University is squeezed in term of its material and human potentials to absorb all of them.

As to confront these situations it has been decided to permit the private sector for establishing of private universities plus lay down the rules that guarantee the educational standard for these universities, whether in respect of their curriculums or standard of the teaching staff so that they shall provide the same educational degrees as they are provided by Kuwait University and shall be equal to them, if the conditions of this equalization are fulfilled.

For this purpose, the decree for the law of facilities was prepared and article (1) thereof contained the provision for permission to establish private universities and higher institutes or branches of foreign universities, under a decree that shall be issued on its presentation by the Minister of Higher Education.

The article (2) defined the objective of establishing private universities, and so it stated: it is contribution to realization of the objectives of the higher education and applied education whereby to realize interconnection between this objective and needs of the advanced society.

Article (3) set forth that the decree issued for establishment of private university must state its legal entity and regulatory provisions for them, colleges and higher institutes, according to which they shall be constituted and formation of Board of Trustees and its power and the university's financial resources and degrees to be granted by it and conditions for obtaining them.

Article (4) held a provision that the private university shall enjoy a status of an independent body corporate and its related provisions described its representation before third parties and the court and whatever of its right for ownership to the property and funds and signing of contracts, provided that they should not be in conflict with its objectives.

As well as article (5) held the provision that the private university shall be subject supervision of the Ministry of Higher Education in whatever related to implementation of the law's provisions and its bylaw, and provided that the said bylaw should define the procedures that warrant the University's compliance with those provisions and the bylaw authorized the council of ministers for dissolution of the Board of Trustees and appoint a provisional

Board of Trustee for management of the university for the period of one year and it can renew it for another one year, should the matter require it.

And article (6), about organization of the private colleges and higher institutes and branches of foreign universities – made reference to the aforesaid article.

And article (7) referred to promulgation of the bylaw of this law, by decision of the Council of Ministers, on the presentation of Minister of Higher Education.

For realization of this objective and as the public interest requires speedy promulgation of this organization of the private universities and private colleges and higher institutes and branches of foreign universities as to absorb the increasing number of secondary school graduates.

(Translated)

List of Figures

List of Tables

Bibliography

Abd-El Bary, P. (1993). *Portrait of Kuwait*. Kuwait: The Kuwait Bookshops Co. Ltd.

Abouammoh, A. M. (2009). *The role of education: trends of reforms and EU-GCC understanding*.

Abu-Hakima, A. M. (1965). *History of eastern Arabia, 1750-1800: the rise and development of Bahrain and Kuwait* (1st ed.). Beirut: Khayats.

Abu-Hakima, A. M. (1983). *The modern history of Kuwait 1750-1965*. London: Luzac.

Al-Hawat, Ali (2007). *Funding higher education in Arab countries, thoughts and reflections on the Topic*. Proceedings, 2nd Regional Research Seminar for Arab States, 25th_ 26th May 2007, Rabat, Morocco: UNESCO.

Al-Qana'i, Y. (1987). *Safahat min tarikh al-kuwayt (pages from the Kuwait History)*. Kuwait: Alsalasil Library.

Al Abduljader, F. (2009). Educational policies in the State of Kuwait: the reality and the ambition. *Al Mua'llem*, 1551.

Al douahees, E. (2006). *Improving scientific research in the Arabian Gulf*.

Al hajeri, A. (2004). Citizenship and political participation in the State of Kuwait the case of the national assembly (1963-1996). (PhD), University of Durham, Institute for Middle Eastern and Islamic studies.

Al Mughni, H. (1993). *Women in Kuwait: the politics of gender*. Saqi Books.

Al Mughni, H. (2010). Kuwait. In S. Kelly & J. Breslin (Eds.), *Women's rights in the Middle East and North Africa: progress amid resistance*. New York: Rowman & Littlefield.

Al Rayyes, F. (2014). Caricature. Al-Qabas *newspaper*, Wednesday, 9-4-2014. http://www.alqabas.com.kw/.

Al-Atiqi, I. M., & Al harbi, L. M. (2009). Meeting the challenge: quality systems in private higher education in Kuwait. *Quality in higher education*, 15(1), 5–16.

Al-Atiqi, I. M., Alharbi, L. M., & Ali, F. M. (n.d.). *The evolution of private higher education in Kuwait*. Kuwait: Private Universities Council – Kuwait (PUC).

Al-Atiqi, I. M., Al-Rashed, A. A., & Al-Ali, F. M. (2010). The contribution of private universities in higher education equity in Kuwait. *Towards an Arab higher education space: international challenges and societal responsibilities*, 111–123.

Al-Atiqi, I. M., & El-Azma, M. (2007). *Funding and financial performance of private higher education institutions in Kuwait*. Paper presented at the

UNESCO Forum on Higher Education, Research and Knowledge, Rabat, Morocco. http://unesdoc.unesco.org/images/0015/001577/157785e.pdf.

Al-Muhareb, H., Aaref, J., Eshfaq, M., Altaf, M., & Al-rahman, h. (2009). *Kuwait education directory* (3rd ed.). Kuwait: Q8 Media for Advertising & Publishing.

Al-Rashid, A.-a. (1995). *Tārīkh al-Kuwayt (the history of Kuwait)*. Kuwait: That Alsalasil.

Altbach, P. G. (1991). Patterns in higher education development. *Prospects*, 21(2), 189–203.

Altbach, P. G. (1999a). The logic of mass higher education. *Tertiary education & management*, 5(2), 107–124.

Altbach, P. G. (1999b). Private higher education: themes and variations in comparative perspective. *Prospects*, 29(3), 310–323.

Altbach, P. G. (1999c). *Private Prometheus: private higher education and development in the 21st century.* (Contributions to the study of education, Vol. 77). London & Westport, CT.: Greenwood Press.

Altbach, P. G., & Levy, D. C. (2005). *Private higher education: a global revolution.* Rotterdam: Sense Publishers.

Appadurai, A. (1996). *Modernity at large: cultural dimensions of globalization* (Public worlds, Vol. 1). Minneapolis, MN: University of Minnesota Press.

Cataloging-in-Publication Data International Monetary Fund. Articles of agreement of the International Monetary Fund (1944) Washington, D.C.: International Monetary Fund, 2011.

Ball, S. J. (1990a). *Foucault and education: disciplines and knowledge.* London: Routledge.

Ball, S. J. (1990b). *Politics and policy-making in education: explorations in policy sociology.* London: Routledge.

Ball, S. J. (2004). *Education for sale! The commodification of everything?* Paper presented at the King's Annual Education Lecture (17th June, 2004), Institute of Education, University of London.

Ball, S. J. (2006). *Education policy and social class: the selected works of Stephen J. Ball.* London & New York: Routledge.

Ball, S. J. (2008). *The education debate.* England: Bristol The Policy Press.

Ball, S. J. (2009). Privatising education, privatising education policy, privatising educational research: Network governance and the 'competition state'. *Journal of education policy*, 24(1), 83–99.

Ball, S. J., Goodson, I., & Maguire, M. (2007). *Education, globalisation and new times.* London: Routledge.

Baz, A. A. S. (1981). Political elite and political development in Kuwait (PhD thesis). George Washington University.

Beitz, C. R. (1979). *Political theory and international relations*, Princeton, NJ: Princeton University Press.

Belfield, C. R., & Levin, H. M. (2002). *Education privatization: causes, consequences and planning implications* (Vol. 74). Paris: International Institute for Educational Planning.

Bloom, D., Hartley, M., & Rosovsky, H. (2006). Beyond private gain: Public benefits of higher education. In J. F. Forest & P. G. Altbach (Eds.), *International handbook of higher education* (pp. 293–308). Dordrecht: Springer.

Bok, D. (2004). The benefits and costs of commercialization of the academy. In D. Stein (Ed.), *Buying in or selling out? The commercialization of the American Research University*. New Jersey: Rutgers University Press.

Bollag, B. (2006). America's hot new export: higher education. *Chronicle of higher education*, 52(24), A44.

Braun, V., & Clarke, V. (2006). Using thematic analysis in psychology. *Qualitative research in psychology*, 3(2), 77–101.

Bray, M. (2002). The costs and financing of education: trends and policy implications. In M. Bray (Ed.), *Education in developing Asia* (Vol. 3). Hong Kong: Asian Development Bank Comparative Education Research Centre The University of Hong Kong.

Breneman, D. W., & Finn, C. E. (1978). *An uncertain future Public policy and private higher education* (pp. 1–61): Washington, DC: Brookings Institution.

Brown, R., & Carasso, H. (2013). *Everything for sale? The marketisation of UK higher education*. London: Routledge.

Buckner, E. (2013). How university admissions distort some Arab societies. Retrieved 13-Jun-2013, from http://www.al-fanar.org/2013/05/how-university-admissions-distorts-some-arab- societies/#comment-1044.

Bush, T. (2003). *Theories of educational management* (3rd ed.). London: Sage.

Bush, T. (2011). *Theories of educational leadership and management* (4th ed.). London: Sage.

Camilleri, A. F. (2008). *The risks of privatisation of higher education*. Paper presented at the SSU Higher Education Conference, Sonoma State University: North Bay. http://www.eric.ed.gov.ezp.lib.unimelb.edu.au/contentdelivery/servlet/ERICServlet?accno=ED50 4317.

Castells, M. (1996). *The rise of the network society* (Vol. 1). Cambridge, MA: Blackwell.

Castells, M. (1999). Information technology, globalization and social development. *UNRISD Discussion paper No.* 114, United Nations Research Institute for Social Development.

Castells, M. (2010). *The rise of the network society* (2nd ed., Vol. 1). Chichester: Wiley-Blackwell.

Cerny, P. G. (1997). Paradoxes of the competition state: the dynamics of political globalization. *Government and opposition*, 32(2), 251–274.

CIA. (2018). The world fact book. Retrieved 21-05-2018, from https://www.cia.gov/library/publications/resources/the-world-factbook/geos/ku.html.

Clark, B. R. (1998). *Creating entrepreneurial universities: organizational pathways of transformation. Issues in higher education.* Oxford, NY: Pergamon; ERIC.

Coffman, J. (2005). Higher education in the Arabian Gulf: privatization and Americanization. In P. G. Altbach & D. C. Levy (Eds.), *Private higher education: a global revolution* (pp. 255–259). Rotterdam: Sense publishers.

Crystal, J. (1990). *Oil and politics in the Gulf: rulers and merchants in Kuwait and Qatar* (Vol. 24). England: Cambridge University Press.

CSB. (2015). Central Statistical Bureau. Kuwait. http://www.csb.gov.kw/Default_EN.aspx.

Curs, B. R., Bhandari, B., & Steiger, C. (2011). The roles of public higher education expenditure and the privatization of the higher education on U.S. states economic growth. *Journal of education finance*, 36(4), 424–441.

Dakhli, M., & El Zohairy, D. (2013). Emerging trends in higher education in the GCC: a critical assessment. In I. Alon, V. Jones & J. R. McIntyre (Eds.), *Innovation in business education in emerging markets* (p. 43). Basingtoke, UK: Palgrave Macmillan.

Dale, R. (1999). Specifying globalization effects on national policy: a focus on the mechanisms. *Journal of education policy*, 14(1), 1–17.

Dar, L. (2012). The political dynamics of higher education policy. *Journal of higher education*, 83(6), 769–794.

David Kin-keung, C. (2012). A comparison of Singapore and Hong Kong on their strategies for developing regional education hubs. *Sociology study*, 2(1), 1–25.

Degefa, D. (2011). *Privatization of higher education in Sub-Saharan Africa: global pressures, national responses and local realities.* Saarbrücken, Germany: LAP Lambert Acad. Publ.

Denzin, N. K., & Lincoln, Y. S. (2005). *The SAGE handbook of qualitative research* (3rd ed.). Thousand Oaks, CA.: Sage Publications.

Denzin, N. K., & Lincoln, Y. S. (2011). *The SAGE handbook of qualitative research.* California, USA: Sage.

Dolowitz, D., & Marsh, D. (1996). Who learns what from whom: a review of the policy transfer literature. *Political studies*, 44(2), 343–357.

Dolowitz, D. P., & Marsh, D. (2000). Learning from abroad: the role of policy transfer in contemporary policy-making. *Governance*, 13(1), 5–23.

Donn, G., & Al Manthri, Y. (2010). *Globalisation and higher education in the Arab Gulf States*. Oxford, UK: Symposium Books.

Draper, T. (1987). American Hubris: From Truman to the Persian Gulf. *The New York review of books*, 40–48.

Education International (EI), & Public Services International (PSI). (1999). The WTO and the Millennium Round: what is at stake for public education? *Common concerns for workers in education and the public sector*. Belgium & France.

El Naggar, D. (2009). New World Bank country office in Kuwait marks a new phase of partnership with the Arab World. *Middle East and North Africa*. Retrieved 01-12-2014 from http://web.worldbank.org/archive/website01051/WEB/0__CON-4.HTM.

Ellingson, L. (2009). *Engaging crystallization in qualitative research*. Thousand Oaks, CA: Sage.

Ellingson, L. (2011). Analysis and representation across the continuum. In N. K. Denzin & Y. S. Lincoln (Eds.), *The SAGE handbook of qualitative research* (pp. 595–610). Los Angeles, London, New Delhi, Singapore & Washington DC: Sage Publications.

Ellingson, L. (2013). Analysis and representation across the continuum. In N. K. Denzin & Y. S. Lincoln (Eds.), *Collecting and interpreting qualitative materials* (Vol. 3). US: Sage Publications.

El-Ojeili, C., & Hayden, P. (2006). *Critical theories of globalization*. New York: Palgrave Macmillan.

Enders, J. (2004). Higher education, internationalisation, and the nation-state: recent developments and challenges to governance theory. *Higher education*, 47(3), 361–382.

Eta, E. A. (2014). Policy borrowing and transfer, and policy convergence: justifications for the adoption of the Bologna Process in the CEMAC region and the Cameroonian higher education system through the LMD reform. *Comparative education*, 51(2), 1–18. (https://files.eric.ed.gov/fulltext/ED438281.pdf).

Eta, E. A. (2015). Policy borrowing and transfer, and policy convergence: justifications for the adoption of the Bologna Process in the CEMAC region and the Cameroonian higher education system through the LMD reform. *Comparative education*, 51(2), 161–178.

Falk, R. (1993). The making of global citizenship. In J. Brecher, J. B. Childs & J. Cutler (Eds.), *Global visions beyond the new world order*. Boston: South End Press.

Faubion, J. D. (2000). *Power / Michel Foucault* (R. Hurley, Trans. Vol. 3). New York: New Press.

Fraenkel, J. R., & Wallen, N. E. (2006). *Student mastery activities to accompany: how to design and evaluate research in education* (6th ed.). Boston, MA: McGraw-Hill.

Friedman, M. (1962). *Capitalism and freedom*. Chicago, IL: University of Chicago Press.

Gall, M. D., Gall, J. P., & Borg, W. R. (2003). *Educational research: an introduction* (7th ed.). Boston, MA: Allyn and Bacon.

Gasiorowski, M. J. (1991). *US foreign policy and the Shah: building a client state in Iran*. Ithaca, NY: Cornell University Press.

Gaziel, H. H. (2012). Privatisation by the back door: the case of the higher education policy in Israel. *European journal of education*, 47(2), 290–298.

GCC. (2006). Comprehensive development of education in the Gulf Cooperation Council countries: a study of the directives stated in the Supreme Council Resolution. The 23rd session (Doha, December 2002) On Education. Riyadh: GGC.

GCC. (2012a). The cooperation council for the Arab States of the Gulf. Retrieved 3-07-2012, from http://www.gcc-sg.org/eng/.

GCC. (2012b). *GCC women challenging the status quo*. Dubai: Al Masah Capital Management Limited.

GCC. (2012c). *Statistical bulletin* (Vol. 20). Riyadh: The Cooperation Council for The Arab States Of Gulf Secretariat General: Information Sector - Statistical Department.

Geiger, R. L. (1986). *Private sectors in higher education: structure, function, and change in eight countries*. Ann Arbor, MI: University of Michigan Press.

Geiger, R. L. (1988). Public and private sectors in higher education: A comparison of international patterns. *Higher education*, 17(6), 699–711.

Gewirtz, S., Ball, S. J., & Bowe, R. (1995). *Markets, choice, and equity in education*. Buckingham: Philadelphia Open University Press.

Ghabra, S. (1997). Kuwait and the dynamics of socio-economic change. *Middle East journal*, 51(3), 358–372.

Ghabra, S. (2011). *Kuwait: a study of the dynamics of state and society (Arabic)*. Kuwait: Aafaq BookStore.

Ginsburg, M., Espinoza, O., Popa, S., & Terano, M. (2005). Globalisation and higher education in Chile and Romania: the roles of the International Monetary Fund, World Bank, and World Trade Organization. In J. Zajda, K. Freeman, M. Geo-Jaja, S. Majhanovic, V. Rust, J. Zajda & R. Zajda (Eds.), *International handbook on globalisation, education and policy research* (pp. 221–234). Netherlands: Springer.

Gonzalez, A. (1997). Philippines. In G. A. Postiglione & G. C. Mak (Eds.), *Asian higher education: an international handbook and reference guide* (pp. 265–283). Westport, CT: Greenwood Publishing Group.

Greaves, H. R. G. (1960). Political theory today. *Political science quarterly*, 75(1), 1–16.

Green, A. (1997). *Education, globalization and the nation state*. London: Macmillan.

GUST. (2011). Gulf University for Science and Technology official website. Retrieved 19-09-2011, from http://www.gust.edu.kw/content/about-gust.

Held, D. (1991). *Political theory today*. Stanford, California: Stanford University Press.

Henig, J. R. (1989). Privatization in the United States: theory and practice. *Political science quarterly*, 104(4), 649–670.

Heyman, S. J. (1992). Positive and negative liberty. *Chicago-Kent law review*, 68(1), 81–90.

Holzhacker, D., Chornoivan, O., Yazilitas, D., Dayan-Ochir, K., & Institute for Higher Education, P. (2009). *Privatization in higher education: cross-country analysis of trends, policies, problems, and solutions*. Issue Brief. Washington, DC: Institute for Higher Education Policy.

International Monetary Fund. (1999). IMF concludes Article IV consultation with Kuwait. *Public Information Notice (PIN) No. 99/11*. Retrieved 20-12-2013, from http://www.imf.org/external/np/sec/pn/1999/pn9911.htm.

International Monetary Fund. (2000). IMF concludes Article IV consultation with Kuwait. *Public Information Notice (PIN) No. 00/27*. Retrieved 20-12-2013, from http://www.imf.org/external/np/sec/pn/2000/pn0027.htm .

International Monetary Fund. (2004). Kuwait: 2003 Article IV consultation – staff report; Public information notice on the Executive Board discussion; and Statement by the Executive Director for Kuwait. *Staff country reports*. Retrieved 10-1-2014, from http://www.elibrary.imf.org.ezp.lib.unimelb.edu.au/doc/IMF002/04157-9781451822304/04157- 9781451822304/Other_formats/Source_PDF/04157-9781452739724.pdf.

International Monetary Fund. (2008) *World economic outlook. World economic and financial surveys, April*. Washington, DC: IMF.

Ismael, J. S. (1982). *Kuwait: social change in historical perspective*. Syracuse, NY: Syracuse University.

Jamshidi, L., Arasteh, H., NavehEbrahim, A., Zeinabadi, H., & Rasmussen, P. D. (2012). Developmental patterns of privatization in higher education: a comparative study. *Higher education: The international journal of higher education and educational planning*, 64(6), 789–803.

Johansson, P. O. (1991). *An introduction to modern welfare economics*. Cambridge, UK: Cambridge University Press.

Johnson, B., & Christensen, L. B. (2012). *Educational research: quantitative, qualitative, and mixed approaches* (4th ed.). Thousand Oaks, CA.: Sage Publications,

Johnson, G. W., & Watson, D. J. (1991). Privatization: provision or production of services? Two case studies. *State & local government review*, 23(2), 82–89.

Kanbur, S. R., Sandler, T., & Morrison, K. M. (1999). *The future of development assistance: common pools and international public goods* (Vol. 25). Washington, DC: Overseas Development Council.

Karoly, L. (2010). *The role of education in preparing graduates for the labor market in the GCC countries*. Paper presented at the 15th annual conference of the Emirates Center for Strategic Studies and Research on Education and the Requirements of the GCC Labour Market, United Arab Emirates: Abu Dhabi. Retrieved 18-01-2014 from http://www.rand.org/pubs/working_papers/2010/RAND_WR742.pdf.

King, E. M., & Hill, M. A. (1993). *Women's education in developing countries: barriers, benefits, and policies*. Baltimore: Published for the World Bank [by] the Johns Hopkins University Press.

King, R., Marginson, S., & Naidoo, R. (2011). Handbook on globalization and higher education Retrieved 06-01-2014 from http://UNIMELB.eblib.com.au/patron/FullRecord.aspx?p=775923.

Kinninmont, J. (2012). *Kuwait's Parliament: an experiment in semi-democracy*. London: Chatham House.

Kogan, M., Marianne Bauer, Ivar Bleiklie & Mary Henkel (Ed.). (2000). *Transforming higher education: a comparative study* (Vol. 57). London & Philadelphia: Jessica Kingsley Publishers.

Kolderie, T. (1986). The two different concepts of privatization. *Public administration review*, 46(4 July/August), 285–291.

Kuwait Security Overview. (2012) *Kuwait defence & security report* (pp. 70–73). London: Business Monitor International.

Kuwait University. (2011). During a press conference headed by KU President in Khaldiya. Retrieved 17-09-2011, from http://www.kuniv.edu/ku/News/KU_007548.

Kuwait University. (2012). The Kuwait University. Retrieved 3-07-2012, from http://www.kuniv.edu/ku.

Kuwait University. (2018). The Kuwait University. Retrieved 1-09-2018, from http://www.kuniv.edu/ku.

Kvale, S., & Brinkmann, S. (2009). *InterViews: learning the craft of qualitative research interviewing* (2nd ed.). Los Angeles: Sage.

Lal, D. (1998). The world economy at the end of the millennium (working papers number 786). Retrieved 6-02-2014, from http://www.econ.ucla.edu/workingpapers/wp786.pdf.

Lane, J. E., & Kinser, K. (2011). Reconsidering privatization in cross-border engagements: the sometimes public nature of private activity. *Higher education policy*, 24(2), 255–273.

Lawn, M. (2006). Soft governance and the learning spaces of Europe. *Comparative European politics*, 4(2–1), 272–288.

Lawn, M., & Lingard, B. (2002). Constructing a European policy space in educational governance: the role of transnational policy actors. *European educational research journal*, 1(2), 290–307.

Lefrere, P. (2007). Competing higher education futures in a globalising world. *European journal of education*, 42(2), 201–212.

Levin, H. M. (1997). The economics of educational choice. In E. Cohn (Ed.), *Market approaches to education: vouchers and school choice.* Oxford: Pergamon.

Levin, H. M., & Driver, C. E. (1997). Cost of an educational voucher system. *Education economics*, 5(3), 265–283.

Levy, D. (2009). Growth and typology. In S. Bjarnason, K.-M. Cheng, J. Fielden, M.-J. Lemaitre, D. Levy & N. V. Varghese (Eds.), *A new dynamic: private sector education* (pp. 1–28). Paris: UNESCO.

Levy, D. C. (1986). *Higher education and the state in Latin America: private challenges to public dominance.* Chicago: University of Chicago Press.

Levy, D. C. (2006). The unanticipated explosion: private higher education's global surge. *Comparative education review*, 50(2), 217–240.

Levy, D. C. (2010). The global growth of private higher education. *ASHE higher education report*, 36(3), 121–133.

Levy, D. C. (2011). Public policy for private higher education: a global analysis. *Journal of comparative policy analysis*, 13(4), 383–396.

Levy, D. C. (2013). The decline of private higher education. *Higher education policy*, 26(1), 25–42.

Luijten-Lub, A. (2007). Choices in internationalisation: how higher education institutions respond to internationalisation, europeanisation, and globalisation. (PhD), University of Twente, Enschede.

Lundqvist, L. (1988). Privatization: towards a concept for comparative policy analysis. *Journal of public policy*, 8(1), 1–19.

Maassen, P. (2000). The changing roles of stakeholders in Dutch university governance. *European journal of education*, 35(4), 449–464.

Marginson, S. (2004). Competition and markets in higher education: a 'glonacal' analysis. *Policy futures in education*, 2(2), 175–244.

Marginson, S. (2007). The public/private divide in higher education: a global revision. *Higher education*, 53(3), 307–333.

Marginson, S. (2008). Global field and global imagining: Bourdieu and worldwide higher education. *British journal of sociology of education*, 29(3), 303–315.

Marginson, S. (2010). *The limits of market reform in higher education.* Paper presented at the Higher Education Forum. Research Institute for

Higher Education, Hiroshima University. Japan. Volume 7. Retrieved 07-03-2010 from http://rihejoho.hiroshima-u.ac.jp/pdf/101732.pdf.

Marginson, S. (2011). Higher education and public good. *Higher education quarterly*, 65(4), 411–433.

Marginson, S. (2012). The 'public' contribution of universities in an increasingly global world. In B. Pusser, K. Kempner, S. Marginson & I. Ordorika (Eds.), *Universities and the public sphere: Knowledge creation and state building in the era of globalization* (pp. 7–26). New York & London: Routledge.

Marginson, S., & Rhoades, G. (2002). Beyond national states, markets, and systems of higher education: A glonacal agency heuristic. *Higher education*, 43(3), 281–309.

Massy, W. F. (2004). Markets in higher education: do they promote internal efficiency? In P. Teixeira, D. Dill, A. Amaral & B. B. Jongbloed (Eds.), *Markets in higher education: rhetoric or Reality?* (pp. 13–36). Dordrecht, Boston, MA. & London: Kluer academic publishers.

McEntee, G. W. (1987). The case against privatization. *American city & county*, 102, 48.

MCS (2018). Kingdom of Saudi Arabia: Ministry of Civil Service, Retrieved 3-07-2018, from https://www.mcs.gov.sa/En/InformationCenter/Events/Pages/default.aspx.

Meleis, A. I., El-Sanabary, N., & Beeson, D. (1979). Women, modernization, and education in Kuwait. *Comparative education review*, 23(1), 115–124.

Mengistu, B., & Hail-Mariam, Y. (1989). Privatization in theory and practice: the issues to be considered. *Journal of applied business research (JABR)*, 5(4), 43–51.

Merriam, S. B. (2009). *Qualitative research: a guide to design and implementation*. San Francisco, CA: Jossey-Bass.

Miller-Idriss, C., & Hanauer, E. (2011). Transnational higher education: offshore campuses in the Middle East. *Comparative education*, 47(2), 181–207.

Mills, A. (2009). New private universities in Kuwait pin their hopes on U.S. partners. *Chronicle of Higher Education*, 55(37), A24.

Moe, R. C. (1987). Exploring the limits of privatization. *Public administration review*, 47(6), 453–460.

MOHE. (2012). Ministry of Higher Education Kuwait. Retrieved 24-06-2012 from https://www.mohe.edu.kw/site/.

Morgan, D. L. (2008). Snowball sampling. In L. M. Given (Ed.), *The SAGE encyclopedia of qualitative research methods* (pp. 816–817). Thousand Oaks, CA: SAGE Publications, Inc.

Norton, A. R. (1993). The future of civil society in the Middle East. *Middle East Journal*, 47(2), 205–216.

Nyborg, P. (2002). *International competition: implications for educational providers and students, Workshop IV: GATS in the light of increasing internationalisation of higher education. Quality assurance and recognition.* Paper presented at the OECD/US Forum on Trade in Educational Services, Council of Europe: Committee for Higher Education and Research.

Nye, J. (2004). Soft power – The means to success in world politics. New York: Public Affairs.

Oanda, I. O., Chege, F. N., & Wesonga, D. M. (2008). *Privatisation and private higher education in Kenya: implications for access, equity, and knowledge production*. Dakar: Codesria.

Olsen, J.P. (2002) 'The many faces of europeanization', *ARENA working papers WP 01/2* http://www.arena.uio.no/publications.

OECD. (2008). Making reforms succeed: moving forward with the MENA investment policy agenda. *Private sector development in the Middle East and North Africa*. Paris: Organisation for Economic Co-operation and Development (OECD).

Olds, K. (2007). Global assemblage: Singapore, foreign universities, and the construction of a 'Global Education Hub'. *World development*, 35(6), 959–975. doi: http://www.elsevier.com/wps/find/journaldescription.cws_home/386/description#description.

O'Toole, J., & Beckett, D. (2009). *Educational research: creative thinking and doing / John O'Toole and David Beckett*. South Melbourne, VIC.: Oxford University Press.

PAAET. (2018). The Public Authority for Applied Education and Training official website. Retrieved 02-09-2018, from http://www.paaet.edu.kw/.

Pachuashvili, M. (2008). Private-public dynamics in post-communist higher education. *Die Hochschule*, 2(17), 84–93.

PACI. (2018). Public Authority for Civil Information. http://www.paci.gov.kw/en/

Palley, T. I. (2004). From Keynesianism to neoliberalism: shifting paradigms in economics. *Foreign Policy in Focus Special Report*, 3. Retrieved 15-03-2014 from https://fpif.org/from_keynesianism_to_neoliberalism_shifting_paradigms_in_economics/

Paper presented at the workshop entitled: *The EU and the GCC: challenges and prospects under the Swedish presidency of the EU*. Sweden: Lund (8th to 9th of June). Center for Higher Education Research and Studies (CHERS). http://faculty.ksu.edu.sa/abouammoh/arabic/Lists/lahvdu%20fpedm/Attachments/1/01%20Aboua mmoh%20The%20Role%20of%20Education%20Trends%20of%20Reforms%20and%20EU-GCC%20Uniderstanding.pdf.

Patton, M. Q. (2002). *Qualitative research and evaluation methods* (3rd ed.). London: Sage Publications.

Paul, S. (1985). Privatisation and the public sector: relevance and limits. *Economic and political weekly*, 20(8), M4–M8.

Phillips, D., & Ochs, K. (2003). Processes of policy borrowing in education: Some explanatory and analytical devices. *Comparative education*, 39(4), 451–461.

Pirie, M. (1985). *Dismantling the state: the theory and practice of privatization*. Dallas, TX: National Center for Policy Analysis.

Psacharopoulos, G. (1994). Returns to investment in education: a global update. *World development*, 22(9), 1325–1343.

PUC. (2011). Private Universities Council official website. Retrieved 19-09-2011, from http://www.puc.edu.kw/en/index.php.

PUC. (2018). Private Universities Council official website. Retrieved 19-09-2011, from http://www.puc.edu.kw/UniversityListPage.aspx.

Qalʿajī, Q. (1970). *al-Nizam al-Siyāsī wa al-Iqtisadī fī Dawlat al-Kuwayt*. Kuwait: Dār al-Kātib al-Arabī.

Reynolds, A. A. (2005). Educational technology in the Middle East. In C. Howard, J. Boettcher, L. Justice, K. Schenk, P. Rogers & G. Berg (Eds.), *Encyclopedia of distance learning* (pp. 717–723). Hershey, PA: IGI Global. Retrieved 30-01-2014 from http://services.igi- global.com/resolvedoi/resolve.aspx?doi=10.4018/978-1-59140-555-9.ch104.

Rizvi, F. (2005). International education and the production of cosmopolitan identities. *RIHE international publication series* 9, pp. 77–92. Retrieved 01-01-2019 from http://hdl.handle.net/2142/3516.

Rizvi, F. (2006). The ideology of privatization in higher education: a global perspective. In D. M. Priest & E. P. St. John (Eds.), *Privatization and public universities* (pp. 65–84). Bloomington, IN & Indianapolis, IN: Indiana University Press.

Rizvi, F., & Lingard, B. (2010). *Globalizing education policy*. New York: Routledge.

Rizvi, F., & Lingard, B. (2011). Social equity and the assemblage of values in Australian higher education. *Cambridge journal of education*, 41(1), 5–22.

Roderick, G., & Stephens, M. (2011). *Higher education for all?* (Vol. 82). New York: Routledge.

Romani, V. (2009). *The politics of higher education in the Middle East: problems and prospects*. Waltham, MA: Brandeis University (Crown Center for Middle East Studies).

Rugh, W. A. (2002). Arab education: tradition, growth and reform. *Middle East journal*, 56(3), 396–414.

Sabry, M. (2009). Funding policy and higher education in Arab countries. *Comparative & international higher education*, 1, 11–12.

Saleh, A. (2014). KU brace for students admission crisis: Seats 'not enough', *Kuwait times*.

Salter, B., & Tapper, T. (1994). *The state and higher education*. London & New York: Routledge Flamer, Taylor & Fraincis Group.

Salter, B., & Tapper, T. (2013). *The state & higher education*. London and New York: Routledge Flamer, Taylor & Francis Group.

Samuelson, P. A. (1954). The pure theory of public expenditure. *The review of economics and statistics*, 36(4), 387–389.

Sanyal, B. C. (1998). Diversification of sources and the role of privatization in financing higher education in the Arab States Region. IIEP contributions, (30). United Nations Educational, Scientific and Cultural Organization, Paris International Inst for Educational Planning.

Sassen, S. (1996). *Losing control?: sovereignty in an age of globalization*. New York: Columbia University Press.

Saunders, D. B. (2010). Neoliberal ideology and public higher education in the United States. *Journal for critical education policy studies*, 8(1), 41–77.

Sauvé, P. (2002). *Trade, education and the GATS: what's in, what's out, what's all the fuss about?* Paper presented at the OECD/US Forum on Trade in Educational Services, Washington, D.C.. Retrieved 13-01-2014 from http://www.oecd.org/edu/skills-beyond-school/2088515.pdf.

Savas, E. S. (1982). *Privatizing the public sector: how to shrink government*. Chatham, NJ: Chatham House Publishers.

Savas, E. S. (1987). *Privatization: the key to better government*. Chatham, NJ: Chatham House Publishers.

Savas, E. S. (2000). *Privatization and public-private partnerships*. New York: Seven Bridges Press, ILC.

Savas, E. S. (2005). *Privatization in the city: successes, failures, lessons*. Washington, D.C.: CQ Press.

Scholte, J. A. (2000). *Globalization: a critical introduction*. New York: St. Martin's Press.

Scholte, J. A. (2008). Defining globalisation. *World economy*, 31(11), 1471–1502.

Shuhaiber, S. K. (1981). Political development in Kuwait, continuity and change in an Arab Independent Gulf State (PhD thesis). University of Oxford.

Shultziner, D., & Tétreault, M. A. (2012). Representation and democratic progress in Kuwait. *Representation*, 48(3), 281–293.

Sinclair, S. (2002). GATS: how the WTO's new services threaten democracy. Ottawa, Canada: Canadian Centre for Policy Alternatives.

Singh, P., & McWilliam, E. (2001). *Designing educational research: theories, methods and practices*. Flaxton, QLD.: Post Pressed. 2001.

Slantcheva Snejana & Levy Daniel C. (2007). *Private Higher Education in Post-Communist Europe: In Search of Legitimacy*, NY: Palgrave.

Smith, S. C. (1999). *Kuwait, 1950-1965: Britain, the al-Sabah, and oil*. Oxford, NY.: Published for the British Academy by Oxford University Press.

Steiner-Khamsi, G. (2004). Globalization in education: real or imagined? In G. Steiner-Khamsi (Ed.), *The global politics of educational borrowing and lending* (pp. 1–6). New York: Teachers College Press.

Steiner-Khamsi, G. (2012). Understanding policy borrowing and lending. In G. Steiner-Khamsi & F. Waldow (Eds.), *World yearbook of education: policy borrowing and lending in education* (pp. 3–17). London: Routledge.

Stiglitz, J. E. (1999). Knowledge as a global public good. In I. Kaul, I. Grunberg & M. A. Stern (Eds.) *Global public goods: international cooperation in the 21st century* (pp. 308–325). Published for the United Nations Development Programme (UNDP). New York, Oxford: Oxford University Press.

Taber, K. S. (2012). Prioritising paradigms, mixing methods, and characterising the 'qualitative' in educational research. *Teacher development*, 16(1), 125–138.

Tan, A. M. (2002). *Malaysian private higher education: globalisation, privatisation, transformation, & marketplaces*. London: Asean Academic Press Ltd.

Taylor, S., Rizvi, f., Lingard, B., & Henry, M. (1997). *Educational policy and the politics of change*. London: Routledge.

Teichler, U. (1996). Comparative higher education: potentials and limits. *Higher education*, 32(4), 431–465.

Teixeira, P., Dill, D., Amaral, A., & Jongbloed, B. B. (2004). Introduction. In P. Teixeira, D. Dill, A. Amaral & B. B. Jongbloed (Eds.), *Markets in higher education: rhetoric or reality?* (Vol. 6, pp. 1–12). Dordrecht, Boston, MA. & London: Kluer academic publishers.

Tétreault, M. A. (1991). Autonomy, necessity, and the small state: ruling Kuwait in the twentieth century. *International organization*, 45(4), 565–591.

Tétreault, M. A. (1995). Patterns of culture and democratization in Kuwait. *Studies in comparative international development*, 30(2), 26–44.

Tétreault, M. A. (2011). Identity and transplant-university education in the Gulf: The American University of Kuwait. *Journal of Arabian studies*, 1(1), 81.

The Constitution of Kuwait. (1962). The constitution of Kuwait, retrieved 06-01-2014 from http://www.pm.gov.kw/en/state_Of_Kuwait/kuwaitConstitution.jsp#Part_III_Public_Rights_and_ Duties.

The Economist Intelligence Unit. (2009). The GCC in 2020: the Gulf and its people. *The economist*. A report from the Economist Intelligence Unit written in cooperation with the IBM Institute for Business Value.

(2015). The need of economic diversification and eliminate the total reliance on oil (Arabic). (January 22). *Al Kuwaityah*. Retrieved from http://www.alkuwaityah.com/products/435/11.pdf.

The Task Force on Higher Education and Society. (2000). *Higher education in developing countries: peril and promise*. Washington, D.C.: The World Bank.

The World Bank. (2008). The road not travelled: education reform in the Middle East and North Africa. *MENA development report*. Washington, D.C.: The World Bank.

The World Bank. (2013). Kuwait. Retrieved 17-01-2014, from http://web.worldbank.org/WBSITE/EXTERNAL/COUNTRIES/MENAEXT/EXTGC/0,,content MDK:22288046~menuPK:6409357~pagePK:141137~piPK:141127~theSitePK:6130003,00.html.

Thornborough, T. (1990). Kuwaiti higher education troubled even before Iraq's invasion. *Chronicle of higher education*, 36(48), A27.

Tilak, J. B. G. (1988). Higher education in Sub-Saharan Africa (Book Review). *Kyklos*, 41(2), 335.

Tilak, J. B. G. (1991). The privatization of higher education. *Prospects*, 21(2), 227–239.

Tilak, J. B. G. (1996). The privatization of higher education. In Z. Morsy & P. G. Altbach (Eds.), *Higher education in an international perspective: critical issues* (pp. 59–71). New York & London: International Bureau of Education.

Tilak, J. B. G. (2000). Higher education in developing countries. [Book Review]. *Minerva: a review of science, learning & policy*, 38(2), 233–240.

Tilak, J. B. G. (2008). Transition from higher education as a public good to higher education as a private good: the saga of Indian experience. *Journal of Asian public policy*, 1(2), 220–234.

Tilak, J. B. G. (2009a). Higher education: a public good or a commodity for trade? *Prospects*, 38(4), 449–466.

Tilak, J. B. G. (2009b). Trends in private higher education in Asia. *Higher education review*, 41(2), 48–77.

Tilak, J. B. G. (2011). Trade in higher education: the role of general agreement on trade in services (GATS). *Fundamentals of educational planning*. Retrieved 5-01-2014, from http://unesdoc.unesco.org/images/0021/002149/214997e.pdf.

Tolmacheva, M. (2011). *Bringing the American college model to the Arabian Gulf*. New Challenges for Intercultural Education.

Tolmacheva, M. (2011a). *Bringing the American college model to the Arabian Gulf: new challenges for intercultural education*. Paper presented at the 4th International Barcelona Conference on Higher Education, Barcelona.

Umakoshi, T. (2004). Private higher education in Asia: transitions and development. In P. G. Altbach & T. Umakoshi (Eds.), *Asian universities: historical perspectives and contemporary challenges* (pp. 33–49). Baltimore: Johns Hopkins University Press.

UNDP. (2002). Creating opportunities for future generations. *Arab human development report*. New York: United Nations Development Programme, Regional Bureau for Arab States (RBAS).

UNDP. (2003). *Building a knowledge society Arab human development report* (p. 217). New York: United Nations Development Programme, Arab Fund For Economic And Social Development.

UNESCO. (2009). A new dynamic: private sector education. In S. Bjarnason, K.-M. Cheng, J. Fielden, M.-J. Lemaitre, D. Levy & N. V. Varghese (Eds.), *World conference on higher education*. Paris: UNESCO.

UNESCO. (2012). Gross enrolment ratio (%) and gender parity index of GER. Retrieved 9-12-2013, from http://stats.uis.unesco.org/unesco/TableViewer/tableView.aspx?ReportId=3345&IF_Language=e ng.

UNESCO. (2013). Enrolment in tertiary public and private institutions. Retrieved 10-12-2013, from http://stats.uis.unesco.org/unesco/TableViewer/tableView.aspx?ReportId=3563&IF_Language=e ng.

UNESCO, & IBE. (2011). *World data on education 7th edition 2010/2011*. Paris: United Nations Educational, Scientific and Cultural Organisation and International Bureau of Education.

Unknown. (2001). Kuwait: private universities one step closer. *Middle East Business Intelligence*, 20(1), 7.

Varghese, N. V. (Ed.). (2006). *New trends in higher education: growth and expansion of private higher education in Africa*. Paris: IIEP/UNESCO.

Verger, A., Edwards Jr, D. B., & Altinyelken, H. K. (2014). Learning from all? The World Bank, aid agencies and the construction of hegemony in education for development. *Comparative education*, 50(4), 381–399.

Wangenge-Ouma, G. (2008). Globalisation and higher education funding policy shifts in Kenya. *Journal of higher education policy and management*, 30(3), 215–229.

Williams, G. (2004). The higher education market in the United Kingdom. In P. Teixeira, D. Dill, A. Amaral & B. B. Jongbloed (Eds.), *Markets in higher education: rhetoric or reality?* (Vol. 6, pp. 241–269). Dordrecht, Boston, MA. & London: Kluer academic publishers.

World Bank. (2000). *The task force on higher education and society, higher education in developing countries: peril and promise*. Washington, D.C.: World Bank.

WTO. (1994a). Annex 1B: general agreement on trade in services (GATS). Retrieved 13-01-2014, from http://www.wto.org/english/docs_e/legal_e/26-gats.pdf.

WTO. (1994b). GATS_Kuwait schedule of specific commitments. Retrieved 14-01-2014, from http://www.wto.org/.

WTO. (1995). GATS_Kuwait schedule of specific commitments-supplement 1. Retrieved 14-01- 2014, from http://www.wto.org/.

WTO. (1998). GATS_Kuwait schedule of specific commitments-supplement 2. Retrieved 14-01- 2014, from http://www.wto.org/.

WTO. (2012). *Trade policy review report by Kuwait*. Genève, Switzerland: World Trade Organization.

WTO. (2013). The general agreement on trade in services (GATS). Retrieved 08-01-2014 from https://www.wto.org/english/tratop_e/serv_e/gsintr_e.pdf.

WTO. (2014). The general agreement on trade in services (GATS): objectives, coverage and disciplines. Retrieved 08-01-2014, from http://www.wto.org/english/tratop_e/serv_e/gatsqa_e.htm.

Yarrow, G. (1986). Privatization in theory and practice. *Economic policy*, 1(2), 323–377.

Yetiv, S. (2002). Kuwait's democratic experiment in its broader international context. *Middle East journal*, 56(2), 257–271.

Zahlan, R. S. (1989). *The making of the modern Gulf states: Kuwait, Bahrain, Qatar, the United Arab Emirates, and Oman*. London: Unwin Hyman.

Index

Higher Education Research and Policy (HERP)

Edited by Marek Kwiek

Vol. 1 Marek Kwiek / Andrzej Kurkiewicz (eds.): The Modernisation of European Universities. Cross-National Academic Perspectives. 2012.

Vol. 2 Marek Kwiek / Peter Maassen (Eds.): National Higher Education Reforms in a European Context. Comparative Reflections on Poland and Norway. 2012.

Vol. 3 Marek Kwiek: Knowledge Production in European Universities. States, Markets, and Academic Entrepreneurialism. 2013.

Vol. 4 Pavel Zgaga / Ulrich Teichler / John Brennan (eds.): The Globalisation Challenge for European Higher Education. Convergence and Diversity, Centres and Peripheries. Second Revised Edition. 2016.

Vol. 5 Jelena Branković / Maja Kovačević / Peter Maassen / Bjørn Stensaker / Martina Vukasović (eds.): The Re-Institutionalization of Higher Education in the Western Balkans. The Interplay between European Ideas, Domestic Policies, and Institutional Practices. 2014.

Vol. 6 Hamish Coates (ed.): Higher Education Learning Outcomes Assessment. International Perspectives. 2014.

Vol. 7 Gabriella Pusztai: Pathways to Success in Higher Education. Rethinking the Social Capital Theory in the Light of Institutional Diversity. 2015.

Vol. 8 Pavel Zgaga / Ulrich Teichler / Hans G. Schuetze / Andrä Wolter (eds.): Higher Education Reform: Looking Back – Looking Forward. 2nd revised edition 2019.

Vol. 9 Ahoud Al-Asfour: Higher Education Privatization in Kuwait. A Study in the Processes of Policy Production. 2019.

www.peterlang.com

www.ingramcontent.com/pod-product-compliance
Ingram Content Group UK Ltd.
Pitfield, Milton Keynes, MK11 3LW, UK
UKHW011005120926
8556IPUK00027B/106

9 783631 772966